The *Ultimate*
SPANISH VERB
Review and Practice

The *Ultimate*
SPANISH VERB
Review and Practice

MASTERING VERBS AND SENTENCE BUILDING
FOR CONFIDENT COMMUNICATION

Ronni L. Gordon, Ph.D., and David M. Stillman, Ph.D.

McGraw·Hill

New York   Chicago   San Francisco   Lisbon   London   Madrid   Mexico City
Milan   New Delhi   San Juan   Seoul   Singapore   Sydney   Toronto

1 2 3 4 5 6 7 8 9   VLP/VLP   0 9 8 7 6 5

ISBN 0-07-141673-0
Library of Congress Control Number 2005931717

By the same authors

*The Ultimate Spanish Review and Practice: Mastering Spanish Grammar for Confident
    Communication*
*The Ultimate Spanish Review and Practice: Mastering Spanish Grammar for Confident
    Communication,* CD Edition
The Big Red Book of Spanish Verbs

*The Ultimate French Review and Practice: Mastering French Grammar for Confident
    Communication*
*The Ultimate French Review and Practice: Mastering French Grammar for Confident
    Communication,* CD Edition
The Big Blue Book of French Verbs

McGraw-Hill books are available at special quantity discounts to use as premiums and
sales promotions, or for use in corporate training programs. For more information, please
write to the Director of Special Sales, Professional Publishing, McGraw-Hill, Two Penn
Plaza, New York, NY 10121-2298. Or contact your local bookstore.

This book is printed on acid-free paper.

Contents

Preface

The Verb was the storm-center. This discovery made plain the right
and wise course to pursue in order to acquire certainty and exactness
in understanding the statements which the newspaper was daily
endeavoring to convey to me: I must catch a Verb and tame it.

—Mark Twain, "Italian With Grammar"

The Ultimate Spanish Verb Review and Practice: Mastering Verbs and Sentence Building for Confident Communication is designed to provide advanced elementary through advanced learners of Spanish with a powerful tool for reviewing and mastering Spanish verb forms and turning these forms into the building blocks of meaningful sentences. We present the forms of Spanish verbs through verb paradigms in the seven simple tenses, the seven compound tenses, and the progressive tenses, and proceed to show how these verb forms function in phrases, clauses, and sentences. This highly productive sentence-building feature, unique to our book, moves the student effectively from verb forms to communication.

We use a contrastive approach in presenting grammar, comparing Spanish verb tenses and structures to the usage of their English counterparts. Grammar explanations of verb formation and usage are clear, concise, and well-organized. Copious examples, many presented in dialogue format, reflect authentic, everyday language usage. Charts and tables are clear and easy to read. Verb lists are presented in structural and semantic groupings and include the latest additions to the lexicon, as in the case of verbs related to the computer and technology.

All Spanish tenses and moods are presented in the 15 efficiently organized chapters of **The Ultimate Spanish Verb Review and Practice.** Each chapter treats one or more tenses, such as the preterit, or type of verb, such as stem-changing or irregular verbs. Following the presentation of verb paradigms and tenses is a section called *Building Sentences,* in which the chapter material is functionally expanded. As students master each tense, they learn to expand the forms of that tense into real sentences that can be used for communication through the addition of different elements, such as other verbs, objects, and subordinate clauses, and the transformation of statements into questions. The flexible organization of the chapters permits the student to study them in any order.

The Ultimate Spanish Verb Review and Practice provides a large number of varied exercises that are designed to facilitate the student's mastery of the Spanish verb system and sentence building. Exercise types include writing verb forms, rewriting sentences, translation into Spanish and English, building sentences, replacement, expansion, writing dialogue exchanges, and identifying types of sentences and verb endings. Useful current vocabulary is incorporated in the exercises. Some exercises provide helpful hints marked **¡Ojo!** that aid the learner in proceeding correctly and efficiently. The Answer Key at the end of the book allows students to monitor their progress as they work through the exercises.

Several chapters have *language boxes* that present information about interesting lexical, historical, and cultural aspects of the Spanish language. These brief language notes are designed to enhance the learner's knowledge and appreciation of the language by presenting etymology, borrowing, punctuation, verb formation, tense formation, and other features.

Our acclaimed grammar review and workbook, **The Ultimate Spanish Review and Practice: Mastering Spanish Grammar for Confident Communication**, provides learners with a highly effective tool for review and progress in the Spanish language. We apply the same successful pedagogy to **The Ultimate Spanish Verb Review and Practice**, with the knowledge that students will benefit measurably from its application. This book is ideal for learners working on their own and as an ancillary for students using a textbook in a classroom setting.

We have every confidence that with **The Ultimate Spanish Verb Review and Practice**, you too will be able to catch a Verb and tame it!

Ronni L. Gordon, Ph.D.
David M. Stillman, Ph.D.

Introduction

Verbs are presented in conjugation paradigms that summarize the forms of a verb in each tense. Spanish verbs change their form for person and number. Verbs are said to have three persons: the speaker, the person spoken to, and the third person, referring neither to the speaker nor the person spoken to. Spanish, like English, has two numbers: singular and plural.

The persons of the verb and their corresponding subject pronouns in English are as follows:

	SINGULAR	PLURAL
FIRST PERSON	*I*	*we*
SECOND PERSON	*you*	*you*
THIRD PERSON	*he, she, it*	*they*

The persons of the verb and their corresponding subject pronouns in Spanish are as follows:

	SINGULAR	PLURAL
FIRST PERSON	yo	nosotros/nosotras
SECOND PERSON	tú	vosotros/vosotras
THIRD PERSON	él/ella	ellos/ellas
THIRD PERSON (*you*)	usted	ustedes

Differences Between English and Spanish

- In English, subject pronouns are required to show who the subject of the verb is, since verbs have only two forms in the present tense. In Spanish, however, verb forms are complete in themselves. Subject pronouns are added for emphasis or contrast.

Ella pregunta y **él** contesta.	*She asks and he answers.*
Ellos empiezan a trabajar cuando **nosotros** terminamos.	*They start to work when we finish.*

- English has only one form for *you*; Spanish has four. **Tú** is a singular form and is informal. The **tú** form of the verb is used to address one person with whom you have an informal relationship: a family member, a close friend, a fellow student, etc. **Vosotros** is the plural of **tú**. The **vosotros** form of the verb is used to address two or more people with whom you have an informal relationship.

  tú, vosotros (INFORMAL ADDRESS)

Esteban, ¿cuándo regresas?	*Esteban, when are you coming back?*
Mamá, papá, ¿cuándo regresáis?	*Mom, Dad, when are you coming back?*

Usted is used to address one person with whom you have a formal relationship: a stranger, a customer, a superior at work, etc. **Ustedes** is the plural of **usted**. It is used to address two or more people with whom you have a formal relationship. **Usted** is used with the third-person singular forms of the verb. **Ustedes** is used with the third-person plural forms of the verb. **Usted** and **ustedes** are often abbreviated **Ud.** and **Uds. Vd.** and **Vds.** are also used as abbreviations.

usted, ustedes (FORMAL ADDRESS)

Usted puede esperar aquí, señor.	*You can wait here, sir.*
Ustedes pueden esperar aquí, señores.	*You can wait here, gentlemen/ ladies and gentlemen.*

In Spain, four forms of *you* are used: **tú, Ud., vosotros,** and **Uds.** In Spanish America, **vosotros** is not used. It is replaced by **ustedes.** Thus, in Spanish America, **ustedes** is used to address all groups consisting of two or more people, whether the relationship is formal or informal.

Mamá, papá, ¿cuándo regresan?	*Mom, Dad, when are you coming back?*

- Spanish has no subject pronoun for *it*. All nouns, whether animate or inanimate, are referred to as either **él** or **ella.** Thus, masculine nouns such as **el muchacho** and **el lápiz** are referred to as **él**, while feminine nouns such as **la mujer** and **la ciudad** are referred to as **ella.**

- Spanish makes a gender distinction in the third-person plural. (Note that English *they* does not.) **Ellos** refers to masculine plural nouns, while **ellas** refers to feminine plural nouns. **Ellos** also refers to groups of males and females, while **ellas** refers to groups consisting of females only.

—¿Quiénes son esas personas? ¿Lucas y Anita?	*"Who are those people? Lucas and Anita?"*
—No, no son **ellos.** Son Alejandro y Catalina.	*"No, it's not they. It's Alejandro and Catalina."*
—¿Rebeca y Luisa están ya?	*"Are Rebeca and Luisa here already?"*
—No, **ellas** no, pero están Julia y Marta.	*"No, they're not. But Julia and Marta are here."*

- The Spanish pronouns **nosotros** and **vosotros** also show gender distinctions. **Nosotros** and **vosotros**, like **ellos**, refer to groups of males and females, while **nosotras** and **vosotras** refer to groups consisting of females only.

—Carlos y Diana, **vosotros** sois hermanos, ¿verdad?	*"Carlos and Diana, you're brother and sister, aren't you?"*
—No, **nosotros** somos primos.	*"No, we're cousins."*
—Pilar y Sara, **vosotras** sois hermanas, ¿verdad?	*"Pilar and Sara, you're sisters, aren't you?"*
—No, **nosotras** somos primas.	*"No, we're cousins."*

The Present Tense of Regular Verbs

Subject + verb, subject + verb + direct object
Negative sentences

Regular verbs in Spanish are divided into three groups called *conjugations*. The ending of the infinitive tells which conjugation a verb belongs to.

INFINITIVE

The infinitive is a form of the verb unmarked for person or tense. English infinitives have the word *to* before the verb: *to speak, to eat, to live.*

Spanish infinitives end in **-ar**, **-er**, or **-ir**. When you remove the infinitive ending, you are left with the *stem* of the verb.

Conjugation of -ar Verbs

Spanish verbs of the first conjugation have infinitives ending in **-ar**. **-Ar** verbs are conjugated as follows.

hablar (STEM **habl-**) *to speak*

(yo)	habl**o**	(nosotros/nosotras)	habl**amos**
(tú)	habl**as**	(vosotros/vosotras)	habl**áis**
(él/ella/usted)	habl**a**	(ellos/ellas/ustedes)	habl**an**

NOTES

1 · The vowel **a** is present in all the endings of the present tense of -ar verbs except the **yo** form.

2 · The forms of the singular (**hablo, hablas, habla**) and the third-person plural form (**hablan**) are stressed on the stem, as indicated by the underlined vowel. The **nosotros** and **vosotros** forms are stressed on the ending: **hablamos, habláis.**

Common -ar verbs

acabar *to finish*	**ahorrar** *to save*
aceptar *to accept*	**alcanzar** *to reach, overtake*
acompañar *to go with, accompany*	**almacenar** *to store*
aconsejar *to advise*	**alquilar** *to rent*
aguantar *to put up with, stand, tolerate*	**analizar** *to analyze*

andar *to walk, go*
apagar *to turn off, shut off*
aparcar *to park*
aprovechar *to take advantage of*
archivar *to file*
armar *to set up, put together*
arrastrar *to drag*
arreglar *to arrange, fix up*
aumentar *to increase*
averiguar *to find out*
avisar *to let know, tell, notify*
ayudar *to help*
bailar *to dance*
bajar *to go down; to lower, turn down;
    to download*
besar *to kiss*
borrar *to erase*
buscar *to look for*
calcular *to calculate, work out*
cambiar *to change*
caminar *to walk*
cantar *to sing*
cargar *to load; to upload*
celebrar *to celebrate*
cenar *to have dinner*
charlar *to chat*
cocinar *to cook*
colocar *to put, place*
comprar *to buy*
contestar *to answer*
cortar *to cut*
crear *to create*
cruzar *to cross*
cursar *to study, take (a course on)*
dejar *to let, leave*
desarrollar *to develop*
desayunar *to have breakfast*
descansar *to rest*
descargar *to download*
desear *to want*
dibujar *to draw*
diseñar *to design*
disfrutar *to enjoy*
doblar *to turn* (change direction);
    to dub (film)
durar *to last*
echar *to throw*

empujar *to push*
enseñar *to teach; to show*
ensayar *to test, try out; to rehearse*
entrar *to go/come in, enter; to input*
entregar *to hand in/over*
escuchar *to listen to*
esperar *to wait, hope, expect*
estacionar *to park*
estornudar *to sneeze*
estudiar *to study*
explicar *to explain*
felicitar *to congratulate*
firmar *to sign*
funcionar *to work, function* (machine)
ganar *to earn, win*
gastar *to spend, waste*
grabar *to record .*
gritar *to shout*
guardar *to keep; to put away; to save*
    (computer file)
hablar *to speak*
instalar *to install*
invitar *to invite*
llamar *to call*
llegar *to arrive*
llevar *to carry; to wear*
llorar *to cry*
luchar *to fight, struggle*
mandar *to send, order*
manejar *to drive*
marcar *to dial; to mark*
mascar *to chew*
mirar *to look at*
nadar *to swim*
navegar *to surf* (the Web)
necesitar *to need*
pagar *to pay*
parar *to stop*
pasar *to spend* (time); *to pass*
patinar *to skate*
pegar *to stick, glue; to hit*
pintar *to paint*
pisar *to stand on, step on*
practicar *to practice; to go in for,
    play* (as a sport)
preguntar *to ask* (a question)
preparar *to prepare*

presentar *to present, introduce*	**terminar** *to finish, end*
programar *to program*	**tirar** *to throw*
pulsar *to press, push* (button)	**tocar** *to play a musical instrument;*
quitar *to take away, remove*	*to touch*
regresar *to come back, return*	**tomar** *to take; to drink*
reparar *to repair, fix*	**trabajar** *to work*
repasar *to review*	**trotar** *to jog*
sacar *to take out; to remove*	**usar** *to use; to wear*
saludar *to greet, say hello to*	**utilizar** *to use, utilize*
tardar *to take/be a long time*	**viajar** *to travel*
telecargar *to load, upload*	**visitar** *to visit*
telefonear *to telephone*	

A Practice the forms of regular -**ar** verbs by completing each sentence with the correct form of the verb in parentheses.

1. (mandar) Yo _____ el correo electrónico ahora.

2. (estudiar) Alejandro _____ administración de empresas.

3. (tomar) Nosotros _____ el tren de las nueve.

4. (entrar) Uds. _____ en la sala de exposición.

5. (escuchar) Tú _____ unos discos compactos.

6. (hablar) Vosotros _____ por teléfono celular.

7. (tocar) Mirián _____ la flauta.

8. (llevar) Yo _____ mi computadora portátil.

9. (navegar) Ellos _____ en la Red.

10. (regresar) ¿A qué hora _____ Verónica y David?

11. (alquilar) Ud. _____ videos los fines de semana.

12. (mirar) Tú y yo _____ la televisión.

13. (llegar) Mis amigos no _____ hasta el miércoles.

14. (trabajar) ¿Ud. _____ en una empresa multinacional?

15. (guardar) Tú _____ los datos.

16. (viajar) Nosotras _____ a España en junio.

17. (enseñar) ¿La profesora Alonso _____ ingeniería informática?

18. (estacionar) Uds. _____ el coche en el parqueo, ¿verdad?

19. (esperar) ¿Vosotras _____ delante del cine?

20. (charlar) Los colegas _____ en el cibercafé.

21. (pasar) Yo _____ todo el día en el museo.

22. (cambiar)   El turista español _____ los euros por dólares.

23. (entregar)   ¿Cuándo _____ Jaime su informe?

24. (doblar)   Tú _____ a la derecha.

25. (funcionar) La máquina no _____ bien.

26. (durar)   ¿La película _____ dos horas?

27. (desayunar) Nosotros no _____ fuerte.

28. (necesitar) Ud. _____ unos disquetes.

B *Answer the questions, using the following strings of elements. Include subject pronouns in your responses.*

MODELO   ¿Qué toman?

tú / un taxi   *Tú tomas un taxi.*

ellos / un café   *Ellos toman un café.*

yo / historia   *Yo tomo historia.*

1. ¿Qué buscan?

   a. nosotros / las llaves _____

   b. él / su teléfono móvil _____

   c. Uds. / la tienda de videos _____

2. ¿Qué compran?

   a. yo / unos libros de texto _____

   b. vosotros / un condominio _____

   c. Ud. / zapatos de tenis _____

3. ¿Qué estudian?

   a. tú / informática _____

   b. ella / programación _____

   c. tú y yo / mercadeo _____

4. ¿Qué graban?

   a. Uds. / una película _____

   b. ellas / un programa de televisión _____

   c. él / una canción francesa _____

5. ¿Qué hablan?

   a. Ud. / inglés _____

   b. vosotras / italiano _____

   c. ellos / chino _____

6. ¿Qué llevan?

    a. tú / una maleta _____

    b. yo / mi portafolio _____

    c. Uds. / el equipaje _____

C *Rewrite each of the following sentences, changing the subject to the plural. You are in Spain, where the plural form of informal* **tú** *is* **vosotros** *and the plural form of formal* **Ud.** *is* **Uds.**

    MODELOS   Hablas inglés.   *Habláis inglés.*_____

               Habla inglés.   *Hablan inglés.*_____

1. Alquilas el video. _____

2. Escucha las noticias. _____

3. Tomas café en Starbucks. _____

4. Telecarga los documentos. _____

5. Estacionas detrás del banco. _____

6. Cambia de opinión. _____

7. Averigua la información. _____

8. Mandas el correo electrónico. _____

9. Pulsa el botón. _____

10. Llegas a las siete. _____

D *Rewrite each of the following sentences, changing the subject to the plural. You are in Spanish America, where both the plural form of informal* **tú** *and the plural form of formal* **Ud.** *are* **Uds.**

    MODELOS   Hablas inglés.   *Hablan inglés.*_____

               Habla inglés.   *Hablan inglés.*_____

1. Crea un sitio Web. _____

2. Regresas al anochecer. _____

3. Ganas una beca. _____

4. Aprovecha la oferta. _____

5. Arrastra el ratón. _____

6. Compras jeans en una tienda GAP. _____

7. Trabajas en el centro. _____

8. Prepara los sándwiches. _____

9. Lleva una computadora portátil. _____

10. Desarrollas un plan. _____

E *Complete each sentence with the correct form of the verb in parentheses, omitting the subject pronoun.*

MODELO   (ellos / caminar) _*Caminan*_ por la zona histórica.

1. (él / aceptar) _____ la pasantía (*internship, assistantship*).

2. (nosotros / averiguar) _____ los detalles.

3. (yo / sacar) _____ los billetes.

4. (Uds. / practicar) _____ el béisbol.

5. (tú / firmar) ¿No _____ los documentos?

6. (vosotros / preparar) ¿Qué _____?

7. (ella / escuchar) _____ la radio.

8. (Ud. / descargar) ¿_____ los ficheros?

9. (Juan / marcar) _____ el número de teléfono.

10. (ellas / crear) ¿_____ una base de datos?

11. (Claudia / celebrar) _____ su cumpleaños.

12. (mi novio y yo / bailar) _____ salsa en la discoteca.

13. (el conferenciante / contestar) _____ las preguntas.

14. (los miembros del equipo / trotar) _____ todas las tardes.

15. (ellos / llevar) _____ una mochila.

F *Identify the subject(s) of each sentence by writing the correct subject pronoun(s). Write all possibilities.*

1. Disfrutamos la vida. _____

2. Acaban la novela. _____

3. Dejo un recado. _____

4. ¿Paga las cuentas? _____

5. Cocinas muy bien. _____

6. ¿Usa anteojos? _____

7. Ahorráis mucho dinero. _____

8. Echan la basura. _____

9. Apago la luz. _____

10. ¿Por qué lloras? _____

11. Telecarga los programas. _____

12. Estacionamos frente al cine. _____

13. Toco el clarinete. _____

14. Alquiláis videos. _____

15. ¿Qué deseas? _____

Conjugation of -er and -ir Verbs

In the present tense, second-conjugation **-er** verbs and third-conjugation **-ir** verbs are conjugated alike, except for a difference in the vowel of the **nosotros** and **vosotros** endings. **-Er** and **-ir** verbs are conjugated as follows.

comer (STEM **com-**) *to eat*

(yo)	como	(nosotros/nosotras)	comemos
(tú)	comes	(vosotros/vosotras)	coméis
(él/ella/usted)	come	(ellos/ellas/ustedes)	comen

vivir (STEM **viv-**) *to live*

(yo)	vivo	(nosotros/nosotras)	vivimos
(tú)	vives	(vosotros/vosotras)	vivís
(él/ella/usted)	vive	(ellos/ellas/ustedes)	viven

NOTES

1 · Stress is a very important feature of the Spanish verbal system. The forms of **-er** and **-ir** verbs, like those of **-ar** verbs, are stressed on the stem in the singular and the third-person plural (**ellos/ellas/ustedes**) forms, and on the ending in the **nosotros** and **vosotros** forms. Examine the following forms, in which the stressed vowel is underlined.

(yo)	como	(nosotros/nosotras)	comemos
(tú)	comes	(vosotros/vosotras)	coméis
(él/ella/usted)	come	(ellos/ellas/ustedes)	comen

(yo)	vivo	(nosotros/nosotras)	vivimos
(tú)	vives	(vosotros/vosotras)	vivís
(él/ella/usted)	vive	(ellos/ellas/ustedes)	viven

2 · The vowel of the infinitive of **-ir** verbs (**i**) appears only in those forms where the ending is stressed (vivimos, vivís). With the exception of the **yo** form, the vowel **e** appears in all other present tense endings of **-ir** verbs.

3 · The **yo** form ending is **-o** in all three conjugations.

Common -er verbs

aprender *to learn*	**comprender** *to understand*
beber *to drink*	**correr** *to run*
comer *to eat*	**coser** *to sew*

creer *to believe, think*
deber *ought, must, to be supposed to;*
  to owe
leer *to read*
meter *to put in, insert*

prender *to turn on*
romper *to break*
toser *to cough*
vender *to sell*

Common -ir verbs

abrir *to open*
añadir *to add*
aplaudir *to applaud*
asistir a *to attend*
compartir *to share*
cumplir *to fulfill, carry out; to keep one's*
  word; to turn _____ years old
describir *to describe*
difundir *to publicize, broadcast, spread*
discutir *to discuss, argue*
escribir *to write*

imprimir *to print*
insistir (en) *to insist (on)*
interrumpir *to interrupt*
ocurrir *to happen*
permitir *to permit, allow*
recibir *to receive*
resistir *to resist, stand, endure*
subir *to go up, raise; to upload*
sufrir *to suffer*
transmitir *to transmit, broadcast*
vivir *to live*

G *Practice the forms of regular -**er** and -**ir** verbs by completing each sentence
with the correct form of the verb in parentheses.*

1. (comer)   Ellos _____ en un restaurante hoy.

2. (leer)   Yo _____ un libro de historia inglesa.

3. (asistir)   Nosotros _____ a un concierto esta noche.

4. (imprimir)   ¿Jaime _____ su informe?

5. (meter)   Tú _____ tantas cosas en el maletín.

6. (discutir)   Uds. _____ sobre política.

7. (vender)   Carmen _____ su coche.

8. (escribir)   Ud. _____ poesía, ¿verdad?

9. (correr)   Vosotros _____ en la carrera.

10. (compartir) Las chicas _____ un apartamento.

11. (toser)   ¿Quién _____?

12. (beber)   Los invitados _____ vino de California.

13. (vivir)   Yo _____ en el centro.

14. (aprender)   Nosotros _____ a esquiar.

15. (subir)   Vosotras _____ al tercer piso.

16. (comprender) ¿Daniel y Elisa _____ chino?

17. (recibir)   Ud. _____ muchos paquetes.

18. (ocurrir)   ¿Qué _____ aquí?

19. (creer) ¿Uds. _____ eso?

20. (interrumpir) ¡Cuánto _____ esos niños!

21. (insistir) ¿Por qué _____ tú, en ese punto?

22. (deber) Tú _____ un dineral (*fortune*).

23. (transmitir) Esta estación de televisión _____ a toda hora.

24. (resistir) Marco Antonio no _____ el calor.

25. (abrir) El centro comercial _____ a las nueve y media.

H *Identify the subject(s) of each sentence by writing the correct subject pronoun(s). Write all possibilities.*

1. ¿Qué crees? _____

2. Añade sal y pimienta. _____

3. No permitimos esto. _____

4. Comparto sus ideas. _____

5. Cosen un botón. _____

6. ¿Por qué rompéis la cita? _____

7. No comprendemos su motivo. _____

8. ¿Todavía sufre de dolor de cabeza? _____

9. ¿Dónde vivís? _____

10. Imprimen el informe en su nueva impresora. _____

11. Corro en la carrera. _____

12. Escribes mensajes electrónicos. _____

13. Subimos en el ascensor. _____

14. ¿Bebes vino tinto o blanco? _____

15. Come demasiado. _____

I *Write sentences using the following strings of elements. Omit the subject.*

MODELO nosotros / correr / en la pista universitaria

Corremos en la pista universitaria.

1. yo / discutir / la idea con ellos _____

2. ellas / vivir / en esta vecindad _____

3. Roberto / vender / cosas en eBay _____

4. nosotros / abrir / las maletas _____

5. vosotros / beber / vino con la carne _____

   6. Ud./aprender/latín y griego _____

   7. Paloma y Esteban/subir/en la escalera mecánica

       _____

   8. tú/no comprender/la teoría _____

   9. Uds./compartir/una pizza _____

  10. ella/deber/una fuerte cantidad de dinero

       _____

  11. Miguel y yo/comer/de todo _____

  12. ¿vosotras/asistir/al partido de fútbol? _____

  13. nosotras/leer/varias revistas electrónicas

       _____

  14. tu hermana/prender/las luces _____

  15. tú/escribir/un artículo para el periódico

       _____

Verbs with Spelling Changes

Verbs Ending in **-ger** and **-gir**

Second- and third-conjugation verbs ending in **-ger** and **-gir** change **g** to **j** before **a** and **o**. Thus, in the present tense, they show this change in the **yo** form.

coger *to take, grasp, catch*

(yo)	cojo	(nosotros/nosotras)	cogemos
(tú)	coges	(vosotros/vosotras)	cogéis
(él/ella/usted)	coge	(ellos/ellas/ustedes)	cogen

fingir *to pretend*

(yo)	finjo	(nosotros/nosotras)	fingimos
(tú)	finges	(vosotros/vosotras)	fingís
(él/ella/usted)	finge	(ellos/ellas/ustedes)	fingen

Verbs ending in -ger

acoger *to welcome, receive* (people)	**proteger** *to protect*
coger[1] *to take, grasp, catch*	**recoger** *to collect, gather; to pick up*
encoger *to shrink*	**sobrecoger** *to surprise*
escoger *to choose*	

_____

[1]This verb is taboo in much of South America; **tomar** and **agarrar** are used instead.

Verbs ending in -gir

afligir *to afflict*	**restringir** *to restrict*
corregir[2] *to correct*	**resurgir** *to rise up again; to reappear*
dirigir *to direct; to lead, conduct; to address*	**rugir** *to roar; to bellow; to shout*
elegir[2] *to choose, elect*	**sumergir** *to submerge*
exigir *to demand*	**surgir** *to arise, come out, spring up; to appear, emerge*
fingir *to feign, pretend*	**teledirigir** *to direct by remote control*
infligir *to inflict*	**transigir** *to compromise, give in*
infringir *to infringe*	**ungir** *to anoint*
refulgir *to shine, glitter*	**urgir** *to be urgent/pressing*
regir[2] *to govern, manage*	

In the verb lists and vocabulary of this book, verbs that have this spelling change will be marked as follows.

escoger (g > j/o,a)
fingir (g > j/o,a)

Verbs Ending in -guir

Verbs ending in **-guir** lose the **u** before **a** and **o**.

distinguir *to distinguish*

(yo)	disting**o**	(nosotros/nosotras)	distinguimos
(tú)	distingues	(vosotros/vosotras)	distinguís
(él/ella/usted)	distingue	(ellos/ellas/ustedes)	distinguen

conseguir[3] *to get; to manage*	**perseguir**[3] *to pursue*
distinguir *to distinguish*	**proseguir**[3] *to pursue, proceed, continue with*
extinguir *to extinguish*	**seguir**[3] *to follow*

Verbs Ending in -uir

Verbs ending in **-uir** (but not **-guir**) insert a **y** between the stem and those present tense endings that are unstressed. Note that this spelling change reflects the pronunciation of these verbs. The **y** is clearly sounded where it appears.

construir *to build*

(yo)	construyo	(nosotros/nosotras)	construimos
(tú)	construyes	(vosotros/vosotras)	construís
(él/ella/usted)	construye	(ellos/ellas/ustedes)	construyen

---

[2]The vowel of the stem changes from **e** to **i** in the singular and the third-person plural. You will see other verbs with this change in Chapter 2.

[3]The vowel of the stem changes from **e** to **i** in the singular and the third-person plural. You will see other verbs with this change in Chapter 2.

atribuir *to attribute*   **incluir** *to include*
concluir *to conclude*   **influir** *to influence*
construir *to build*   **instituir** *to institute*
destruir *to destroy*   **instruir** *to instruct*
diluir *to dissolve; to dilute* **sustituir** *to substitute*
huir *to flee*

J *Complete each sentence with the correct form of the verb in parentheses.*
All verbs end in **-ger**, **-gir**, **-guir**, *or* **-uir**.

1. (seguir)   ¿Por qué no _____ (tú) nuestros consejos?

2. (escoger)   Yo _____ un regalo para la cumpleañera.

3. (exigir)   Yo no _____ demasiado, ¿verdad?

4. (construir)   Se _____ un centro comercial en la carretera.

5. (recoger)   Yo _____ el equipaje en la aduana.

6. (huir)   Ellos _____ del huracán.

7. (conseguir)   Uds. no _____ convencernos.

8. (corregir)   Felipe _____ sus faltas.

9. (coger)   Vosotros _____ un taxi en la esquina.

10. (elegir)   ¿Cuál marca _____ Ud.?

11. (destruir)   La humedad _____ la madera.

12. (proteger)   ¿Cómo se _____ el medio ambiente?

13. (extinguir)   Nosotros _____ el fuego de campamento.

14. (perseguir)   ¿Paloma _____ sus objetivos?

15. (dirigir)   Un director norteamericano _____ la compañía.

16. (acoger)   Nosotros _____ a nuestros amigos con mucho cariño.

17. (surgir)   ¿Por qué _____ tantos conflictos?

18. (distinguir) Yo no _____ el perfil (*skyline*) de la ciudad por la niebla.

19. (diluir)   Tú _____ la pólvora en el agua.

20. (urgir)   Este asunto _____.

Uses of the Present Tense

The Spanish present tense is used to express general actions or states.

—¿Dónde trabaja tu hermana?   *"Where does your sister work?"*
—Enseña matemáticas en una   *"She teaches math at a university."*
  universidad.

It can also express actions going on at the present time, a function for which English usually prefers the present progressive tense (see Chapter 14).

—¿Los chicos **trotan**?	*"Are the kids **jogging**?"*
—No, ahora **navegan** en la Red.	*"No, now **they're surfing** the Web."*

Note that Spanish has no equivalent for the English auxiliary *do, does* in questions or negative sentences.

—¿Qué idioma **estudias**? ¿El alemán?	*"What language **do you study**? German?"*
—No, **no estudio** alemán. Curso francés.	*"No, **I don't study** German. I take French."*

Spanish can use the present tense to express future time when another element of the sentence makes it clear that the verb is referring to the future. Note that English often uses the present progressive to express the future.

—¿A qué hora **llegan** mañana?	*"What time **are you arriving** tomorrow?"*
—**Llegamos** a las diez. Y al llegar, te **llamamos**.	*"**We're arriving** at ten. And when we arrive, **we'll call** you."*

The present tense can be used to express past actions once the conversation makes clear that the past is being referred to. This may occur in both speech and writing, and it has parallels in English. This use of the present to refer to the past is called the *historical present*.

No te puedes imaginar lo que pasó anoche. **Entro** en el teatro, **busco** mi asiento, **me siento** y **levanto** la vista. Y ¿a quién **veo** sentado a mi lado? A Fernando mi ex-novio. ¡Y acompañado de mi mejor amiga!	*You can't imagine what happened last night. I go into the theater, I look for my seat, I sit down and look up. And whom do I see sitting next to me? Fernando, my ex-boyfriend. And he was with my best friend!*

Spanish uses the present tense to refer to actions that began in the past but are continuing into the present. English uses a *have/has been doing something* construction for this function. The Spanish construction consists of the following elements.

- **¿cuánto tiempo hace que** + verb in present tense?

    This construction is used to ask a question about how long something has been going on. The word **tiempo** can be omitted in the question.

¿**Cuánto hace que** Ud. vive en esta vecindad?	*How long have you been living in this neighborhood?*

- **hace** + time expression + **que** + verb in present tense OR
  verb in present tense + **hace** + time expression

    These constructions are used to tell how long something has been going on.

—¿**Cuánto tiempo hace que** Ud. vive en esta vecindad?	*"How long have you been living in this neighborhood?"*
—**Hace un año que vivo** aquí.	*"I've been living here for a year."*
—**Vivo** aquí **hace un año**.	*"I've been living here for a year."*

- **Desde** is added to specify the starting point of an action that began in the past and continues into the present.

—¿**Desde cuándo** vives al lado de los Vega?	"*Since when have you been living next door to the Vegas?*"
—Somos vecinos **desde** septiembre.	"*We've been neighbors since September.*"

- When the verb is *to be*, Spanish often prefers to use the verb **llevar** to express *have/has been* with expressions of time.

—¿Cuánto tiempo **llevas** aquí?	"*How long have you been here?*"
—**Llevo un año** en Madrid.	"*I've been in Madrid for one year.*"
—**Llevamos más de dos años** en esta universidad.	"*We've been at this university for more than two years.*"

- **Tener** can also be used with this meaning, especially in Spanish America.

¿**Tienes mucho tiempo** con esta empresa?	*Have you been with this company for a long time?*
Tienen dos años en Nueva York.	*They've been in New York for two years.*

K *How long has this been going on?* Form a question from the elements given, and then answer it in two ways.

MODELO   Ud./esperar el tren (quince minutos)

¿Cuánto tiempo hace que Ud. espera el tren?

Hace quince minutos que espero el tren.

Espero el tren hace quince minutos.

1. Carolina/navegar en la Red (dos horas)

_____

_____

_____

2. tú/estudiar administración de empresas (un año)

_____

_____

_____

3. Uds./vivir en Londres (cuatro años)

_____

_____

_____

4. los Soriano / viajan por Europa (seis semanas)

_____

_____

_____

5. vosotros / asistir a estas conferencias (un par de meses)

_____

_____

_____

6. Ud. / descargar los documentos (media hora)

_____

_____

_____

7. nosotros / discutir los trámites (*steps, procedures*) (una semana)

_____

_____

_____

8. yo / exigir la colaboración de todos (varios días)

_____

_____

_____

L **Translation.** *Express the following sentences in Spanish.* **¡Ojo!** *There might be more than one way to express an answer.*

1. *Are you (tú) working in the office tomorrow?*

_____

2. *No, I'm spending the day at home.*

_____

3. *Are you (Ud.) attending the concert tonight?*

_____

4. *Yes, and before that I'm having dinner with some friends.*

_____

5. *How long have you (Uds.) been building the house?*

_____

6. *We've been building the house for a year.*

_____

7. *How long have they been in the United States?*

_____

8. *They've been here for fifteen years.*

_____

9. *Since when have you (Ud.) been pursuing your studies?*

_____

10. *I've been taking engineering courses since January.*

_____

BUILDING SENTENCES   **Subject + verb, subject + verb + direct object**

The subject is the element of the sentence that determines the ending of the verb. In the following sentences, **Juan** and **los chicos** are subjects.

Juan navega en la Red.

Los chicos nadan en la piscina.

In many Spanish sentences, the subject is not expressed, but is indicated solely by the ending of the verb.

Siempre **tomo** café por la mañana.	*I always **have** coffee in the morning.*
¿A qué hora **comes**?	*At what time **do you eat**?*
Asistimos a todos los conciertos.	*We attend all the concerts.*

In the third person, the subject is omitted when context clarifies who or what it is.

—¿Dónde están los asesores?	*"Where are the consultants?"*
—Creo que **llegan** pronto.	*"I think **they're arriving** soon."*
—¿Por qué no llevas tu reloj?	*"Why aren't you wearing your watch?"*
—**No funciona.**	*"**It doesn't work.**"*

A complete Spanish sentence may consist of a verb form by itself.

—¿Qué haces?	*"What are you doing?"*
—**Leo.**	*"**I'm reading.**"*
—Mañana estáis ocupados, ¿verdad?	*"Tomorrow you're busy, right?"*
—Sí. **Trabajamos.**	*"Yes, we are. **We're working.**"*

The idea or action expressed by the verb may affect or be directed at a person or thing. That person or thing is the object of the verb. Spanish treats objects that refer to animate beings differently from objects referring to things. If a noun is not the subject of a sentence and it both refers to an inanimate object and follows the verb directly without a preposition, it is called a *direct object*. In the sentences below, the direct objects are in boldface.

Queremos modernizar **nuestra cocina**.	*We want to modernize **our kitchen**.*
Necesito comprar **sellos**.	*I need to buy **stamps**.*
¿Lavas **el carro**?	*Are you washing **the car**?*

Transitive and Intransitive Verbs

Spanish verbs that take a direct object are called *transitive verbs*. In most cases these verbs *must* appear with a direct object. In the verb lists in this book, transitive verbs that take an inanimate direct object (an object that is a thing) are followed by **algo**.

preparar algo *to prepare something*
romper algo *to break something*
ver algo *to see something*

Spanish verbs that cannot be followed by a direct object are called *intransitive verbs*. Most verbs of motion fall into this category.

Mis amigos **salen**.	*My friends **are going out**.*
Regresan a la una para almorzar.	*They're **coming back** at one to have lunch.*
Por la tarde **van** al cibercafé.	*In the afternoon **they're going** to the Internet café.*

Some verbs can be used either intransitively or transitively.

Sube al quinto piso. (INTRANSITIVE)	*He's going up to the fifth floor.*
Sube el equipaje. (TRANSITIVE)	*He's bringing the luggage up.*
Los precios bajan en verano. (INTRANSITIVE)	*Prices fall in the summer.*
Bajan los cuadros. (TRANSITIVE)	*They're taking the paintings down.*
Corro todos los días. (INTRANSITIVE)	*I run every day.*
Corro la milla en quince minutos. (TRANSITIVE)	*I run the mile in fifteen minutes.*

THE VERB regresar

In American Spanish, the verb **regresar** can be used as a transitive verb as well as an intransitive one.

Regresamos a fines del mes.	*We're coming back at the end of the month.*
Regresamos el coche lo antes posible.	*We're returning the car as soon as possible.*

Sometimes transitive verbs appear without an expressed direct object, but have an implied direct object that is understood from context.

Abrimos (la tienda) a las nueve.	***We open** (the store) at nine o'clock.*

Here are some transitive verbs in Spanish that do not take a direct object in English, but do take an inanimate direct object in Spanish. Note that the English verbs have a preposition (*of, for, about, in, at, on, to,* or *into*).

aprobar (o > ue) algo *to approve of something*

No apruebo su conducta.   *I don't approve of his conduct.*

aprovechar algo *to take advantage of something*

Debemos aprovechar las instalaciones   *We should take advantage of the sports*
  deportivas del hotel.   *facilities of the hotel.*

buscar algo *to look for something*

Él busca un apartamento.   *He's looking for an apartment.*

comentar algo *to comment on something*

Todos comentan el acontecimiento.   *Everyone is talking about the event.*

escuchar algo *to listen to something*

Escucho las noticias por la mañana.   *I listen to the news in the morning.*

esperar algo *to wait for something*

Espero el autobús en la esquina.   *I wait for the bus at the corner.*

mirar algo *to look at something*

Siempre miro los anuncios del diario.   *I always look at the newspaper ads.*

pagar algo *to pay for something*

¿Quién paga la comida?   *Who's paying for the meal?*

pedir (e > i) algo *to ask for something*

Ella siempre me pide dinero.   *She always asks me for money.*

pisar algo *to step on something*

No pisar el césped. (*sign*)   *Don't step on the grass.*

profundizar algo *to go into, study something in depth, delve deeply into*

El profesor profundiza el tema.   *The professor goes into the subject in depth.*

solicitar algo *to apply for something*

¿Solicitas aquel puesto?   *Are you applying for that job?*

There are also English transitive verbs whose cognates or equivalents do not take a direct object in Spanish. These verbs have a preposition (typically **a** or **de**, depending on the verb) linking them to their objects.

asistir a algo *to attend something*

Asistimos a muchos conciertos.   *We attend a lot of concerts.*

entrar a/en *to enter*

Entramos al café / en el café.   *We enter the café.*

NOTE: **Entrar** is also used as a transitive verb with a direct object in the expression **entrar datos** *to enter or input data.*

jugar (u > ue) a + the definite article (name of sport or game)
to play (a sport or game)

En verano jugamos al béisbol.   *In the summer we play baseball.*

NOTE: Some speakers omit the preposition **a** and the definite article before the name of the game: **En verano jugamos béisbol.**

renunciar a algo *to give up something, resign from / quit something*

Mi hermano renuncia a su puesto.   *My brother is quitting his job.*

salir de (un lugar) *to leave (a place)*

Los empleados salen de la oficina a   *The employees leave the office at five.*
las cinco.

M *Identify each sentence as having a transitive or intransitive verb.*

	TRANSITIVE	INTRANSITIVE
1. Firma los cheques.	☐	☐
2. Bajan al patio.	☐	☐
3. Recojo las hojas.	☐	☐
4. Descargan los documentos.	☐	☐
5. Diseñas ropa muy elegante.	☐	☐
6. Camináis hacia el metro.	☐	☐
7. Almacenamos la información.	☐	☐
8. Maneja con cuidado.	☐	☐
9. ¿Compras un nuevo módem?	☐	☐
10. Sustituyen este teclado por otro.	☐	☐
11. Busco su dirección electrónica.	☐	☐
12. ¿Él sube al desván?	☐	☐
13. Transmiten las noticias a las seis.	☐	☐
14. Creamos una base de datos.	☐	☐
15. Llegáis para las once.	☐	☐

N **Subject + verb.** *Write sentences using the intransitive verbs and other elements given in the following strings.*

MODELO   Rodrigo y yo / cenar / a las ocho

Rodrigo y yo cenamos a las ocho.

1. tú / cantar / afinadamente (*in tune*)

_____

2. los atletas / correr / en la carrera

   _____

3. Pablo / toser / mucho

   _____

4. ¿Uds. / vivir / en las afueras?

   _____

5. yo / regresar / la semana entrante

   _____

6. el módem / funcionar / bien

   _____

7. nosotros / subir / al tercer piso

   _____

8. los habitantes / huir / del terremoto (*earthquake*)

   _____

9. yo / trotar / por el parque

   _____

10. el gerente / trabajar / de lunes a viernes

    _____

11. ¿vosotros / llegar / en tren?

    _____

12. tú / viajar / por el sudoeste del país

    _____

13. ¿Mercedes y Sofía / estornudar / por su alergia?

    _____

14. un conflicto / surgir / entre los socios

    _____

15. Ud. / bajar / por la escalera

    _____

16. nosotros / participar / en el foro de debate

    _____

17. ¿qué / opinar (Uds.) / de la facultad de educación?

    _____

O ***Subject + verb + direct object.*** *Write sentences using the transitive verbs and direct objects given in the following strings.*

MODELO   Clara / romper / los papeles
         Clara rompe los papeles.

1. Roberto y yo / ahorrar / dinero

   _____

2. yo / regir / la empresa

   _____

3. los jefes / concluir / su conversación

   _____

4. ¿Ud. / conseguir / sus billetes electrónicos (*e-tickets*)?

   _____

5. tú / guardar / el secreto

   _____

6. Uds. / comprar / una cámara digital

   _____

7. vosotros / imprimir / el informe

   _____

8. Beatriz y Alicia / compartir / la computadora

   _____

9. Ud. / leer / la página Web

   _____

10. nosotras / crear / unas carpetas

    _____

11. Marco Antonio / aprender / las fechas de memoria

    _____

12. ¿vosotros / marcar / el número de teléfono?

    _____

13. yo / conseguir / los boletos

    _____

14. los programadores / instalar / un programa de gráficas

    _____

15. tú / recibir / revistas de informática

_____

16. el director de la junta / interrumpir / la reunión

_____

P *Write sentences using the following strings of elements, adding prepositions as needed.*

MODELOS yo / pagar / la cuenta
Pago la cuenta.

yo / entrar / la librería
Entro a/en la librería.

1. Alberto y Daniela / esperar / un taxi

_____

2. ¿Ud. / asistir / el congreso?

_____

3. tú y yo / escuchar / estos discos compactos

_____

4. la jefa / renunciar / su puesto

_____

5. el ingeniero / entrar / los datos

_____

6. vosotras / mirar / los sitios Web

_____

7. Uds. / salir / el hotel

_____

8. los jugadores / pisar / el césped

_____

9. Rafael y yo / jugar / fútbol

_____

10. yo / entrar / el centro comercial

_____

11. mi hermana / subir / su ropa al dormitorio

_____

12. los vecinos / comentar / las noticias del barrio

_____

13. los turistas / visitar / los monumentos

   _____

14. ¿vosotros / aprobar / el plan económico?

   _____

15. ¿tú / buscar / las llaves?

   _____

Q *Translation.* *Express the following sentences in Spanish.*

1. *I'm applying for this job.* _____

2. *Virginia is looking at her e-mail.* _____

3. *Are you (tú) taking advantage of the sales?* _____

4. *We're attending that concert.* _____

5. *They're entering the bookstore.* _____

6. *You (Ud.) are entering data.* _____

7. *Esteban is giving up the project.* _____

8. *What are you (Uds.) looking for?* _____

BUILDING SENTENCES	**Negative sentences**

Sentences are made negative in Spanish by placing the word **no** before the verb. Both declarative sentences and questions may be made negative.

—¿Subes?	*"Are you going upstairs?"*
—**No, no subo.**	*"No, I'm not going upstairs."*
—**No llegan** el viernes?	*"Aren't they arriving on Friday?"*
—**No, no llegan** el viernes.	*"No, they're not arriving on Friday."*

Note in the two responses above that a negative answer to a question may begin with two occurrences of the word **no**. The first is the opposite of **sí** *yes*. The second is the word **no** that negates the verb.

The words **nunca** and **jamás** mean *never*. When they follow the verb, **no** precedes it. For some speakers, **jamás** is more formal or more emphatic than **nunca**.

—¿Nadas **a veces**?	*"Do you sometimes swim?"*
—**No, no nado nunca.**	*"No, I never swim."*
—¿Asisten Uds. **mucho** a los conciertos?	*"Do you attend concerts a lot?"*
—**No, no asistimos jamás** a los conciertos.	*"No, we never attend concerts."*
—¿Trasnocháis **siempre**?	*"Do you always stay up late?"*
—**No, no trasnochamos nunca.**	*"No, we never stay up late."*

The words **nunca** and **jamás** may appear before the verb. In this case, **no** is not used before the verb.

—¿Nadas **a veces**?	*"Do you sometimes swim?"*
—**No, nunca nado.**	*"No, I never swim."*
—¿Asisten Uds. **mucho** a los conciertos?	*"Do you attend concerts a lot?"*
—**No, jamás asistimos** a los conciertos.	*"No, we never attend concerts."*
—¿Trasnocháis **siempre**?	*"Do you always stay up late?"*
—**No, nunca trasnochamos.**	*"No, we never stay up late."*

The phrase **ya no** means *not anymore* and precedes the verb. It can be used as a short response.

—¿Los señores Alba viven al lado?	*"Do the Albas live next door?"*
—**No, ya no viven** al lado.	*"No, they don't live next door anymore."*
—**Ya no.**	*"Not anymore."*

The phrase **todavía no** means *not yet* and precedes the verb. It can be used as a short response.

—Necesito ver al jefe.	*"I have to see the boss."*
—**Todavía no está.**	*"He isn't here yet."*
—¿Uds. firman el contrato?	*"Are you signing the contract?"*
—**Todavía no.**	*"Not yet."*

Nada means *nothing* and usually follows the verb. **No** precedes the verb.

—¿Buscan **algo**?	*"Are you looking for something?"*
—No, **no buscamos nada.**	*"No, we're not looking for anything."*
—¿Compran **algo**?	*"Are they buying anything?"*
—No, **no compran nada.**	*"No, they're not buying anything."*

Nadie means *no one* and often precedes the verb when it is the subject of the sentence. **No** is not used when **nadie** precedes the verb.

—¿Los invitados comen?	*"Are the guests eating?"*
—No, **nadie come.**	*"No, no one is eating."*

Nadie as subject may follow the verb (and often does). In this case, the word **no** is used before the verb.

—¿Los invitados comen?	*"Are the guests eating?"*
—No, **no come nadie.**	*"No, no one is eating."*

Nadie and **alguien** as direct objects of the verb are presented in Chapter 2 (see p. 39).

At the top of the next page is a summary of the most common negative words and their affirmative counterparts.

AFFIRMATIVE WORDS AND EXPRESSIONS

alguna vez *sometime*
algunas veces, a veces *sometimes*
muchas veces, a menudo *often*
mucho *a lot, often*
siempre *always*

algo *something*

alguien *someone, somebody* (as subject)

a alguien *someone, somebody*
  (as direct object)

NEGATIVE WORDS AND EXPRESSIONS

nunca, jamás *never*

nada *nothing*

nadie *no one, nobody* (as subject)

a nadie *no one, nobody*
  (as direct object)

R   *Answer each question in the negative.*

MODELO   ¿Ud. patina sobre hielo?

     No, no patino sobre hielo.

1. ¿Uds. usan una calculadora de bolsillo?

2. ¿Daniel habla por teléfono celular?

3. ¿Echáis las cartas al buzón?

4. ¿Prendes el ordenador (*computer,* Spain)?

5. ¿Tú y tus amigos comparten los gastos?

6. ¿Transmiten el documental esta noche?

7. ¿Ud. corrige las faltas en el manuscrito?

8. ¿Carmen renuncia a su puesto de contable (*accountant*)?

9. ¿Los campistas extinguen el fuego de campamento?

10. ¿Uds. influyen en la decisión?

S *Answer each question, using the negative words and expressions that correspond to their affirmative counterparts. ¡Ojo! There might be more than one way to express your answers.*

MODELO ¿Dibujas animales a veces?

No, no dibujo animales nunca/jamás. / No, nunca/jamás dibujo animales.

1. ¿Uds. solicitan algo?

_____

2. ¿Alguien grita?

_____

3. ¿Los novios salen a bailar muchas veces?

_____

4. ¿Exiges algo?

_____

5. ¿Ud. espera a alguien?

_____

6. ¿Los niños lloran mucho?

_____

7. ¿Laura siempre llega puntualmente?

_____

8. ¿Montáis a caballo a menudo?

_____

9. ¿Tus amigos trasnochan algunas veces?

_____

10. ¿Pablo llega tarde alguna vez?

_____

T *Translation. Express the following sentences in Spanish.*

1. *Don't you (tú) stay up late anymore?*

_____

2. *We don't repair the computer often.*

_____

3. *Jaime isn't saving the files yet.*

_____

4. *You (Uds.) never have dinner before eight o'clock.*

_____

5. *They're not looking at anything.*

    _____

6. *No one is taking advantage of the opportunity.*

    _____

7. *Nothing is happening.*

    _____

8. *I'm not choosing anything.*

    _____

9. *We often rent videos.*

    _____

10. *Sometimes they watch baseball games on the computer.*

    _____

11. *Someone is looking for you (tú).*

    _____

12. *She never interrupts anyone.*

    _____

Stem-changing Verbs; Special Verbs Ending in **-iar** and **-uar**

BUILDING SENTENCES

Verb + infinitive construction
Personal a

Stem-changing **-ar** and **-er** Verbs

Many Spanish verbs change the vowel of the stem in the present tense in those forms where the vowel of the stem is stressed. For **-ar** and **-er** verbs, the changes that occur are **e > ie** and **o > ue**.

In the present tense, the change in the vowel of the stem takes place only in those forms where the stress falls on the stem. There is *no* change in the vowel of the stem in those forms where the stress falls on the ending (the infinitive and the **nosotros** and **vosotros** forms).

Study the present tense forms of **pensar** *to think,* **querer** *to want,* **contar** *to count, to tell,* and **volver** *to return.*

pensar (e > ie) *to think*		querer (e > ie) *to want*	
pienso	pensamos	quiero	queremos
piensas	pensáis	quieres	queréis
piensa	piensan	quiere	quieren

contar (o > ue) *to count; to tell*		volver (o > ue) *to return*	
cuento	contamos	vuelvo	volvemos
cuentas	contáis	vuelves	volvéis
cuenta	cuentan	vuelve	vuelven

Common verbs that pattern like **pensar** and **querer** (e > ie)

acertar *to be on target, guess right*
apretar *to squeeze, be tight; to grip*
ascender *to go up, rise; to promote, be promoted*
atravesar *to cross*
cerrar *to close*
comenzar *to begin*

confesar *to confess, admit*
defender *to defend*
descender *to go down*
despertar(se) *to wake up*
empezar *to begin*
encender *to light, turn on* (appliance)
encerrar *to lock in; to contain*

entender *to understand*
gobernar *to govern, manage, direct*
helar[1] *to freeze*
merendar *to have an afternoon snack*
nevar[1] *to snow*

perder *to lose; to miss* (train, etc.)
quebrar *to break*
recomendar *to recommend*
sentar(se) *to seat, sit down*

Common verbs that pattern like **contar** and **volver** (o > ue)

acordarse *to remember*
acostar(se) *to put to bed, go to bed*
almorzar *to have lunch*
conmover *to move* (emotionally)
costar *to cost*
demostrar *to show*
devolver *to return (something),*
  give (something) back
doler *to hurt, ache*
encontrar *to find*
envolver *to wrap up*
jugar (u > ue) *to play*
llover[2] *to rain*

mostrar *to show, display*
oler (o > hue) *to smell*
poder *can, be able*
probar(se) *to try, taste; to try on*
recordar *to remember; to remind*
resolver *to solve, resolve, decide*
rodar *to roll; to film, shoot a film*
rogar *to ask, request; to beg, plead*
soler *to usually do something,*
  be accustomed to doing something
tronar[2] *to thunder*
volar *to fly*

A *Practice the forms of stem-changing verbs that pattern like **pensar** and **querer** (e > ie) by completing each sentence with the correct form of the verb in parentheses.*

1. (querer)   Yo _____ una computadora portátil.

2. (pensar)   Nosotros _____ mucho en el futuro.

3. (comenzar)   La película _____ a las diez de la noche.

4. (entender)   Tú no _____ mi genial idea.

5. (recomendar) ¿Ud. _____ esta marca?

6. (perder)   Ellos _____ el tren a menudo.

7. (encender)   Vosotros _____ las luces.

8. (gobernar)   El presidente _____ el país muy hábilmente.

9. (descender)   Tú _____ en ascensor.

10. (empezar)   Yo _____ a navegar en la Red.

11. (cerrar)   ¿Estas farmacias nunca _____?

12. (nevar)   _____ casi todos los días en invierno.

13. (atravesar)   Nosotros _____ la calle en la esquina.

14. (defender)   Los soldados _____ la frontera.

---

[1]Impersonal verb conjugated only in the third-person singular: **hiela, nieva.**

[2]Impersonal verb conjugated only in the third-person singular: **llueve, truena.**

15. (ascender)   La temperatura _____ rápidamente.

16. (helar)   El frío _____ el agua del lago.

17. (despertar)   Nadie se _____ temprano los fines de semana.

18. (sentar)   Los invitados se _____ en la sala.

B *Practice the forms of stem-changing verbs that pattern like* **contar** *and* **volver** *(o > ue) by completing each sentence with the correct form of the verb in parentheses.*

1. (volver)   Ellos _____ de vacaciones el sábado.

2. (encontrar)   Yo no _____ los disquetes.

3. (envolver)   Pilar y yo _____ los regalos.

4. (almorzar)   ¿Tú _____ en la cafetería hoy?

5. (devolver)   Ud. nos _____ el coche mañana.

6. (costar)   Este televisor de plasma _____ una fortuna.

7. (merendar)   Vosotros _____ a las cuatro.

8. (demostrar)   Marco Antonio _____ interés en la inteligencia artificial.

9. (llover)   Siempre _____ por aquí en abril.

10. (poder)   ¿Ud. _____ terminar el informe para el lunes?

11. (probar)   Nosotras _____ muchos platos exóticos.

12. (recordar)   Ellas no _____ nada del acontecimiento.

13. (oler)   Algo _____ mal en la cocina.

14. (resolver)   Yo _____ todos los problemas.

15. (volar)   Estas aves _____ al sur de Estados Unidos.

16. (mostrar)   La agencia _____ unas casas amuebladas.

17. (acostar)   Tú te _____ demasiado tarde.

18. (acordar)   ¿Vosotros no os _____ de la fecha?

The verb **jugar** *to play* is anomalous in that it changes the stem vowel **u** to **ue** in the present tense. The **u** remains in the **nosotros** and **vosotros** forms.

jugar (u > ue) *to play*

j**ue**go	jugamos
j**ue**gas	jugáis
j**ue**ga	j**ue**gan

LA LENGUA ESPAÑOLA jugar

The reason for the apparently anomalous change **u** > **ue** in this verb is its medieval form. **Jugar** was pronounced **jogar** in Medieval and early Renaissance Spanish. Thus, the original pattern **jogar** > **juego** was not irregular at all.

NOTES

1 · **Jugar** is used with the preposition **a** and the definite article to indicate the game or sport played.

> **jugar al tenis** *to play tennis*
> **jugar al baloncesto** *to play basketball*
> **jugar a las cartas** *to play cards*
> **jugar al escondite** *to play hide-and-seek*
>
> —¿A qué juegan?   *"What are they playing?"*
> —Juegan al béisbol.   *"They are playing baseball."*

Some speakers omit the preposition **a** and the definite article before the name of the game: **jugar béisbol, jugar tenis, jugar baloncesto, jugar cartas**, etc.

2 · The verb **tocar**, not **jugar**, is used for *to play a musical instrument*.

> tocar el piano, la flauta, el violin,   *to play the piano, the flute, the violin,*
> el saxofón, el clarinete, la guitarra   *the saxophone, the clarinet, the guitar*

3 · **Jugar** also means *to gamble, bet*. The noun **el juego** *game* also means *gambling*. **Perder su dinero en el juego** means *to gamble one's money away*.

C *Write sentences using the verb* **jugar** *and the following strings of elements.*

MODELO   Paco / jugar / golf   *Paco juega (al) golf.*

1. Uds. / jugar / béisbol _____

2. yo / jugar / en un equipo de tenis

   _____

3. los jugadores / jugar / limpio (*play fairly*) _____

4. él / jugar / sucio (*play dirty/foul*) _____

5. tú / jugar / baloncesto _____

6. nosotros / jugar / fútbol americano / en otoño

   _____

7. vosotros / jugar / juegos electrónicos

   _____

8. los campeones / jugar / el partido / el sábado

   _____

Stem-changing -ir Verbs

In addition to the stem changes **e > ie** and **o > ue**, some **-ir** verbs have a third change: **e > i**. Here are the present tense forms of **sentir** *to regret, to feel*, **pedir** *to ask for, order,* and **dormir** *to sleep*. **Pedir** changes **e** to **i** in those forms of the present tense where the stress falls on the stem.

sentir (e > ie) *to regret; to feel*		**pedir (e > i)** *to ask for, order*	
siento	sentimos	pido	pedimos
sientes	sentís	pides	pedís
siente	sienten	pide	piden

dormir (o > ue) *to sleep*	
duermo	dormimos
duermes	dormís
duerme	duermen

The verb **morir** *to die* is conjugated like **dormir**.

Common verbs that pattern like sentir (e > ie)

advertir *to notify, warn, inform, point out*	**hervir** *to boil*
	mentir *to lie*
convertir *to convert*	**preferir** *to prefer*
convertirse en *to become*	**referirse (a)** *to refer (to)*
divertirse *to have a good time*	**sentar(se)** *to seat, sit down*

Common verbs that pattern like pedir (e > i)

conseguir[1] *to get, obtain*	**reír(se)** *to laugh*
despedir *to fire*	**reñir** *to quarrel; to scold*
despedirse (de) *to say good-bye*	**repetir** *to repeat; to have a second helping*
gemir *to groan, moan*	
impedir *to prevent*	**seguir**[1] *to follow, continue*
medir *to measure*	**servir** *to serve*
perseguir[1] *to pursue, chase, aim for, go after*	**sonreír(se)** *to smile*
proseguir[1] *to pursue, proceed, carry on with*	**vestir(se)** *to dress*

Note that **reír** *to laugh* and **sonreír** *to smile* have **í** as the stem vowel in the singular and the third-person plural.

reír *to laugh*		**sonreír** *to smile*	
río	reímos	sonrío	sonreímos
ríes	reís	sonríes	sonreís
ríe	ríen	sonríe	sonríen

---

[1]Verbs ending in **-guir** such as **seguir, conseguir, perseguir,** and **proseguir** drop the letter **u** in writing before the first-person singular ending **-o: sigo, consigo, persigo, prosigo.**

NOTES

1 · You cannot predict from the infinitive which verbs will have a stem change and which will not. For instance, **volver** has a stem change (**vuelvo**, etc.) but **comer** does not (**como**, etc.). It is therefore necessary to memorize which verbs have a stem change.

2 · In the verb lists and vocabulary of this book, stem-changing verbs will be marked as follows.

pedir (e > i)
pensar (e > ie)
volver (o > ue)

D   *Complete each sentence with the correct form of the stem-changing -ir verb that patterns like* **sentir (e > ie)**.

1. (sentir)   Yo lo _____ mucho.

2. (preferir)   ¿Tú _____ los aretes (*earrings*) de oro o los de plata?

3. (divertir)   Ellos se _____ mucho en la fiesta.

4. (referir)   Ella no se _____ a nada.

5. (hervir)   El agua no _____ todavía.

6. (mentir)   Nosotros nunca _____.

7. (convertir)   La ciudad se _____ en una importante capital cosmopolita.

8. (advertir)   Ellos _____ en la radio que hay embotellamientos.

E   *Complete each sentence with the correct form of the stem-changing -ir verb that patterns like* **pedir (e > i)**.

1. (pedir)   Uds. _____ mucho dinero por la casa de campo.

2. (servir)   ¿Ella _____ pescado o pollo?

3. (vestir)   Sara y Laura se _____ de azul.

4. (despedir)   Yo me _____ de mis colegas.

5. (seguir)   Tú _____ por la avenida hasta llegar al semáforo.

6. (reír)   Nosotros nos _____ de sus chistes.

7. (impedir)   Vosotros _____ el progreso del equipo.

8. (sonreír)   El bebé _____ mucho.

9. (repetir)   Él _____ las palabras dos veces.

10. (medir)   Nosotros _____ la foto con una regla.

11. (conseguir)   Yo _____ los billetes en la taquilla.

12. (perseguir)   Uds. _____ el doctorado en ingeniería mecánica.

F *Complete each sentence with the correct form of* **dormir (o > ue)**.

1. Yo _____ mucho los fines de semana.

2. ¿Tú no _____ bien en este dormitorio?

3. Ellos _____ entre siete y ocho horas.

4. Nosotros _____ la siesta hoy.

5. Uds. _____ profundamente.

6. Elena _____ en casa de sus abuelos.

7. ¿Ud. _____ en un saco de dormir?

8. Vosotros _____ mal en ese motel.

Special Verbs Ending in **-iar** and **-uar**

Some verbs ending in **-iar** and almost all verbs ending in **-uar** stress the vowel before the **a** of the infinitive in the singular and the third-person plural. An accent mark is written over the **i** and **u** in those forms.

enviar *to send*		**continuar** *to continue*	
envío	enviamos	continúo	continuamos
envías	enviáis	continúas	continuáis
envía	envían	continúa	continúan

Verbs that pattern like **enviar**

confiar (en) *to trust, rely on*	**guiar** *to guide, lead, drive*
criar *to raise, bring up*	**resfriarse** *to catch a cold*
desafiar *to challenge, dare, defy*	**rociar** *to sprinkle, spray, water*
espiar *to spy on, keep watch*	**vaciar** *to empty*
esquiar *to ski*	**variar** *to vary*
fiarse (de) *to trust*	

Verbs that pattern like **continuar**

acentuar *to accent, stress, emphasize*	**evaluar** *to evaluate, assess*
actuar *to act, perform, behave*	**graduarse** *to graduate*
efectuar *to effect, carry out, do, execute*	**insinuar** *to hint*

You cannot tell from the infinitive which verbs have stressed **i** or **u** in the singular and third-person plural and which do not. The verbs **enviar**, **esquiar**, **actuar**, and **graduarse** *do* have these respective changes, while verbs such as **estudiar**, **iniciar**, **limpiar**, and **averiguar** do not.

In the verb lists and vocabulary of this book, verbs that have stressed **i** or **u** will be marked as follows.

    efectuar (efectúo)
    resfriarse (me resfrío)

G   *Complete each sentence with the correct form of the special verb ending in* **-iar** *or* **-uar**.

1. (confiar)   Nosotros _____ en su buena voluntad.

2. (enviar)   Uds. _____ unos mensajes electrónicos.

3. (continuar)   ¿Tú _____ con el proyecto?

4. (graduar)   Yo me _____ el año próximo.

5. (variar)   Ellos nunca _____ su rutina.

6. (resfriar)   Ud. se _____ todos los años.

7. (insinuar)   ¿Vosotros _____ algo?

8. (fiar)   Ella se _____ de sus amigos.

9. (evaluar)   Nosotros _____ bien la situación.

10. (guiar)   El guía _____ a los turistas por el museo.

11. (efectuar)   Los gerentes _____ muchos cambios.

12. (esquiar)   Yo _____ en las Montañas Rocosas.

13. (acentuar)   Tú siempre _____ lo más interesante.

14. (vaciar)   ¿Uds. _____ las cajas?

15. (actuar)   Ella _____ en una comedia musical.

16. (espiar)   Los espías _____ a sus enemigos.

17. (criar)   Vosotros _____ ganado en la hacienda.

18. (rociar)   El jardinero _____ las flores.

BUILDING SENTENCES   **Verb + infinitive construction**

Some Spanish verbs can be followed directly by an infinitive to form a verb + infinitive construction. In the following list, **hacer algo** represents any infinitive.

conseguir (e > i) hacer algo *to succeed in doing something,*
  manage to do something
creer hacer algo *to think/believe something done*
deber hacer algo *ought to do something, should do something*
decidir hacer algo *to decide to do something*
dejar hacer algo *to let/allow to do something*
desear hacer algo *to want to do something*
elegir (e > i) hacer algo *to choose to do something*
escoger (escojo) hacer algo *to choose to do something*
esperar hacer algo *to hope to do something*
evitar hacer algo *to avoid doing something*
fingir (finjo) hacer algo *to pretend to do something*
hacer (irreg.) hacer algo *to make do something, to have something done*

impedir (e > i) hacer algo *to prevent from doing something*
intentar hacer algo *to try to do something*
lamentar hacer algo *to regret doing something*
lograr hacer algo *to succeed in doing something, manage to do something*
mandar hacer algo *to order to do something*
merecer (merezco) hacer algo *to deserve to do something*
necesitar hacer algo *to need to do something*
oír (irreg.) **hacer algo** *to hear something done*
olvidar hacer algo *to forget to do something*
ordenar hacer algo *to order to do something*
parecer (parezco) hacer algo *to seem to do something*
pedir (e > i) hacer algo *to ask to do something*
pensar (e > ie) hacer algo *to intend/plan to do something*
permitir hacer algo *to allow to do something*
poder (o > ue) hacer algo *to be able to do something, can do something*
preferir (e > ie) hacer algo *to prefer to do something*
pretender hacer algo *to claim/try to do something*
procurar hacer algo *to try to do something*
prohibir (prohíbo) hacer algo *to prohibit from doing something*
prometer hacer algo *to promise to do something*
querer (e > ie) hacer algo *to want to do something*
recordar (o > ue) hacer algo *to remember to do something*
resolver (o > ue) hacer algo *to resolve to do something*
saber (irreg.) **hacer algo** *to know how to do something*
sentir (e > ie) hacer algo *to be sorry for / regret doing something*
soler (o > ue) hacer algo *to usually do something, be accustomed to doing something*
temer hacer algo *to be afraid to do something*
ver hacer algo *to see something done*

—¿**Sabe Ud. reparar** esta máquina?	*"Do you know how to repair this machine?"*
—Lo siento pero **no puedo ayudarle**.	*"I'm sorry, but I can't help you."*
—¿**Logran terminar** el informe para la fecha tope?	*"Can they manage to finish the report by the deadline?"*
—**Procuran terminarlo** pero **temen no poder respetar** el plazo fijado.	*"They're trying to finish it, but they're afraid they can't meet the deadline."*
—**Espero verte** en la tertulia.	*"I hope to see you at the get-together."*
—**Quiero ir**, pero no sé si puedo.	*"I want to go, but I don't know if I can."*
—¿**Piensas venir** a la oficina hoy?	*"Do you intend to come to the office today?"*
—No, **prefiero trabajar** en casa.	*"No, I prefer to work at home."*
—**Siento molestarla**, señora.	*"I'm sorry to bother you, ma'am."*
—No es ninguna molestia. **Necesito hablar** con Ud.	*"It's no bother. I need to speak with you."*

H **Sentence expansion.** *Practice the* verb + infinitive *construction, expanding each sentence with the verb in parentheses.*

MODELO   Archivan los documentos. (necesitar)
Necesitan archivar los documentos.

1. Ahorramos mucho dinero. (lograr)

   _____

2. No averiguan nada. (poder)

   _____

3. Interrumpo su conversación. (sentir)

   _____

4. Llueve por aquí en abril. (soler)

   _____

5. Escribe el informe en un solo día. (conseguir)

   _____

6. Construyen unos rascacielos. (hacer)

   _____

7. ¿Manejáis en la autopista? (temer)

   _____

8. Vuelves lo antes posible. (procurar)

   _____

9. Compro un organizador personal. (querer)

   _____

10. No pierde el tren. (esperar)

    _____

11. No mienten más. (prometer)

    _____

12. Aprovecho las rebajas navideñas. (pensar)

    _____

13. ¿Bebes el vino tinto o el blanco? (preferir)

    _____

14. Pide los billetes electrónicos. (olvidar)

    _____

15. No encienden la videocasetera. (recordar)

    _____

16. Aparcan en esta zona en hora punta (*rush hour*). (prohibir)

    _____

17. Corremos en el maratón. (decidir)

    _____

18. Ese carro cuesta una fortuna. (deber)

    _____

19. ¿Creáis sitios Web? (saber)

    _____

20. Envío el paquete por el FedEx. (escoger)

    _____

I **Translation.** *Express the following sentences in Spanish.*

1. *I want to surf the Web.*

   _____

2. *We hope to begin the project next week.*

   _____

3. *He can read his e-mail at the Internet café.*

   _____

4. *Do you (Uds.) intend to travel by plane or by train?*

   _____

5. *They usually spend the weekends in New York.*

   _____

6. *You (tú) shouldn't interrupt the meeting.*

   _____

7. *She prefers to buy clothing in department stores.*

   _____

8. *Do you (vosotros) know how to download music?*

   _____

BUILDING SENTENCES | **Personal a**

You have seen that direct object nouns that refer to things, not people, directly follow the verb without a preposition.

Nosotros resolvemos **el problema**.	*We are solving **the problem**.*
Hacen reparar **la computadora**.	*They have **the computer** repaired.*
¿Cuándo envías **los paquetes**?	*When are you sending **the packages**?*
Repito **las palabras** interminablemente.	*I repeat **the words** ad nauseam.*

However, when the direct object noun refers to a specific, definite animate being (a person or a higher animal), it is linked to the verb by **a**. This function of **a** is called *personal **a***. An animate direct object noun is considered definite if it is preceded by the definite article (**el, la, los, las**), a demonstrative adjective (forms of **este, ese, aquel**), or a possessive adjective (forms of **mi, tu, su, nuestro, vuestro**).

No comprendemos **a la profesora**.	*We don't understand **the professor**.*
Los abuelos cuidan **a los niños**.	*The grandparents are looking after **the children**.*
¿Conoces **a aquel señor**?	*Do you know **that man**?*
Baño **a mi perro** todos los días.	*I bathe **my dog** every day.*

NOTE

The personal **a** contracts with the definite article **el** to form the contraction **al**.

Buscamos **al** profesor Estrada.	*We're looking for Professor Estrada.*
No veo **al** dependiente.	*I don't see the salesperson.*

Proper names of people are also considered definite and are preceded by personal **a** when they function as direct objects.

Quiero ver **a Juan**.	*I want to see **Juan**.*
¿Recuerdas **a Laura Martínez**?	*Do you remember **Laura Martínez**?*

When **quién** is the direct object of the verb, it is also preceded by **a**. Personal **a** is required before **alguien** and **nadie**, and before **alguno, ninguno** (**ningun-**), **cualquiera** (**cualquier**), and **¿cuántos?** when they modify a noun referring to people or are used as pronouns referring to people.

—¿**A quién** buscas?	*"**Whom** are you looking for?"*
—No busco **a nadie**.	*"I'm not looking for **anyone**."*
—¿Esperan **a alguien**?	*"Are they waiting for **somebody**?"*
—No, no esperan **a nadie**.	*"No, they're not waiting for **anybody**."*
—Sí, esperan **a algunos colegas**.	*"Yes, they're waiting for **a few colleagues**."*
—¿Ud. conoce **a algunos** de los gerentes?	*"Do you know **any** of the managers?"*
—No, no conozco **a ninguno**.	*"No, I don't know **any**."*
—No, no conozco **a ningún gerente**.	*"No, I don't know **any (managers)**."*
—¿Puedo llevar **a cualquier amigo**?	*"May I bring **any friend**?"*
—Claro, puedes invitar **a cualquiera**.	*"Of course, you may invite **anyone**."*

—¿**A cuántas personas** debemos llamar? *"**How many people** should we call?"*
—Debéis llamar **a veinte personas**. *"You should call **twenty people**."*

—¿**A cuántos candidatos** eligen este año? *"**How many candidates** are they electing this year?"*
—Eligen **a siete**. *"They're electing **seven**."*

When a direct object animate noun is preceded by the indefinite article (**un, una, unos, unas**), it is usually not preceded by a personal **a**.

Necesitamos **un mozo**. *We need **a waiter**.*
El autobús recoge **unos turistas** delante del museo. *The bus picks up **some tourists** in front of the museum.*

However, personal **a** is sometimes used before an animate noun preceded by the indefinite article in order to indicate that the person referred to is a known individual.

Cuando queremos vender propiedades, llamamos **a un agente**. *When we want to sell property, we call an agent.*

The above sentence implies the identity of the agent is known. Compare it with the following sentence.

Para vender propiedades es mejor llamar **un agente**. *To sell property it's better to call an agent.*

J *Complete each sentence by adding personal **a** where necessary. If none is needed in the sentence, write an X in the blank. **¡Ojo!** Don't forget to use the contraction **al**.*

1. Pienso comprar _____ una nueva impresora.

2. ¿_____ quién llevas al cine?

3. Felipe intenta solicitar _____ ese puesto.

4. Esperamos ver _____ nuestros familiares el domingo.

5. Encuentras _____ el arquitecto en su oficina.

6. No conocen _____ ningún programador.

7. Necesitan buscar _____ unos consultores.

8. ¿_____ cuántos empleados despiden este año?

9. Deciden no visitar _____ nadie este fin de semana.

10. ¿No deseáis probar _____ el helado de coco?

11. ¿Buscáis _____ alguien?

12. Invito _____ Sofía al concierto.

13. Suelen escuchar _____ las noticias en el canal tres.

14. ¿No entiendes _____ la profesora?

15. Prefiero alquilar _____ una película policíaca.

16. Llevan _____ los turistas por el barrio histórico.

17. Los señores Martínez crían _____ sus hijos muy bien.

18. Debemos saludar _____ los recién llegados.

19. Resuelven no variar _____ el horario.

20. Puedes contratar _____ cualquiera de las traductoras.

21. Traigo _____ algunos informes.

22. Los policías persiguen _____ el ladrón.

K **Translation.** *Express the following sentences in Spanish.*

1. *Whom do you (tú) want to invite to the dance?*

   _____

2. *They plan to see the (male) engineer.*

   _____

3. *Isabel doesn't help anybody.*

   _____

4. *I'm waiting for someone.*

   _____

5. *The firm should hire programmers.*

   _____

6. *Do you (Uds.) know Roberto Murillo?*

   _____

7. *We're looking for our dog.*

   _____

8. *The restaurant needs a (male) chef.*

   _____

9. *How many soccer players do you (Ud.) know?*

   _____

10. *I don't know any (soccer players).*

    _____

11. *Sir, are you looking for me?*

    _____

12. *No, Miss, I'm not looking for you.*

    _____

Irregular Verbs (Part I)

Many Spanish verbs do not follow the conjugation patterns presented in Chapters 1 and 2. These are called *irregular verbs*. It should be noted, however, that there are patterns even among the irregular verbs. Many irregular verbs are irregular only in the first-person singular (**yo**) form of the present tense. The other five present-tense forms of such verbs are regular.

Verbs with Irregular Stems in -g-

A common irregularity is the appearance of a **g** before the -**o** ending of the first-person singular. We call these verbs *g verbs*. The verb **hacer** *to do, make* is typical of this category of irregular verbs.

hacer *to do, make*

ha**go**	hacemos
haces	hacéis
hace	hacen

Compounds of **hacer**, such as **deshacer** *to undo* and **rehacer** *to redo*, are conjugated like **hacer**.

Expressions with hacer

hacer un viaje / una excursión *to take/go on a trip*
hacer las maletas *to pack*
hacer cola *to line up, stand in line*
hacer planes *to make plans*
hacer ejercicio to *exercise*
hacer el desayuno / el almuerzo / la cena *to make breakfast/lunch/dinner*
hacer la compra *to do the shopping*
hacer una pregunta *to ask a question*
hacer el papel de *to play the part/role of*
hacer algo pedazos *to break/smash/tear something to pieces*
hacer (un) clic al / en el botón / en el enlace / en el icono *to click on the button / on the link / on the icon* (computer)
hacer un login / un logon / un logoff *to log in / log on / log off*
hacer investigaciones *to do research*
hacer una lista *to make a list*

Weather expressions with hacer (used only in the third-person singular)

¿Qué tiempo hace? *What's the weather like?*
Hace buen/mal tiempo. *The weather's good/bad.*
Hace (mucho) calor/frío/fresco. *It's (very) warm/cold/cool.*
Hace (poco) sol/viento. *It's (not very) sunny/windy.*
¿Qué temperatura hace? *What's the temperature?*
Hace 70 grados. *It's seventy degrees.*

Here are some other verbs that have a **g** before the **-o** ending of the first-person singular. Note that their conjugations may have stem changes in other persons.

caer *to fall*

ca**ig**o	caemos
caes	caéis
cae	caen

Compounds of **caer**, such as **decaer** *to decline, weaken, deteriorate* and **recaer** *to fall again, backslide, relapse,* are conjugated like **caer**.

Expressions with caer

caer en un error *to make a mistake*
caer en una trampa *to fall into a trap*
caer enfermo *to fall ill*

Mi cumpleaños cae en sábado. *My birthday falls on a Saturday.*
Cae por la casa sin llamar. *She drops by without calling.*
El sol cae. *The sun is setting.*
La noche cae. *It's nightfall.*
La lluvia/nieve cae. *The rain/snow is falling.*
Las manzanas caen del árbol. *The apples fall from the tree.*

decir *to say, tell*

di**g**o	decimos
dices	decís
dice	dicen

Expressions with decir

decir la verdad / una mentira *to tell the truth / a lie*
decir algo sin querer *to say something without meaning to*
decir que sí/no *to say yes/no*

Compounds of **decir**, such as **desdecir** *to fall short of, not live up to,* **maldecir** *to curse,* and **predecir** *to predict,* are conjugated like **decir**.

oír *to hear*

oigo	oímos
oyes	oís
oye	oyen

Note that in **oímos** an accent mark is added to indicate that the **i** represents a full syllable and not the second part of the diphthong **oi**.

Expressions with oír

oír un ruido *to hear a noise*
oír música *to listen to music*
oír hablar de *to hear of*
oír decir que *to hear that*
oír misa *to hear mass*
oír mal *to misunderstand, be hard of hearing*

poner *to put*

pongo	ponemos
pones	ponéis
pone	ponen

Compounds of **poner**, such as **componer** *to compose, fix,* **descomponer** *to break, make malfunction,* **disponer** *to dispose,* **imponer** *to impose,* **oponer** *to oppose,* **posponer** *to postpone,* **proponer** *to propose,* **reponerse** *to get well, recover,* and **suponer** *to suppose,* are conjugated like **poner**.

Expressions with poner

poner al día *to bring up to date*
poner la mesa *to set the table*
poner una película *to show a film*
poner la televisión *to turn on the television*
poner fin a algo *to put an end to something*
poner a alguien por las nubes *to praise someone highly / to the skies*

salir *to go out, leave*

salgo	salimos
sales	salís
sale	salen

Expressions with salir

salir al cine *to go out to the movies*
salir a comer *to go out to eat*
salir a pasear / de paseo *to go out for a walk*
salir de viaje *to go on a trip, leave on a trip*

salir bien/mal *to turn out well/badly, work out well/badly*
salir para un lugar *to leave for a place*
salir ganando/perdiendo *to win/lose, wind up winning/losing*
salir a alguien *to take after/resemble someone*

tener *to have*

tengo	tenemos
tienes	tenéis
tiene	tienen

Compounds of **tener**, such as **contener** *to contain,* **detener** *to stop, arrest, detain,* **mantener** *to maintain, keep, support* (economically), **obtener** *to obtain, get,* **retener** *to retain,* and **sostener** *to support,* are conjugated like **tener**.

Expressions with **tener**

tener (mucha) hambre/(mucha) sed *to be (very) hungry/(very) thirsty*
tener (mucho) calor/(mucho) frío *to be (very) warm/(very) cold*
tener éxito *to be successful*
tener confianza en *to have confidence in*
tener (mucha) prisa *to be in a (big) hurry*
tener sueño *to be sleepy*
tener (poca) paciencia *to (not) be patient*
tener (muchos) celos *to be (very) jealous*
tener ganas de *to feel like doing something*
tener miedo *to be afraid*
tener razón *to be right*
tener suerte *to be lucky*
¿Cuántos años tienes? *How old are you?*
tener _____ años *to be _____ years old*
tener lugar *to take place*
tener que + infinitive *to have to do something*
tener que ver con *to have to do with*

traer *to bring*

traigo	traemos
traes	traéis
trae	traen

Compounds of **traer**, such as **atraer** *to attract,* **contraer** *to contract,* and **distraer** *to distract, amuse, entertain,* are conjugated like **traer**.

Expressions with **traer**

traer noticias *to bring news*
traer flores *to bring flowers*
traer buena/mala suerte *to bring good/bad luck*

valer *to be worth*

valgo	valemos
vales	valéis
vale	valen

Expressions with valer

valer mucho/poco *to be worth a lot/little*
valer un mundo / un ojo de la cara *to be worth a fortune*
(no) valer para ese trabajo *(not) to be suitable for / good at that work/job*
¿Cuánto vale? *How much does it cost?*
valer la pena *to be worth it, worth the trouble*
más vale ir *it's better to go*

venir *to come*

vengo	venimos
vienes	venís
viene	vienen

Compounds of **venir**, such as **convenir** *to agree, be convenient or fitting*, **devenir** *to happen, become*, **prevenir** *to prevent, warn*, and **provenir** *to come, arise, originate from*, are conjugated like **venir**.

Expressions with venir

venir temprano/tarde *to come early/late*
venir en coche / en taxi *to come by car/taxi*
venir cansado/entusiasmado *to arrive tired/excited*
venir con cuentos *to tell tall stories / gossip / fibs*

A *Complete each dialogue exchange with the correct forms of the verbs in parentheses.*

1. —Teodoro y yo _____ al cine esta noche. (salir)

   —¿Ah sí? ¿Qué película _____? (poner)

2. —¿Sabes que _____ 90 grados? (hacer)

   —Por eso nosotros _____ tanto calor. (tener)

3. —La nieve _____ todo el día. (caer)

   —Y _____ mucho frío y viento. (hacer)

4. —¿Tú _____ música? (oír)

   —No, yo no _____ nada por el ruido del tráfico. (oír)

5. —Yo _____ hambre. (tener)

   —Yo también. Ahora yo _____ el almuerzo. (hacer)

6. —¿Cuándo _____ Sara y Manuel a la casa? (venir)

   —¿Quién sabe? Seguro que _____ por la casa como de costumbre. (caer)

7. —¿Uds. _____ lo que yo _____? (oír / decir)

   —Sí, nosotros _____ lo que tú _____. (oír / decir)

8. —¿Tú me _____ al día? (poner)

   —Sí, te _____ todas las noticias. (traer)

9. —Vosotros _____ muy cansados. (venir)

   —Es verdad que _____ mucho sueño. (tener)

10. —Marisol siempre _____ ganando. (salir)

    —Es que la chica _____ mucha suerte. (tener)

11. —¿Qué (ellos) _____ del tiempo? (decir)

    —Según el parte meteorológico, _____ muy buen tiempo. (hacer)

12. —¿Tu cumpleaños _____ en viernes? (caer)

    —Sí, esa noche yo _____ a bailar en una discoteca. (salir)

13. —Javier _____ mucho éxito en los negocios. (tener)

    —En efecto. Y sus colegas lo _____ por las nubes. (poner)

14. —¿Nosotros _____ la tele ahora? (poner)

    —No quiero. Más _____ salir al teatro. (valer)

15. —Yo _____ la mesa si tú _____ la comida. (poner, hacer)

    —¡Yo no _____ para ese trabajo! (valer)

B *Write sentences using the following strings of elements.*

    MODELO   nosotros / decir / que no   *Decimos que no.*_____

1. yo / oír / hablar del nuevo centro comercial

   _____

2. Uds. / venir / en taxi _____

3. él / tener / veintiséis años _____

4. yo / posponer / la reunión un par de días

   _____

5. nosotros / traer / dos botellas de vino a la fiesta

   _____

6. ¿quién / decir / tal cosa? _____

7. yo / salir / para la oficina / temprano _____

8. en otoño/las hojas/caer/de los árboles

   _____

9. ¿tú/salir/al cine esta noche? _____

10. yo/no valer/para esas cosas _____

11. yo/hacer/clic/al botón _____

12. ¿Ud./oír/las noticias? _____

C *Complete each sentence by selecting the correct verb from the two given, and writing its correct form.*

1. (poner | caer)   Cada vez que Cristóbal viaja en avión, _____ enfermo.

2. (hacer | traer)   Yo _____ cola para sacar los billetes.

3. (oír | venir)   Tú siempre _____ con cuentos. ¡Basta ya!

4. (decir | poner)   ¿Cuándo _____ Uds. fin a los chismes?

5. (tener | salir)   Su pregunta no _____ nada que ver con el tema.

6. (valer | decir)   ¿Cómo se _____ eso en español?

7. (oír | caer)   Nosotros _____ unos ruidos muy desagradables.

8. (traer | salir)   ¿Con quiénes (vosotros) _____ a pasear?

9. (traer | poner)   Por desgracia yo no _____ dinero.

10. (valer | poner) Su sortija _____ un ojo de la cara.

11. (hacer | tener) Carmen _____ poca paciencia.

12. (venir | hacer) ¿Qué actor _____ el papel de don Juan?

Verbs Ending in -cer

Verbs that end in a vowel + **-cer** have **zc** in the **yo** form. The rest of the conjugation is regular.

conocer *to know*	
cono**zc**o	conocemos
conoces	conocéis
conoce	conocen

The verbs **desconocer** *to not know, be unaware or ignorant of* and **reconocer** *to recognize* are conjugated like **conocer**.

NOTE

See Chapter 4 (p. 60) for the uses of **conocer** vs. **saber**, two verbs that mean *to know*.

merecer *to deserve*		**parecer** *to seem*	
merezco	merecemos	parezco	parecemos
mereces	merecéis	pareces	parecéis
merece	merecen	parece	parecen

Verbs conjugated like **merecer** and **parecer**

aborrecer *to hate*	**envejecer** *to grow old*
agradecer *to thank, be grateful*	**establecer** *to establish*
amanecer *to wake up in the morning*	**estremecer** *to shake, startle*
aparecer *to appear*	**fallecer** *to die* (formal)
carecer *to lack*	**favorecer** *to favor, flatter*
compadecer *to feel sympathy, feel sorry for*	**fortalecer** *to fortify, make strong*
	humedecer *to dampen, moisten*
convalecer *to convalesce*	**obedecer** *to obey*
crecer *to grow*	**ofrecer** *to offer*
desaparecer *to disappear*	**padecer** *to suffer, endure, bear*
desobedecer *to disobey*	**palidecer** *to turn pale*
embellecer *to beautify, embellish*	**perecer** *to perish*
enflaquecer *to lose weight, get thinner*	**permanecer** *to remain, stay*
enfurecer *to make furious, infuriate*	**pertenecer** *to belong*
enloquecer *to drive crazy or mad*	**prevalecer** *to prevail, take root*
enriquecer *to make rich or wealthy*	**resplandecer** *to shine, blaze, glow*
enternecer *to soften, make tender, touch*	**restablecer** *to reestablish, restore*
entristecer *to make sad*	

In the verb lists and vocabulary of this book, verbs that have **zc** in the **yo** form will be marked as follows.

merecer (yo merezco)

Verbs that end in -**cer** preceded by a consonant do *not* have **zc** in the **yo** form. However, the final **c** of the stem changes to **z** in this form.

torcer (o > ue) *to twist*	
tuerzo	torcemos
tuerces	torcéis
tuerce	**tue**rcen

The verb **retorcer** *to twist, wring* is conjugated like **torcer**.

vencer *to defeat, beat*	
venzo	vencemos
vences	vencéis
vence	vencen

The verbs **convencer** *to convince* and **ejercer** *to exercise, practice, be in practice* (profession) are conjugated like **vencer**.

The verbs **mecer** *to rock* (a child), *to swing* (in a swing) and **cocer** (**o > ue**) *to cook* have **z**, not **zc**, in the first-person singular.

mecer *to rock* (a child), *to swing* (in a swing)

mezo	mecemos
meces	mecéis
mece	mecen

cocer (**o > ue**) *to cook*

cuezo	cocemos
cueces	cocéis
cuece	cuecen

Verbs ending in **-ucir** have **zc** in the **yo** form. The rest of the conjugation is regular.

conducir *to drive*

conduzco	conducimos
conduces	conducís
conduce	conducen

lucir *to shine; to seem (look); to sport (wear)*

luzco	lucimos
luces	lucís
luce	lucen

traducir *to translate*

traduzco	traducimos
traduces	traducís
traduce	traducen

Verbs conjugated like conducir, lucir, and traducir

deducir *to deduce, infer, deduct*
inducir *to lead, induce*
introducir *to introduce, show in, cause*
producir *to produce*
reducir *to reduce*
relucir *to shine, glitter, gleam*
reproducir *to reproduce*
seducir *to seduce, tempt, attract*

D *Complete each sentence with the correct form of the verb in parentheses.*

1. (conocer) Yo _____ a ese locutor.

2. (torcer) La patinadora se _____ el tobillo patinando.

3. (vencer) Los campeones _____ fácilmente a los otros equipos.

4. (permanecer) Nosotros _____ en Chicago todo el mes.

5. (introducir) Yo _____ datos en la base de datos.

6. (favorecer) El color rojo te _____ mucho.

7. (cocer) Yo _____ la carne a fuego lento (*on low heat, slowly*).

8. (conducir) Tú _____ muy rápidamente.

9. (obedecer) Esos niños malcriados no _____ a sus papás.

10. (amanecer) ¿A qué hora vosotras _____ los días de trabajo?

11. (ofrecer) Yo les _____ mi amistad.

12. (producir) La compañía _____ fibra óptica.

13. (agradecer) Yo le _____ sus atenciones.

14. (aparecer) Blanca, tu nombre no _____ en la lista.

15. (reducir) Yo _____ mis gastos poco a poco.

16. (traducir) Yo _____ los documentos del español al inglés.

17. (ejercer) Arturo es ingeniero pero ya no _____.

18. (resplandecer) Sus pendientes de oro _____.

19. (reproducir) Yo _____ el documento en blanco y negro (*black and white*).

20. (establecer) La cadena _____ una sucursal en las afueras.

BUILDING SENTENCES | **Questions**

Yes/No Questions

Yes/no questions expect either *yes* or *no* as an answer. They do not begin with an interrogative word. The most common way to form *yes/no questions* in Spanish is to change the intonation of the sentence so that your voice rises abruptly at the end, rather than falls as it does in statements.

In writing, this is shown by the addition of a pair of question marks, an inverted question mark at the beginning of the question and a traditional one at the end.

¿Tienes hambre?	*Are you hungry?*
¿Luz y Paco salen de viaje?	*Are Luz and Paco leaving on a trip?*
¿Este país produce acero?	*Does this country produce steel?*

The subject may also be placed after the verb, either before the direct object or after it. To focus on the subject, place it at the end of the sentence, since in Spanish the element that comes last in a sentence is emphasized. The subject is in boldface in each of the following questions.

¿Mece **la madre** a su hijo?	*Does the mother rock her child?*
¿Conducen **Uds.** un coche deportivo?	*Do you drive a sports car?*
¿Reproduce bien los colores **aquella cámara digital**?	*Does that digital camera reproduce colors well?*
¿Tiene mucho trabajo **María Elena**?	*Does María Elena have a lot of work?*

SIGNOS DE PUNTUACIÓN

The Spanish custom of placing an inverted question mark (¿) at the beginning of questions and an inverted exclamation point (¡) at the beginning of exclamations can be seen as parallel to other punctuation that affects an entire phrase or sentence, such as quotation marks, which appear both at the beginning and end of the material quoted.

E *Translate the English yes/no questions into Spanish. The underlined words are emphasized.*
¡Ojo! Think about word order.

1. *Does <u>Mirián</u> play the flute?* _____

2. *Are they translating <u>the reports</u>?* _____

3. *Are <u>Raquel and Daniel</u> making dinner?*

   _____

4. *Are you (Uds.) listening to <u>classical music</u>?*

   _____

5. *Are <u>you</u> (tú) coming in a taxi?* _____

6. *Am <u>I</u> setting the table?* _____

7. *Is Jorge driving <u>a sports car</u>?* _____

8. *Are <u>you</u> (Ud.) asking a question?* _____

9. *Are <u>Julia and I</u> bringing the cake?* _____

10. *Does Miguel's birthday fall on <u>Friday</u>?*

    _____

Spanish adds phrases such as **¿no?**, **¿verdad?**, **¿no es verdad?**, and **¿no es cierto?** to statements to turn them into questions. These phrases are called *tags*. *Tag questions* signal that the speaker expects the answer *yes*. If the statement is negative, only **¿verdad?** can be used as a tag. Similarly, English uses tags such as *isn't it?* and *are you?* to turn statements into questions.

Hace calor hoy, ¿no es cierto?	*It's warm today, isn't it?*
Uds. no tienen prisa, ¿verdad?	*You're not in a hurry, are you?*

F *Write tag questions, using the following strings of elements.*

   MODELO   todos / venir / en taxi / ¿no es verdad?

   _*Todos vienen en taxi, ¿no es verdad?*_____

1. Miguel / buscar / un sitio para aparcar (*parking space*) / ¿no es cierto?

   _____

2. Uds. / hacer / una excursión el domingo / ¿no?

   _____

3. tú / no conocer / nuestro barrio / ¿verdad?

   _____

4. Pilar / tener / confianza en sí misma / ¿no es verdad?

   _____

5. aquellos terrenos / pertenecer / a tu familia / ¿no?

   _____

6. yo / no necesitar / pagar con contante (*cash*) / ¿verdad?

   _____

7. nosotros / deber / digitalizar (*digitize*) los documentos / ¿no es cierto?

   _____

8. Ud. / no conseguir convencerlo / ¿verdad?

   _____

Information Questions

Information questions begin with an interrogative word and ask for a piece of information.

Common interrogative words

¿Qué? *What?*	**¿Dónde?** *Where?*
¿Quién? *Who?* (singular)	**¿Adónde?** *Where?* (= to what place)
¿Quiénes? *Who?* (plural)	**¿Cuándo?** *When?*
¿A quién? *Whom?* (singular)	**¿A qué hora?** *At what time?*
¿A quiénes? *Whom?* (plural)	**¿Cómo?** *How?*
¿De quién? *Whose?* (singular)	**¿Cuánto?, ¿Cuánta?** *How much?*
¿De quiénes? *Whose?* (plural)	**¿Cuántos?, ¿Cuántas?** *How many?*
¿Cuál?, ¿Cuáles? *Which one(s)?*	**¿Por qué?** *Why?*
	¿Para qué? *Why?, For what purpose?*

Note that all question words have a written accent.

In information questions, the subject usually follows the verb.

¿Cuántos días por semana **trabaja Juan**?	*How many days a week does Juan work?*
¿Por qué **no vienen tus amigos**?	*Why aren't your friends coming?*

Some of the interrogative words are used differently from their English equivalents.

NOTES

1 · **¿Cómo?**, in addition to its meaning of *how,* is used to ask for repetition when you don't hear what someone says or to express surprise at what you just heard. Its English equivalent in these cases is *what?*

¿Cómo dices?	*What are you saying?*
¿Cómo?	*What?*

2 · Before a noun, **¿qué?** is usually used for *which.*

> **¿Qué libro quieres?**   *Which book do you want?*

However, in parts of Latin America, **¿cuál?**, **¿cuáles?** may be used before nouns.

> **¿Cuál libro quieres?**   *Which book do you want?*
> **¿Cuáles libros quieres?**   *Which books do you want?*

3 · Spanish makes a distinction between **¿qué?** and **¿cuál?** that does not exist in English.

¿Cuál? asks for identification or selection.

> **¿Cuál** es la importancia de este artículo?   *What is the importance of this article?*
> **¿Cuál** es la capital de Chile?   *What is the capital of Chile?*
> **¿Cuál** es la marca de computadora que   *What is the brand of computer that you*
>   piensa comprar?   *intend to buy?*
> **¿Cuál** es la fecha de hoy?   *What is today's date?*
> **¿Cuál** es la diferencia entre estas   *What is the difference between these*
>   calculadoras?   *calculators?*

¿Qué? asks for a definition.

> **¿Qué** es la informática?   *What is computer science?*
> **¿Qué** es un nanosegundo?   *What is a nanosecond?*

4 · **¿Dónde?** asks about location. **¿Adónde?** asks direction and is used with verbs of motion.

> **¿Dónde** viven tus primos?   *Where do your cousins live?*
> **¿Adónde** van los empleados?   *Where are the employees going?*

Many speakers, however, use **¿dónde?** with both meanings.

5 · In questions with **¿de quién(es)?**, the subject is placed after the verb. The resulting word order is thus different from English.

> **¿De quién** es este teléfono celular?   *Whose cell phone is this?*

6 · Spanish speakers use **quiénes** instead of **quién** when they are certain the reference is plural.

> **¿Quiénes** salen al cine? ¿Inés y Raúl?   *Who's going out to the movies? Inés and*
>   *Raúl?*

7 · A preposition used with an interrogative word in Spanish always precedes it: **¿con quién?**, **¿para dónde?**, **¿en qué?**, etc. It cannot be placed at the end of a question as in English.

> **¿Con quién** sale Gabriel?   *Whom is Gabriel going out with?*
> **¿Para dónde** camináis?   *Where are you walking / headed toward?*
> **¿En qué calle** viven?   *What street do they live on?*
> **¿Sobre qué** van a hablar Uds.?   *What are you going to talk about?*

G *Create information questions based on the statements. ¡Ojo! Some items may have more than one possible question.*

1. Viven en San Francisco.

   _____

2. Tengo dos hijos.

   _____

3. San Juan es la capital de Puerto Rico.

   _____

4. Van al centro comercial.

   _____

5. Leo este libro.

   _____

6. La ofimática es la informática aplicada a la oficina.

   _____

7. Conocemos a su hermano.

   _____

8. Las cosas salen bien.

   _____

9. Salen para el campo.

   _____

10. Camina por el parque.

    _____

11. El comercio electrónico son las transacciones comerciales por Internet.

    _____

12. Esta cámara digital cuesta quinientos dólares.

    _____

13. Llegan Alejandro y Catalina.

    _____

14. Los disquetes son de Carlos.

    _____

15. Vuelvo a las cuatro y media.

    _____

16. Hoy es el veintidós de febrero.

    _____

17. Nicolás quiere bailar con Sofía.

_____

18. No vamos a la playa porque llueve.

_____

19. El cibercafé está en la avenida Sur.

_____

20. Expresan sus ideas muy lógicamente.

_____

21. Juan Ramón estudia justicia criminal.

_____

22. Compran tres tarjetas telefónicas.

_____

H _Write a question that would elicit each of the following responses in instant messaging (**mensaje instantáneo**). ¡Ojo! There are both information and yes/no questions._

1. La reunión tiene lugar el jueves.

_____

2. Necesito comprar una computadora personal.

_____

3. Prefiero la marca IBM.

_____

4. Voy al teatro esta noche.

_____

5. Elena estudia enfermería.

_____

6. Voy a la fiesta con Teodoro.

_____

7. No, no trabajo el viernes.

_____

8. Sí, hago ejercicio ahora.

_____

9. Sí, mañana salimos de paseo.

_____

10. Sí, conduzco yo.

_____

11. Debemos ir a eso de la una.

_____

12. Sí, vamos a estar de vuelta para las seis.

_____

I   **Translation.** *Express the following questions in Spanish.*

1. *Where are they coming from?*

_____

2. *What is the capital of Spain?*

_____

3. *Whom are you (tú) making plans with?*

_____

4. *In what month are you (Uds.) leaving on a trip?*

_____

5. *What's the weather like?*

_____

6. *Is it sunny?*

_____

7. *Is it worth it?*

_____

8. *Why is he in such a hurry?*

_____

9. *What is "telemarketing" (el telemercadeo)?*

_____

10. *Shall I click on the link?*

_____

Irregular Verbs (Part II)

Verb + connector + infinitive construction

Ir, ver, and dar

The verb **ir** *to go* is irregular.

ir *to go*	
voy	vamos
vas	vais
va	van

Expressions with ir

ir a México *to go to Mexico*
ir a pie / a caballo / en bicicleta *to go on foot / on horseback / by bicycle*
ir al médico / al dentista *to go to the doctor / to the dentist*
ir a + infinitive *to be going to do something*
ir bien/mal *to go well/badly*
ir de compras *to go shopping*
ir de mal en peor *to go from bad to worse*
ir de San Francisco a Los Ángeles *to go from San Francisco to Los Angeles*
ir de vacaciones *to go on vacation*
ir de viaje *to go on a trip*
ir en carro/tren/avión/lancha/barco/taxi/metro *to go by car/train/plane/rowboat/ boat/taxi/subway*
ir por algo *to go get something*
Voy por el pan. *I'm going to get the bread.*

The verb **ver** *to see* is irregular in the **yo** form. Its stem in the remaining forms consists solely of the letter **v-**.

ver *to see*	
veo	vemos
ves	veis
ve	ven

The verb **dar** *to give* is irregular in the **yo** form. Its stem in the remaining forms consists solely of the letter **d-**.

dar *to give*

doy	damos
das	dais
da	dan

Note that the **vosotros** forms of **ir**, **ver**, and **dar** have no written accent marks: **vais**, **veis**, **dais**.

Expressions with **ver**

ver televisión/tele *to watch TV*
ver los documentos *to look at the documents*
no ver ni jota *to be as blind as a bat*
no ver por qué *not to see why, not to understand why*
no ver más allá de sus narices *not to be able to see further than the end of one's nose*

Expressions with **dar**

dar al mar / a las montañas *to face the ocean / the mountains*
dar (un) clic al botón / en el enlace / en el icono *to click on the button / on the link / on the icon*
dar con *to find, run across, bump into*
dar consejos *to give advice*
dar la bienvenida *to welcome*
dar las gracias *to thank*
dar mucho trabajo *to give/make a lot of work*
dar un concierto *to give a concert*
dar un paseo / una vuelta *to take a walk*
dar una película *to show a film*

—¿Ves a Carlota a menudo?   *"Do you see Carlota often?"*
—Si, siempre **doy con ella** en el centro.   *"Yes, I always run into her downtown."*

—**No veo por qué ellos dan tantos consejos.**   *"I don't see why they give so much advice."*

—Yo tampoco. No saben nada. **No ven más allá de sus narices.**   *"I don't either. They don't know anything. They aren't able to see further than the end of their noses."*

—¿**Das un paseo** con nosotros?   *"Will you take a walk with us?"*
—No, hoy **veo tele**. Quiero ver el partido.   *"No, today I'm watching TV. I want to see the game."*

Caber and haber

The verb **caber** *to fit* is irregular in the **yo** form.

caber *to fit*

quepo	cabemos
cabes	cabéis
cabe	caben

The verb **haber**, literally *to have*, is used almost exclusively as an auxiliary verb to form the compound tenses (see Chapters 8, 10, and 12).

haber *to have*	
he	hemos
has	habéis
ha	han

Hay, a modified form of **ha**, means *there is, there are*. **Hay** may be followed by either a singular or a plural noun.

Hay un concierto hoy a las ocho.	*There is a concert today at eight o'clock.*
No hay necesidad de comprar más.	*There is no need to buy any more.*
Hay muchas razones por no hacer eso.	*There are many reasons not to do that.*
No hay suficientes aulas.	*There are not enough classrooms.*

The expression **hay que** means *one must / you must do something, it is necessary to do something*.

Hay que hacer una copia de seguridad.	*One must / It's necessary to make a backup copy.*
Hay que seguir una dieta equilibrada.	*You have to follow a balanced diet.*

Haber is used as a conjugated verb in one expression, **haber de** + infinitive *to have to do something*.

Hemos de terminar el proyecto.	*We have to finish the project.*
Has de oír lo que quieren.	*You have to hear what they want.*
Han de salir hoy.	*They have to leave today.*

Sometimes **haber de** is used as a substitute for the future tense. This is common in Mexican usage.

Ha de regresar a las once.	*He will return at eleven.*

Saber and conocer

The verb **saber** *to know* is irregular in the **yo** form. The other persons are formed regularly from the stem **sab-**.

saber *to know*	
sé	sabemos
sabes	sabéis
sabe	saben

Expressions with **saber**

saber algo de memoria *to know something by heart*
saber algo de sobra *to know something all too well*
saber dónde vive Daniel *to know where Daniel lives*
saber inglés y español *to know English and Spanish*

saber lo del accidente *to know about the accident*
saber para quién trabaja Alicia *to know for whom Alicia works*
saber + infinitive *to know how to do something*
no saber lo que pasa *not to know what's happening / what's wrong*
no saber nada de nada *not to know anything at all*
no saber ni jota / ni papa de algo *not to have a clue about something*

The verb **conocer** also means *to know*. It is conjugated like verbs ending in **-cer** (see p. 48).

conocer *to know*

conozco	conocemos
conoces	conocéis
conoce	conocen

Expressions with **conocer**

conocer a alguien de vista *to know someone by sight*
conocer un lugar como la palma de la mano *to know a place like the back of one's hand*

Saber means to know facts, to know something you can state or repeat. It is used before nouns and clauses.

No sé su dirección electrónica.	*I don't know his e-mail address.*
¿Sabes dónde viven?	*Do you know where they live?*
¿Sabe Ud. a qué hora llega el avión?	*Do you know at what time the plane is arriving?*
No sabemos por qué lo dicen.	*We don't know why they say that.*
Sé que Felipe trabaja por aquí.	*I know that Felipe works around here.*

Conocer means to be familiar with a person or place. It is used before nouns, and if the noun refers to people, it is preceded by the personal **a**.

¿Conocen Uds. al director?	*Do you know the director?*
Conocen a Isabel Montero.	*They know Isabel Montero.*
¿A quién conoce Ud. en Barcelona?	*Whom do you know in Barcelona?*
No conozco a nadie en esta ciudad.	*I don't know anyone in this city.*
Conocemos muy bien Buenos Aires.	*We know Buenos Aires very well.*
No conozco Perú.	*I've never been to Peru.*

A *Complete each sentence with the correct form of one of the following verbs:* **ir, dar, ver, saber, caber***. Then write the infinitive of each verb on the line in parentheses.*

1. Esteban _____ de Filadelfia a Nueva York en tren. (_____)

2. Nosotros _____ televisión por cable. (_____)

3. Yo les _____ las gracias por sus atenciones. (_____)

4. No _____ ni una sola cosa más en esta cajita. (_____)

5. ¿Uds. _____ las fechas de memoria? (_____)

6. Yo _____ a la tienda de videos. (_____)

7. Aurelia no _____ ni jota de la tecnología informacional. (_____)

8. Somos tantos pasajeros que yo no _____ en el taxi. (_____)

9. Antonio no _____ más allá de sus narices. (_____)

10. Nuestro hotel _____ a la playa. (_____)

11. _____ una película inglesa en el cine Multiplex. (_____)

12. Yo _____ los contratos detenidamente. (_____)

13. Vosotros _____ clic sobre la imagen. (_____)

14. ¿Tú _____ por la pizza? (_____)

15. ¿Vosotros no _____ los videodiscos por aquí? (_____)

16. Yo no _____ su código postal. (_____)

17. Vosotras nos _____ buenos consejos. (_____)

18. ¿Vosotros _____ de vacaciones a mediados de mayo? (_____)

19. Jaime y yo no _____ hacer funcionar este aparato. (_____)

20. Tú _____ qué pasa con tus propios ojos. (_____)

21. ¿Nosotros _____ al museo el sábado? (_____)

22. _____ trescientas personas en la sala de conciertos. (_____)

B *Complete each dialogue with the correct forms of* **saber** *and* **conocer**.
¡Ojo! Remember the different meanings and uses of the two verbs.

1. —¿Ud. _____ una buena tienda de cómputo?

    —Yo _____ que hay una supertienda en el centro.

2. —¿Tú _____ a los miembros del equipo?

    —Yo _____ a algunos de vista.

3. —¿Ud. _____ por qué Alberto no llama?

    —No, no _____ el motivo.

4. —¿Tú _____ al nuevo consultor?

    —No, no lo _____ pero _____ quién es.

5. —Uds. _____ Nueva York, ¿verdad?

    —No, ni _____ a nadie en la ciudad.

6. —¿Vosotros _____ que yo trabajo para una empresa multinacional?

    —Sí, nosotros _____ la compañía.

7. —¿Lorenzo _____ crear páginas Web?

    —No, no _____ ni jota.

8. —¿Tomás e Isabel _____ italiano?

—Sí, _____ hablarlo con soltura (*fluently*).

C *Write sentences using* **hay** *with the following strings of elements.*
¡**Ojo!** *Remember to use* **que** *when necessary.*

1. hay / una función (*performance*) el sábado a las dos

_____

2. hay / hacer clic en el icono

_____

3. hay / ser un buen ciudadano

_____

4. no hay / necesidad de quedarse

_____

5. hay / conferencias en la feria del libro (*book fair*)

_____

6. hay / una megatienda tecnológica en esta carretera

_____

7. hay / pasar por la aduana (*customs*)

_____

8. ¿hay / alguna dificultad en realizar el proyecto?

_____

9. hay / invertir en varias industrias

_____

10. hay / entrevistar a los candidatos

_____

BUILDING SENTENCES **Verb + connector + infinitive construction**

In Chapter 2 you learned that many Spanish verbs are followed directly by the infinitive to form the verb + infinitive construction.

No puedo salir hoy.	*I can't go out today.*
¿Qué **piensan Uds. hacer** mañana?	*What do you plan to do tomorrow?*
Queremos viajar por Europa este verano.	*We want to travel around Europe this summer.*
Ud. debe cobrar su cheque.	*You should cash your check.*
Necesitas arrastrar y **soltar** en este ejercicio.	*You need to drag and drop in this exercise.*

Remember that the verb **saber** is followed directly by the infinitive with the meaning *to know how to do something.*

¿**Sabe Ud. programar** la computadora?   *Do you know how to program the computer?*

Todos los chicos **saben nadar.**   *All the children know how to swim.*

Verb + *a, de, en, con, por, que* + Infinitive

Some verbs, however, require a *connector* to link them to a following infinitive. The most common connectors are the prepositions **a** and **de**. In the following examples, **hacer algo** represents any infinitive.

Verbs connected by **a** to a following infinitive

acostumbrarse a hacer algo *to be accustomed to doing something*
animar a uno a hacer algo *to encourage someone to do something*
aprender a hacer algo *to learn to do something*
atreverse a hacer algo *to dare to do something*
ayudar a uno a hacer algo *to help someone do something*
comenzar (e > ie) a hacer algo *to begin to do something*
decidirse a hacer algo *to decide to do something*
dedicarse a hacer algo *to devote oneself to doing something*
disponerse a hacer algo *to get ready to do something*
echar(se) a hacer algo *to begin to do something*
empezar (e > ie) a hacer algo *to begin to do something*
enseñar a hacer algo *to teach/show how to do something*
invitar a uno a hacer algo *to invite someone to do something*
ir a hacer algo *to be going to do something*
llegar a hacer algo *to succeed in doing something, manage to do something*
llevar a hacer algo *to be led to do something*
meterse a hacer algo *to start to do something*
negarse (e > ie) a hacer algo *to refuse to do something*
obligar a uno a hacer algo *to force/compel someone to do something*
persuadir a uno a hacer algo *to persuade someone to do something*
ponerse a hacer algo *to begin to do something*
prepararse a hacer algo *to prepare to do something*
renunciar a hacer algo *to renounce / give up doing something*
volver (o > ue) a hacer algo *to do something again*

Verbs of motion connected by **a** to a following infinitive

bajar a hacer algo *to go downstairs to do something*
correr a hacer algo *to run to do something*
entrar a hacer algo *to go in(side) to do something*
pasar a hacer algo *to stop by to do something*
regresar a hacer algo *to go/come back to do something*
salir a hacer algo *to go out(side) to do something*
subir a hacer algo *to go upstairs to do something*
venir a hacer algo *to come to do something*

—**Vuelvo a recordarte** que no tenemos más pasta de dientes en casa.	*"I'm reminding you again that we don't have any more toothpaste in the house."*
—**Salgo a comprarla** ahora mismo.	*"I'm going out to buy it right now."*
—¿Qué hacemos si Rodolfo **viene a pedir** un préstamo?	*"What will we do if Rodolfo comes to ask for a loan?"*
—Lo **animamos a buscar** trabajo.	*"We'll encourage him to look for work."*
—Oye, ¿me **ayudas a instalar** el equipo físico?	*"Hey, will you help me install the hardware?"*
—Está bien. ¿Pero cuándo **aprendes a hacerlo** tú?	*"Okay. But when are you going to learn to do it yourself?"*
—**Empiezo a tener** hambre.	*I'm beginning to get hungry.*
—Ven. Te **invito a comer**.	*Come. I'll treat you (invite you to eat).*

Ir a + infinitive is often a substitute for the future tense, much like English *going to.*

—No sé lo que **vamos a hacer**.	*"I don't know what we will do."*
—No te preocupes. La situación **va a mejorar**.	*"Don't worry. The situation is going to improve."*
—¿Adónde **vas a ir**?	*"Where will you go?"*
—**Voy a estudiar** en Londres.	*"I'm going to study in London."*

Verbs connected by **de** to a following infinitive

acabar de hacer algo *to have just done something*
acordarse (o > ue) de hacer algo *to remember to do something*
alegrarse de hacer algo *to be glad to do something*
arrepentirse (e > ie) de hacer algo *to regret doing something*
avergonzarse (o > üe) de hacer algo *to be ashamed to do something*
cansarse de hacer algo *to get tired of doing something*
dejar de hacer algo *to stop doing something*
desesperar de hacer algo *to despair / lose hope of doing something*
encargarse de hacer algo *to take charge of doing something*
hartarse de hacer algo *to get fed up with / have enough of doing something*
jactarse de hacer algo *to boast about doing something*
olvidarse de hacer algo *to forget to do something*
presumir de hacer algo *to presume to do something*
terminar de hacer algo *to finish doing something*
tratar de hacer algo *to try to do something*

—**Desespero de encontrar** al perro.	*"I am giving up hope of finding the dog."*
—Pero yo **acabo de verlo** en el jardín.	*"But I have just seen him in the garden."*
—Este mes **dejo de fumar**.	*"This month I'm going to stop smoking."*
—Yo también **trato de no fumar**.	*"I'm also trying not to smoke."*
—¿**Te cansas de escribir** tu informe?	*"Are you getting tired of writing your report?"*
—**Acabo de terminarlo**.	*"I have just finished it."*

Verbs connected by **en** to a following infinitive

consentir (e > ie) en hacer algo *to consent/agree to do something*
consistir en hacer algo *to consist of doing something*
demorar en hacer algo *to delay/put off/take long in doing something*
dudar en hacer algo *to hesitate/be hesitant to do something*
empeñarse en hacer algo *to insist on doing something, be determined to do something*
esforzarse (o > ue) en hacer algo *to strive to do something*
insistir en hacer algo *to insist on doing something*
interesarse en hacer algo *to be interested in doing something*
quedar en hacer algo *to agree to do something*
tardar en hacer algo *to take time/delay/take long in doing something*
vacilar en hacer algo *to hesitate to do something*

—Juan **insiste en hablar** con nosotros.	*"Juan insists on talking with us."*
—Debemos **quedar en verlo** mañana.	*"We should agree to see him tomorrow."*
—¿El puesto que te ofrecieron **consiste en redactar** muchos informes?	*"Does the job they offered you consist of writing a lot of reports?"*
—Sí, por eso **dudo en aceptarlo**.	*"Yes, that's why I'm hesitant to accept it."*

Verbs connected by **con** to a following infinitive

amenazar con hacer algo *to threaten to do something*
contar (o > ue) con hacer algo *to count on/rely on doing something*
soñar (o > ue) con hacer algo *to dream of/about doing something*

—Luis no se concentra en la clase. **Sueña con ver** el partido de baloncesto.	*"Luis is not concentrating in class. He's dreaming of seeing the basketball game."*
—Por eso el profesor **amenaza con suspenderlo**.	*"That's why the teacher is threatening to fail him."*

Verbs connected by **por** to a following infinitive

empezar (e > ie) por hacer algo *to begin by doing something*
esforzarse (o > ue) por hacer algo *to strive/work hard to do something*
interesarse por hacer algo *to be interested in doing something*
optar por hacer algo *to opt/choose to do something*
votar por hacer algo *to vote to do something*

—**Optó por renunciar** a su puesto.	*"He opted for quitting his job."*
—Es que su jefe nunca consintió en ascenderlo.	*"The fact is that the boss never agreed to promote him."*
—Siempre **se interesaba por ser** cirujana.	*"She was always interested in being a surgeon."*
—Ahora **se esfuerza por terminar** su residencia en cirugía.	*"Now she's working hard to finish her residency in surgery."*

There are two verbs that use **que** as the connector to a following infinitive.

tener que hacer algo *to have to do something*
hay que hacer algo *one must do something*

—¿Qué **tienes que hacer** hoy?   *"What do you have to do today?"*
—**Tengo que llevar** mi coche al taller.   *"I have to take my car to the mechanic's."*

Hay que is not conjugated. It expresses a general obligation, not a personal one. Sometimes the English passive voice best translates **hay que hacer algo**.

—**Hay que trabajar** mucho hoy.   *"We have / One has to work hard today."*
—Sí, **hay que terminarlo** todo.   *"Yes, everything has to be finished."*

Verb + Preposition + Noun

Many of the verbs listed above take the same preposition before a noun that they require before an infinitive complement.

Ella **se dedica a enseñar**.   *She devotes herself to teaching.*
Ella **se dedica a su familia**.   *She devotes herself to her family.*

Cuento con recibir tu apoyo.   *I'm counting on receiving your support.*
Cuento con tu apoyo.   *I'm counting on your support.*

Votaron por presentar la moción.   *They voted to table the motion.*
Votaron por el otro partido.   *They voted for the other party.*

Se interesa en diseñar.   *He's interested in designing.*
Se interesa en el diseño gráfico.   *He's interested in graphic design.*

Me harto de oírla quejándose.   *I get fed up with hearing her complain.*
Me harto de sus quejas.   *I get fed up with her complaints.*

SPANISH VERBS CORRESPONDING TO ENGLISH ADVERBS

English speakers should remember to use **acabar de hacer algo** *to have just done something* and **volver a hacer algo** *to do something again*. These constructions in Spanish are very different from their English equivalents. There is another construction where the equivalent of an English adverb is a verb in Spanish (see p. 252).

seguir trabajando *to still be working*
seguir enfermo *to still be sick*

D *Complete each sentence with the correct connector. Choose* **a**, **de**, **en**, **con**, **por**, *or* **que**.

1. Emilia acaba _____ graduarse en el instituto de arte culinario.

2. Cuento _____ verlos en la reunión.

3. Hay _____ almacenar los datos.

4. Vuelvo _____ enviar el mensaje electrónico.

5. Samuel insiste _____ dejar la propina.

6. Salgo _____ jugar tenis.

7. Quedan _____ reunirse en el cibercafé.

8. Comienza _____ llover.

9. Victoria sueña _____ realizar sus ambiciones.

10. Terminan _____ hacer un curso a distancia.

11. Tienen _____ ir al supermercado.

12. Gabriel no deja _____ decir tonterías.

13. ¿Te ayudamos _____ subir los paquetes?

14. El proyecto me va _____ quitar mucho tiempo.

15. ¿Vaciláis _____ comprar la casa por el precio?

16. Le enseñan _____ programar.

17. El puesto consiste _____ hacer investigaciones.

18. ¿Por qué tardan _____ regresar del aeropuerto?

19. Magdalena se esfuerza _____ triunfar en la vida.

20. Ellos se encargan _____ la campaña publicitaria.

21. Votan _____ suspender (*adjourn*) la reunión.

22. Se arrepiente _____ portarse tan mal.

E *Complete each sentence with the correct connector in those sentences that require them. If none is needed in a sentence, write an X in the blank.*

1. Quiero _____ darles la bienvenida.

2. Consienten _____ compartir los gastos.

3. Ricardo puede _____ ganar una beca.

4. ¿Aprendes _____ esquiar?

5. Dudamos _____ ponernos en contacto con ellos.

6. Suelo _____ leer las novelas policíacas.

7. ¿Qué tratáis _____ hacer?

8. Sé _____ patinar sobre hielo.

9. Susana empieza _____ estudiar contabilidad.

10. Esperan _____ terminar su maestría este año.

11. ¿Adónde piensas _____ viajar este verano?

12. El jefe amenaza _____ despedirlo.

13. Opta _____ quedarse unos días más.

14. Se empeña _____ tener una firma exitosa.

15. Se avergüenzan _____ contar chismes.

16. Nos acostumbramos _____ vivir en un rancho.

17. Teme _____ subir en el ascensor de la torre.

18. El avión demora _____ despegar.

19. Ese tipo se jacta _____ ser más inteligente que nadie.

20. Al llegar a la oficina me pongo _____ trabajar.

F **Translation.** *Express the following sentences in Spanish.*

1. *There's a cell phone on the table.*

   _____

2. *It is necessary to know English in the world market.*

   _____

3. *They've just gone out to have dinner.*

   _____

4. *Sergio is calling again.*

   _____

5. *Are you (Ud.) beginning to write the report?*

   _____

6. *I don't know the new (male) programmer.*

   _____

7. *Do they know her telephone number?*

   _____

8. *I know how to download the files.*

   _____

9. *We agree to go by car.*

   _____

10. *Ana is counting on seeing Federico at the party.*

    _____

11. *You (tú) are striving to be successful in life.*

    _____

12. *I'm glad to see them.*

    _____

Ser and Estar

Spanish has two verbs that mean *to be*, **ser** and **estar**. Both are irregular.

ser *to be*		**estar** *to be*	
soy	somos	estoy	estamos
eres	sois	estás	estáis
es	son	está	están

Note that the forms of **estar** are all stressed on the endings. The **vosotros** form of **ser**, **sois**, has no accent mark. Compare **vais** (**ir**), **dais** (**dar**), and **veis** (**ver**).

Although **ser** and **estar** both mean *to be* in English, they are not interchangeable. In most cases, the choice between **ser** and **estar** depends on structural factors.

Uses of **ser**

Ser is used to connect nouns and/or pronouns.

Álvaro Domínguez **es** profesor de informática.	*Álvaro Domínguez is a professor of computer science.*
El culpable **es** él.	*He is the guilty one (party).*
Es un edificio muy moderno.	*It's a very modern building.*
Uds. **son** los responsables del lío.	*You are the ones responsible for the mess.*
Tú **eres** el siguiente.	*You're next / the next one.*
Las víctimas **somos** nosotros.	*We're the victims.*

When the predicate of **ser** is plural, **son** is used even when the subject is singular.

El mayor problema **son** <u>los gastos.</u>	*The biggest problem is the expenses.*
Lo importante **son** <u>nuestros planes.</u>	*The important thing is our plans.*
Su felicidad **son** <u>sus hijos.</u>	*Her happiness is her children.*
Nuestro equipo favorito **son** <u>los Medias Rojas.</u>	*Our favorite team is the Red Sox.*

Ser is used with subject pronouns to express *It's me*, etc.

Soy yo.	*It's I.* (colloquial, *It's me.*)
Eres tú.	*It's you.*
Es él/ella/Ud.	*It's he/she/you.* (colloquial, *It's him/her.*)
Somos nosotros/nosotras.	*It's we.* (colloquial, *It's us.*)
Sois vosotros/vosotras.	*It's you.*
Son ellos/ellas/Uds.	*It's they/you.* (colloquial, *It's them.*)

speaker sees as resulting from a change, or conveys the idea that the adjective expresses the speaker's subjective impression.

Compare the following uses of **ser** and **estar**.

Pedro Gómez tiene 90 años. **Es viejo.**	*Pedro Gómez is 90. He's old.*
María ha trabajado duro y ha criado ocho hijos. Ahora, a los 42 años, **está vieja.**	*María has worked hard and raised eight children. Now, at 42, she is/looks/seems/ acts old.*
Laura **es guapa.**	*Laura is good looking. (= is a good-looking girl)*
Marisa tiene un nuevo peinado. ¡Qué **guapa está!**	*Marisa has a new hairdo. How nice she looks!*
El yogur **es bueno** para la salud.	*Yogurt is good for your health.*
Este yogur **está malo.**	*This yogurt is spoiled.*
Luis Mario **es nervioso.**	*Luis Mario is a nervous person.*
Estamos nerviosos porque hoy hay examen.	*We're nervous because there's a test today.*

Only **estar** can be used with the adjective **contento** *happy, glad, satisfied*. **Ser** is used with **feliz** *happy*, although in Spanish America **estar** is common with **feliz** as well. Both **ser** and **estar** occur with **alegre**, though with a slight difference in meaning.

Paula **es alegre.**	*Paula is a cheerful person.*
Veo que **estás** muy **alegre** hoy.	*I see you're very cheerful today.*

Estar can be used before certain adverbs to express conditions of health or well-being.

Estoy bien.	*I'm feeling fine.*
Estás mal.	*You're feeling ill.*
Estamos perfectamente.	*We're doing fine. / We feel terrific.*
En este momento **están muy mal.**	*At this time they're not doing well.*

Estar is used to answer the question **¿Cómo estás/está/estáis/están?** *How are you?*

—¿Cómo está Ud. hoy?	*"How are you today?"*
—Estoy regular. Estoy un poco acatarrado.	*"I'm so-so. I have a slight cold."*

Adjectives and Expressions with ser and estar

Some adjectives have different English translations depending on whether they are used with **ser** or **estar**.

ser aburrido *to be boring*	**estar aburrido** *to be bored*
ser bueno *to be good*	**estar bueno** *to be tasty; to be funny* (of a joke)
ser interesado *to be self-interested*	**estar interesado** *to be interested*
ser listo *to be sharp/clever*	**estar listo** *to be ready*
ser malo *to be bad*	**estar malo** *to be sick*
ser preocupado *to be caring*	**estar preocupado** *to be worried*
ser rico *to be rich*	**estar rico** *to be delicious*
ser verde *to be green; to be risqué*	**estar verde** *to be unripe*
ser vivo *to be sharp/clever/shrewd*	**estar vivo** *to be alive*

Both **ser** and **estar** are used as auxiliary verbs. **Ser** is used to form the passive voice (see Chapter 15), and **estar** is used to form the progressive tenses (see Chapter 14).

Some common expressions with ser

¿De qué color es?	*What color is it?*
¿De qué es la camiseta?	*What is the T-shirt made of?*
¿De quién es la mochila?	*Whose backpack is it?*
¿Para quién es la carta?	*Whom is the letter for?*
Si no fuera por ti,…	*If it weren't for you, . . .*
Érase una vez…	*Once upon a time . . .*
¿Cuál es su nacionalidad?	*What is your nationality?*
¿Cuál es su profesión?	*What is your profession?*
¿De dónde eres?	*Where are you from?*
¿De qué origen es Ud.?	*What is your origin/background?*
¿Cuál es su fecha de nacimiento?	*What is your date of birth?*

Some common expressions with estar

estar de vacaciones	*to be on vacation*
estar reunido	*to be at a meeting*
estar de acuerdo con	*to agree with*
estar comprometido para hacer algo	*to be obliged to do something*
Maya está prometida con Octavio.	*Maya is engaged to Octavio.*
Los prometidos están enamorados.	*The fiancés (engaged couple) are in love.*
Estamos en primavera/verano/otoño/ invierno.	*It's spring/summer/fall/winter.*
estar hecho una sopa	*to be soaked through and through*
estar en la luna	*to be out of it, have one's head in the clouds*
No estoy para quejas.	*I'm not in the mood for complaints.*
Chicos, ¡esténse quietos!	*Kids, don't move around so much! (Stay still!)*
—¿A cuánto está el peso hoy?	*"What's the exchange rate of the peso today?"*
—El peso está a cincuenta centavos de dólar.	*"The peso is at fifty cents to the dollar."*

LA LENGUA ESPAÑOLA   ser and estar

Spanish has two verbs for *to be* because it absorbed two different Latin verbs, **essere** *to be* and **stare** *to stand,* and distributed the functions of *to be* between them. These original meanings explain things such as the use of **ser** for essential, unchanging conditions and the use of **estar** for location. There are examples as early as the fourth century of **stare** encroaching upon the domain of **essere**, so the distribution of the meanings of *to be* between two verbs goes back to Late Latin. It is a feature Spanish shares with Portuguese and Italian, especially southern Italian dialects (although the distribution of functions varies).

A   *Complete each sentence with the correct form of the verb* **ser** *to describe these people.*

1. Ud. _____ honesto y responsable.

2. Mario y Virginia _____ arquitectos.

3. Yo _____ optimista.

4. Uds. _____ protestantes.

5. Nosotros _____ republicanos.

6. Guillermo _____ gracioso.

7. Tú _____ delgado y rubio.

8. Magdalena _____ encantadora.

9. Vosotros _____ artísticos.

10. Los jugadores de baloncesto _____ altísimos.

B   *Create sentences using the verb* **ser** *with the following strings of elements to tell the nationality and origin of these people.*

MODELO   Carlos / México / español
        Carlos es de México. Es de origen español.

1. yo / los Estados Unidos / inglés

2. Matías / Polonia / ruso

3. tú / España / italiano

4. nosotros / Taiwán / chino

5. Ud. / la India / hindú

6. Jacobo y Sara / Israel / turco

7. Uds. / Vietnám / tailandés

8. vosotros / Australia / coreano

9. María Luisa / Chile / alemán

    _____

10. los Madero / Francia / kosovano

    _____

C *Complete each sentence with the correct form of the verb* **estar** *to tell where these people are.*

1. Tú _____ en el centro comercial.

2. Álvaro _____ en el gimnasio.

3. Los usuarios _____ en línea.

4. Yo _____ en Chicago.

5. Uds. _____ en un cibercafé.

6. Nosotros _____ en el aeropuerto.

7. El profesor Pastor _____ en el laboratorio.

8. Carolina y Daniel _____ en Escocia.

9. Vosotras _____ en la peluquería.

10. Ud. _____ en la facultad de ciencias políticas.

D *Create sentences using the verb* **estar** *with the following strings of elements to tell where these places and things are.*

MODELO   el restaurante japonés / lejos de aquí

       El restaurante japonés está lejos de aquí.

1. los grandes almacenes / a la vuelta de la esquina

    _____

2. el club de jazz / por esta avenida

    _____

3. el parqueo / detrás del teatro

    _____

4. los hoteles más lujosos / en frente del jardín público

    _____

5. la piscina del condominio de tiempo compartido (*time share*) / en el patio

    _____

6. la estación de tren / en la zona oeste de la ciudad

    _____

7. los sillones / delante de la ventana

_____

8. los dormitorios / en el segundo piso

_____

9. la librería técnica / a dos cuadras de aquí

_____

10. los monumentos históricos / en la ciudad vieja

_____

11. la tienda de videos / al lado de una pizzería

_____

12. los centros comerciales / en las afueras

_____

E *Complete each sentence with the correct form of either* **ser** *or* **estar**.

1. Isabel _____ de Inglaterra.

2. Todos nosotros _____ perfectamente.

3. El quemador de CD _____ mío.

4. Los muebles de patio _____ de madera y plástico.

5. Los directores _____ reunidos en la sala de conferencias.

6. Cristóbal _____ emprendedor e inteligente.

7. Ud. _____ comprometido para entregar el informe.

8. Los pantalones grises _____ de lana.

9. Yo no _____ de acuerdo con su estrategia.

10. ¡Vosotros _____ hechos una sopa!

11. Nosotros _____ de origen francés.

12. Yo _____ profesora de diseño gráfico.

13. ¿Tú _____ listo para salir?

14. Vosotros _____ los más aplicados.

15. Tú _____ de Santiago, ¿verdad?

16. Marisol _____ enamorada de Adán.

17. Todos nosotros _____ estadounidenses.

18. ¿A cuánto _____ el dólar hoy?

19. _____ las once y media.

20. La fiesta de cumpleaños va a _____ en la casa.

21. Ellos _____ republicanos.

22. Alejandro _____ gracioso y encantador.

23. ¿De quiénes _____ estas maletas?

24. Vais a _____ de vacaciones, ¿verdad?

25. Tú _____ muy contento.

26. ¿Uds. _____ acatarrados?

Yes/No Questions with **ser** or **estar** + Adjective

Statements that consist of a subject, **ser** or **estar**, and an adjective are usually made into *yes/no questions* by placing the subject at the end of the sentence, unlike English, which places it after the verb.

El condominio es caro.
¿Es caro el condominio?

The condominium is expensive.
Is the condominium expensive?

Estos consumidores son ahorrativos.
¿Son ahorrativos estos consumidores?

These consumers are thrifty.
Are these consumers thrifty?

Su hija es traviesa.
¿Es traviesa su hija?

Their daughter is mischievous.
Is their daughter mischievous?

Las tiendas están abiertas.
¿Están abiertas las tiendas?

The stores are open.
Are the stores open?

F Create statements using the correct form of **ser** or **estar** and the following strings of elements. Then create information questions that ask for that same information.

MODELO el traje / azul

El traje es azul.

¿De qué color es el traje?

1. yo / ingeniero genético

_____

_____

2. las siete y media de la mañana

_____

_____

3. el Cine Mediaplex / al lado de un bar

_____

_____

4. los mensajes electrónicos / para Eva

_____

_____

5. los aficionados de béisbol / entusiasmados y nerviosos

_____

_____

6. hoy / el veintitrés de junio

_____

_____

7. estas llaves de coche / de Marcelo

_____

_____

8. el euro / a noventa centavos de dólar

_____

_____

9. los gemelos de Hugo y Silvia / consentidos y malcriados

_____

_____

10. nosotros / de Canadá

_____

_____

G *Create statements using the correct form of* **ser** *or* **estar** *and the following strings of elements. Then create yes/no questions that ask for that same information.* **¡Ojo!** *Remember the differences between* **ser** *and* **estar**.

MODELO   la aspiradora / barata

   La aspiradora es barata.

   ¿Es barata la aspiradora?

1. el coche / descompuesto

_____

_____

2. su ropa / elegante

_____

_____

3. estos platos de comida fusión / ricos (*delicious*)

   _____

   _____

4. las clases de finanzas / fáciles

   _____

   _____

5. los analistas / superinteligentes

   _____

   _____

6. su nuevo abrigo / azul marino

   _____

   _____

7. el museo de arte / abierto

   _____

   _____

8. los mozos / ocupados

   _____

   _____

9. la chica / simpática

   _____

   _____

10. las tiendas / cerradas

    _____

    _____

11. aquellos hoteles / lujosos

    _____

    _____

12. los directores / reunidos

    _____

    _____

13. su buzón de correo electrónico / lleno

    _____

    _____

H *Translation.* *Express the following sentences in Spanish.* ¡**Ojo!** *Review the differences between* **ser** *and* **estar.**

1. *Esteban is a programmer.*

_____

2. *They're on vacation at this time.*

_____

3. *It's nine fifteen.*

_____

4. *The première (el estreno) of the film will be in New York.*

_____

5. *Alicia is worried and tired.*

_____

6. *The program is boring and the TV viewers (los televidentes) are bored.*

_____

7. *The most interesting part of the exhibit is the paintings.*

_____

8. *Julia is married to Miguel. Her sister is divorced.*

_____

9. *Are the windows broken?*

_____

10. *What are your (tú) neighbors like?*

_____

11. *How are you (Uds.)?*

_____

12. *They are of English descent.*

_____

13. *The peaches are not ripe yet.*

_____

14. *All these T-shirts are cotton.*

_____

15. *I'm from the Southwest.*

_____

BUILDING SENTENCES **Sentences with direct object pronouns**

First- and Second-person Object Pronouns

Direct object pronouns replace direct object nouns. In the first and second persons the direct object pronouns are as follows (the corresponding subject pronoun appears in parentheses).

me (yo)   **nos** (nosotros/nosotras)
te (tú)   **os** (vosotros/vosotras)

In Spanish, direct object pronouns are placed before the conjugated verb.

—¿Cuándo **me** llamas?   *"When will you call me?"*
—**Te** llamo mañana, sin falta.   *"I'll call you tomorrow without fail."*

—¿**Nos** necesitan Uds.?   *"Do you need us?"*
—Sí, Uds. siempre **nos** ayudan mucho.   *"Yes, you always help us a lot."*

In verb + infinitive constructions, direct object pronouns may either precede the first verb or follow the infinitive. When they follow the infinitive, they are attached to it in writing.

—¿**Me quieres** ayudar?   *"Do you want to help me?"*
—Sí, quiero, pero no sé si puedo   *"Yes, I do, but I don't know if I can help*
  ayudarte.   *you."*

—Uds. **nos deben** visitar.   *"You should visit us."*
—¿Y cuándo piensan Uds. **invitarnos**?   *"And when do you plan to invite us?"*

In many verb + connector + infinitive constructions, direct object pronouns may either precede the first verb or follow the infinitive.

—Paso por tu casa. **Tengo que verte.**   *"I'm coming by your house. I have to see*
                                 you."
—¿A qué hora **me vienes a ver**?   *"What time are you coming to see me?"*

Third-person Object Pronouns

In the third person, the direct object pronouns are more complicated. Spanish third-person object pronouns refer to people and things, unlike English, where *him/her* are distinguished from *it*. Spanish pronouns reflect the gender and number of the nouns they replace and they refer to both people and things.

MASCULINE SINGULAR NOUNS	MASCULINE PLURAL NOUNS
lo	**los**

FEMININE SINGULAR NOUNS	FEMININE PLURAL NOUNS
la	**las**

—¿Conoces **el centro de la ciudad**?   *"Do you know the downtown area?"*
—No, no **lo** conozco.   *"No, I don't know it." (I haven't been*
                                 there.)

—¿Conoces **a Juan Meléndez**?	*"Do you know Juan Meléndez?"*
—No, no **lo** conozco.	*"No, I don't know **him**."*
—¿Buscas **la nueva revista**?	*"Are you looking for the new magazine?"*
—Sí, necesito ver**la**. (OR **la** necesito ver)	*"Yes, I need to see **it**."*
—¿Buscas **a la profesora Mora**?	*"Are you looking for Professor Mora?"*
—Sí, necesito ver**la**. (OR **la** necesito ver)	*"Yes, I need to see **her**."*
—¿Oyen Uds. **esos anuncios**?	*"Do you hear those announcements?"*
—No, no **los** oímos.	*"No, we don't hear **them**."*
—¿Oyen Uds. **a los niños**?	*"Do you hear the children?"*
—Sí, **los** oímos.	*"Yes, we hear **them**."*
—¿Adónde lleva Ud. **esas cajas**?	*"Where are you carrying those boxes to?"*
—**Las** llevo a la oficina.	*"I'm taking **them** to the office."*
—¿Adónde lleva Ud. **a esas programadoras**?	*"Where are you taking those programmers to?"*
—**Las** llevo a la oficina.	*"I'm taking **them** to the office."*

Third-person object pronouns, like first- and second-person object pronouns, precede the conjugated verb. In both the verb + infinitive and the verb + connector + infinitive constructions, they may either precede the first verb or follow the infinitive, in which case they are attached to it in writing.

¿Me prestas el periódico? **Lo** quiero leer. OR Quiero leer**lo**.	*Will you lend me the newspaper? I want to read it.*
Tengo que hablar con Felisa. **La** voy a llamar esta tarde. OR Voy a llamar**la** esta tarde.	*I have to talk with Felisa. I'm going to call her this afternoon.*

A direct object noun can be moved to the front of the sentence for emphasis or focus. When it is moved, the direct object pronoun must be used along with it. (See "Building Sentences: Word order in Spanish," p. 259.)

Veo a Pablo. No veo a Gloria.	*I see Pablo. I don't see Gloria.*
A Pablo lo veo, a Gloria, no.	*I see Pablo, but not Gloria.*
El pescado lo compro en la pescadería, pero **la carne la compro** en el supermercado.	*I buy fish in the fish store, but I buy meat in the supermarket.*

The Neuter Pronoun lo

The object pronoun **lo** can also serve as a neuter pronoun. It can replace sentences and clauses.

—¿Sabes dónde trabaja Luis Pedro?	*"Do you know where Luis Pedro works?"*
—No, no **lo** sé. (**lo** = dónde trabaja Luis Pedro)	*"No, I don't."*

The neuter pronoun **lo** is mandatory with **ser** and **estar** to replace predicate nouns and adjectives. It does *not* vary for gender and number.

—¿Luisa es una buena estudiante?   *"Is Luisa a good student?"*
—Sí, **lo** es.   *"Yes, she is."*

—¿Esos hombres son astronautas?   *"Are those men astronauts?"*
—Sí, **lo** son.   *"Yes, they are."*

—¿Los chicos están emocionados?   *"Are the kids excited?"*
—Sí, **lo** están.   *"Yes, they are."*

In central Spain, the object pronoun **le** (an indirect object pronoun; see p. 104) replaces **lo** as the direct object of a verb when referring to a person. Thus, the examples given on pp. 82–83 would appear as follows.

—¿Conoces **el centro de la ciudad**?   *"Do you know the downtown area?"*
—No, no **lo** conozco.   *"No, I don't know **it**." (I haven't been there.)*

—¿Conoces **a Juan Meléndez**?   *"Do you know Juan Meléndez?"*
—No, no **le** conozco.   *"No, I don't know **him**."*

In contemporary usage, however, **lo** seems to be encroaching on this use of **le**.

I *Answer the following questions in the affirmative, changing direct object nouns to pronouns in your responses.*

MODELO   ¿Pagas las cuentas? ___Sí, las pago._____

1. ¿Ud. usa anteojos? _____

2. ¿Haces la compra? _____

3. ¿Tere toma cursos de tecnología informacional? _____

4. Paco y Tito reparan sus bicicletas? _____

5. ¿Los navegantes leen estas revistas electrónicas? _____

6. ¿Entráis los datos? _____

7. ¿Uds. conocen al nuevo empleado? _____

8. ¿Ud. aprovecha esta ocasión (*opportunity*)? _____

9. ¿Agustín busca su gorro? _____

10. ¿Los invitados felicitan a la cumpleañera? _____

11. ¿Esperas a las dentistas? _____

12. ¿Traéis el vino? _____

13. ¿Ellos imprimen los papeles? _____

14. ¿Oyes a los cantantes? _____

15. ¿Conduces la furgoneta (*van*)? _____

J *Rewrite each sentence, changing the direct object nouns to pronouns. Write each sentence in two ways, according to the model.*

MODELO   El pintor empieza a pintar la naturaleza muerta (*still life*).

El pintor empieza a pintarla.

El pintor la empieza a pintar.

1. Quiero comprar el coche todo terreno (*SUV*).

   _____

   _____

2. ¿Acabas de grabar la telenovela?

   _____

   _____

3. Vamos a analizar los problemas.

   _____

   _____

4. Ud. debe conocer a la directora de la empresa.

   _____

   _____

5. ¿Comienzas a comprender mis ideas?

   _____

   _____

6. Los aficionados piensan ver el partido de los Patriotas.

   _____

   _____

7. Los usuarios no saben utilizar las herramientas.

   _____

   _____

8. Ramón corre a buscar a los policías.

   _____

   _____

9. Aprendo a tocar el piano.

   _____

   _____

10. Tratamos de ganar la beca.

_____

_____

K **Translation.** *Express the following sentences in Spanish.*

1. *Are you (tú) ordering the meat dish as usual?*

_____

2. *Yes, if I find it on the menu.*

_____

3. *Are you (tú) going to wait for me?*

_____

4. *Yes, I'll see you after the lecture.*

_____

5. *Do you (Uds.) want to listen to these songs?*

_____

6. *No, we've just listened to them.*

_____

7. *Is Cristina the best dancer?*

_____

8. *Yes, she is.*

_____

9. *Where are you (Ud.) taking the (male and female) consultants?*

_____

10. *I'm taking them to meet the (female) boss.*

_____

11. *I see Mauricio over there. Do you (tú) see him?*

_____

12. *I see Laura, but I don't see Mauricio.*

_____

The Preterit

The preterit tense in Spanish is used to express past actions that are seen as completed in the past or as having happened once.

Regular Verbs in the Preterit

The preterit tense of regular verbs has its own set of endings. All of these endings are stressed. Study the endings of the preterit tense of regular **-ar** verbs.

comprar *to buy*	
compré	compramos
compraste	comprasteis
compró	compraron

-Er and **-ir** verbs share the same set of endings in the preterit.

comer *to eat*	
comí	comimos
comiste	comisteis
comió	comieron

vivir *to live*	
viví	vivimos
viviste	vivisteis
vivió	vivieron

Note that the **nosotros** forms of **-ar** and **-ir** verbs are the same in the present and the preterit.

compramos (present OR preterit)	*we buy* OR *we bought*
Compramos un coche todo terreno.	*We're buying an SUV.*
Compramos un coche todo terreno el año pasado.	*We bought an SUV last year.*
vivimos (present OR preterit)	*we live* OR *we lived*
Vivimos en Boston.	*We live in Boston.*
Vivimos en Boston hasta el año pasado.	*We lived in Boston until last year.*

Context clarifies which one is meant. Compare English verbs such as *put, hit,* and *cut,* which have no past tense marker in certain persons.

> *Yesterday we put the car in the garage.*
> *We always put the car in the garage.*

> *I hit a home run in last night's game.*
> *I hit a home run in every game I play.*

> *They cut themselves shaving this morning.*
> *They cut themselves shaving every morning.*

The **nosotros** forms of **-er** verbs are distinct in the present and the preterit.

comemos (present)	*we eat*
comimos (preterit)	*we ate*
bebemos (present)	*we drink*
bebimos (preterit)	*we drank*

A *Identify the subject(s) of each verb in the preterit, and write the correct subject pronoun(s). Then write the infinitive of each verb on the line in parentheses.*

1. _____ vendió (_____)

2. _____ celebré (_____)

3. _____ imprimimos (_____)

4. _____ aprendieron (_____)

5. _____ patinó (_____)

6. _____ vivisteis (_____)

7. _____ corrimos (_____)

8. _____ ahorraron (_____)

9. _____ aprendí (_____)

10. _____ insististe (_____)

11. _____ bebisteis (_____)

12. _____ saludasteis (_____)

13. _____ compartió (_____)

14. _____ disfrutamos (_____)

15. _____ escribí (_____)

16. _____ hablaste (_____)

17. _____ rompiste (_____)

18. _____ transmitieron (_____)

19. _____ utilizó (_____)

20. _____ añadí (_____)

B *Practice the forms of the preterit of regular verbs by completing each sentence with the correct form of the verb in parentheses.*

1. (regresar)   Tú _____ lo antes posible.

2. (asistir)   Yo _____ al concierto de música contemporánea.

3. (correr)   Nosotros _____ a coger el tren.

4. (transmitir)   Los locutores _____ el reportaje del terremoto.

5. (aceptar)   Cristóbal _____ el puesto de gerente de ventas.

6. (recibir)   ¿Vosotros _____ los mensajes electrónicos?

7. (aprender)   Tú _____ japonés.

8. (discutir)   Mis colegas y yo _____ el asunto.

9. (toser)   Ud. _____ toda la noche sin parar.

10. (viajar)   Uds. _____ por el sudoeste del país.

11. (abrir)   Yo _____ una cuenta bancaria.

12. (tomar)   Verónica y Andrés _____ algo en el bar.

13. (vender)   ¿Uds. ya _____ su casa de campo?

14. (insistir)   Octavio _____ en participar en el equipo.

15. (alquilar)   Yo _____ unos videos.

16. (beber)   Los aficionados _____ cerveza durante el partido.

17. (romper)   Magda _____ con su novio.

18. (vivir)   Tú _____ en Santa Fe.

19. (comprar)   ¿Ud. _____ todo lo necesario?

20. (grabar)   Nosotros _____ el documental histórico.

21. (dibujar)   Vosotras _____ un hermoso paisaje.

22. (compartir)   Uds. _____ las ganancias.

23. (comer)   Ud. _____ como un rey.

24. (prender)   Daniel _____ la televisión.

Verbs with Stem Changes in the Preterit

Stem-changing -ar and -er verbs do not have any stem changes in the preterit because the stem is not stressed in any of the forms. Study the preterit of **pensar** *to think*.

pensar

pensé	pensamos
pensaste	pensasteis
pensó	pensaron

Compare the preterit of **pensar** with its present tense.

pienso	pensamos
piensas	pensasteis
piensa	piensan

Here is the preterit of **volver** *to return*.

volver

volví	volvimos
volviste	volvisteis
volvió	volvieron

Compare the preterit of **volver** with its present tense.

vuelvo	volvemos
vuelves	volvéis
vuelve	vuelven

NOTE

See Chapter 2 to review verbs that pattern like **pensar** and **volver**.

-**Ir** verbs having a stem change in the present tense *do* have stem changes in two forms of the preterit tense, the **él/ella/Ud.** form (third-person singular) and the **ellos/ellas/Uds.** form (third-person plural). The verbs **dormir** *to sleep* and **morir** *to die* change **o** to **u** in these forms.

dormir

			morir		
dormí	dormimos		morí	morimos	
dormiste	dormisteis		moriste	moristeis	
durmió	durmieron		murió	murieron	

Verbs having the stem changes **e > i** or **e > ie** in the present change **e** to **i** in the **él/ella/Ud.** form (third-person singular) and the **ellos/ellas/Uds.** form (third-person plural) of the preterit. Compare the present and preterit forms of **sentir** *to feel* and **pedir** *to ask for*.

sentir (present tense)		**sentir** (preterit tense)	
siento	sentimos	sentí	sentimos
sientes	sentisteis	sentiste	sentisteis
siente	sienten	sintió	sintieron

pedir (present tense)		**pedir** (preterit tense)	
pido	pedimos	pedí	pedimos
pides	pedís	pediste	pedisteis
pide	piden	pidió	pidieron

Note that these are some of the few stem changes in Spanish verbs that occur when the stem is *not* stressed.

Verbs conjugated like **sentir** in the present and preterit

advertir *to warn*	**hervir** *to boil*
convertir *to convert, change*	**mentir** *to lie (tell a falsehood)*
divertirse *to have a good time, have fun, enjoy oneself*	**preferir** *to prefer*
	referirse (a) *to refer (to)*

Verbs conjugated like **pedir** in the present and preterit

conseguir *to get, obtain*	**reír(se)** *to laugh*
derretirse *to melt*	**reñir**[1] *to quarrel, scold*
despedir *to fire*	**repetir** *to repeat*
despedirse (de) *to say good-bye (to)*	**seguir** *to follow*
gemir *to groan, moan*	**servir** *to serve*
impedir *to prevent*	**sonreír(se)** *to laugh*
medir *to measure*	**teñir**[1] *to dye*
perseguir *to pursue, chase, aim for, go after*	**vestir(se)** *to dress*
proseguir *to pursue, proceed, carry on with*	

C *Rewrite the verb in each sentence, changing it from present tense to preterit.*

1. Vuelven en el vuelo de las ocho.

   _____

2. Pienso visitarlos en Mallorca.

   _____

---

[1]**Reñir** and **teñir** differ from **pedir** in the third-person singular and plural. They have the expected **i** as the stem vowel, but they lose the **i** of the preterit endings **-ió, -ieron** in these forms: **riñó/riñeron, tiñó/tiñeron**. These verbs are also treated in the section on spelling changes below.

3. Nos divertimos mucho en la fiesta.

_____

4. Moisés pierde el tren.

_____

5. ¿Encuentras tu ordenador (*computer*, Spain) portátil?

_____

6. Ud. prueba la comida tailandesa.

_____

7. Uds. piden un préstamo.

_____

8. Servís unos platos muy sabrosos.

_____

9. Nieva mucho en esta región.

_____

10. Entiendo exactamente lo que pasó.

_____

11. Raquel se viste de buen gusto.

_____

12. Truena fuerte todo el día.

_____

13. Cierran las fronteras.

_____

14. No llueve mucho este año.

_____

15. Los padres riñen a su hijo malcriado.

_____

16. Medís la alfombra persiana.

_____

17. El joven se convierte en un hombre hecho y derecho (*a real man*).

_____

18. ¿Uds. siguen mis consejos?

_____

19. Ella no siente el calor.

_____

20. El hielo se derrite.

_____

21. El agua hierve.

_____

22. Prefieren usar la cámara digital mía.

_____

23. Ese chico nunca miente.

_____

24. El fuego de campamento muere.

_____

25. Patrocinamos la fiesta benéfica (*sponsor the fundraising party*).

_____

Verbs with Spelling Changes in the Preterit

Most verbs with spelling changes are regular in speech. The rules of Spanish spelling, however, cause changes in their written forms.

Spelling Changes with **c, g, z**

-**Ar** verbs whose stems end in **c**, **g**, and **z** have the following spelling changes in the **yo** form of the preterit.

c > qu
g > gu
z > c

Compare the spelling of some of these spelling change verbs in the **yo** form of the present and the preterit.

INFINITIVE	PRESENT TENSE	PRETERIT
buscar	bus**c**o	bus**qué**
sacar	sa**c**o	sa**qué**
llegar	lle**g**o	lle**gué**
pagar	pa**g**o	pa**gué**
comenzar	comien**z**o	comen**cé**
alcanzar	alcan**z**o	alcan**cé**

The reason for this change is that Spanish spells the sounds /k/, /g/, /s/ (spelled **z**) differently before **e** and **i**. Study the spelling of these sounds before the five vowels.

/k/	ca, **que**, **qui**, co, cu
/g/	ga, **gue**, **gui**, go, gu
/s/ (spelled **z**)	za, **ce**, **ci**, zo, zu

Verbs like **buscar**

acercarse *to approach*	**fabricar** *to make, manufacture*
aparcar *to park*	**identificar** *to identify*
arrancar *to pull/root out; to start up* (vehicle)	**indicar** *to indicate*
atacar *to attack*	**justificar** *to justify*
calificar *to grade, give a grade to*	**marcar** *to dial; to mark*
chocar *to crash, collide with*	**mascar** *to chew*
colocar *to put, place*	**masticar** *to chew*
criticar *to criticize*	**pescar** *to fish*
dedicar *to devote*	**practicar** *to practice*
desbancar *to supplant, replace*	**publicar** *to publish*
educar *to educate, bring up, rear, train*	**roncar** *to snore*
embarcarse *to embark, go on board*	**sacar** *to take out*
equivocarse *to be mistaken*	**secar** *to dry*
explicar *to explain*	**tocar** *to touch; to play* (a musical instrument)
	volcar (o > ue) *to tip, knock over, upset*

Verbs like **llegar**

agregar *to add*	**investigar** *to investigate*
ahogarse *to drown*	**jugar (u > ue)** *to play* (a sport)
apagar *to put out, extinguish*	**juzgar** *to judge*
cargar *to load*	**madrugar** *to get up early*
castigar *to punish*	**navegar** *to navigate; to surf* (the Web)
colgar (o > ue) *to hang*	**negar (e > ie)** *to deny*
conjugar *to conjugate*	**pagar** *to pay*
despegar *to take off* (airplane)	**pegar** *to stick; to beat*
encargar *to put in charge, entrust; to order*	**regar (e > ie)** *to water*
	rogar (o > ue) *to beg, ask*
entregar *to hand in/over*	**tragar** *to swallow*
fregar (e > ie) *to scrub, rub*	**vengar** *to avenge*
interrogar *to question, interrogate*	

Verbs like **comenzar**

abrazar *to hug, embrace*	**empezar (e > ie)** *to begin*
actualizar *to bring up to date*	**enlazar** *to tie together, link; to embrace*
adelgazar *to get thin*	**gozar** *to enjoy*
alcanzar *to reach, overtake*	**hipnotizar** *to hypnotize*
almorzar (o > ue) *to have lunch*	**lanzar** *to throw*
alzar *to raise*	**organizar** *to organize*
amenazar *to threaten*	**popularizar** *to popularize*
analizar *to analyze*	**realizar** *to fulfill*
aplazar *to postpone*	**rechazar** *to reject*
bautizar *to baptize*	**rezar** *to pray*
bostezar *to yawn*	**tranquilizarse** *to calm down*
cruzar *to cross*	**trazar** *to draw, sketch, outline, trace*
deslizarse *to slip*	**tropezar (e > ie)** *to trip, stumble*
destrozar *to destroy, ruin*	

D *Answer the questions, using the* **yo** *form of the preterit. Change direct object nouns to pronouns in your responses.* **¡Ojo!** *Be sure to write the correct spelling changes.*

MODELO ¿Vas a pagar la cuenta? *Ya la pagué.*

1. ¿Vas a marcar el número de teléfono? _____

2. ¿Quieres jugar al béisbol? _____

3. ¿Tiene ganas de almorzar? _____

4. ¿Piensa navegar en la Red? _____

5. ¿Puede aparcar el carro? _____

6. ¿Piensas aplazar la reunión? _____

7. ¿Debe conjugar los verbos en pretérito? _____

8. ¿No quieres explicar tu idea? _____

9. ¿Esperas realizar tu proyecto? _____

10. ¿Procuras entregar la tesis? _____

11. ¿Esperas adelgazar? _____

12. ¿Te animan a tocar el piano? _____

13. ¿Va a practicar el español? _____

14. ¿No debes fregar las cacerolas? _____

15. ¿Va a actualizar los datos? _____

16. ¿Piensa organizar los papeles? _____

17. ¿Quiere colgar los cuadros? _____

18. ¿Va a agregar cilantro (*coriander*) a la carne? _____

19. ¿Puedes arrancar la mala hierba (*weeds*)? _____

20. ¿No tienes que apagar las luces? _____

An **-ir** verb whose stem ends in **ñ** drops the **i** of the third-person preterit endings **-ió** and **-ieron**.

INFINITIVE	THIRD-PERSON SINGULAR PRETERIT	THIRD-PERSON PLURAL PRETERIT
gruñir *to grunt, growl*	gruñó	gruñeron
heñir *to knead*	hiñó	hiñeron
reñir *to quarrel*	riñó	riñeron
teñir *to dye*	tiñó	tiñeron

Note that **heñir, reñir,** and **teñir** are stem-changing verbs (**e > i**).

Spelling Changes in -er and -ir Verbs
Whose Stems End in a Vowel

These verbs change the **i** of the third-person preterit endings **-ió** and **-ieron** to **y**. This is not just a spelling convention: The **y** is actually pronounced in these forms. All of the remaining persons have a written accent on the **i** of the preterit ending, not just the **yo** form.

leer *to read*		**oír** *to hear*	
leí	leímos	oí	oímos
leíste	leísteis	oíste	oísteis
leyó	leyeron	oyó	oyeron

Verbs like **leer** and **oír**

caer *to fall*
creer *to believe, think*
poseer *to have, possess*

Verbs ending in **-uir** also change **i** to **y** in the third-person preterit endings, but do not add a written accent on the **i** of the **tú**, **nosotros**, and **vosotros** forms of the preterit.

construir *to build*	
construí	construimos
construiste	construisteis
construyó	construyeron

Verbs like **construir**

atribuir *to attribute, credit*	**incluir** *to include*
concluir *to conclude*	**instruir** *to educate, teach, instruct, train*
contribuir *to contribute*	**intuir** *to have a sense of, feel*
destruir *to destroy*	**obstruir** *to obstruct, hinder, impede*
disminuir *to diminish*	**reconstruir** *to rebuild*
distribuir *to distribute*	**sustituir** *to substitute*
huir *to flee*	

For verbs ending in **-guir**, such as **seguir** and **distinguir**, the **u** is not a pronounced vowel but merely a spelling feature. Such verbs are not conjugated like **construir** in the preterit.

seguir *to follow*		**distinguir** *to distinguish*	
seguí	seguimos	distinguí	distinguimos
seguiste	seguisteis	distinguiste	distinguisteis
siguió	**siguieron**	**distinguió**	**distinguieron**

E *Create sentences from the following strings of elements.* ¡**Ojo!** *Be sure to write spelling changes.*

MODELO   el perro / gruñir   *El perro gruñó.*

1. los muchachos / teñir / las camisetas de rojo

   _____

2. la guerra / destruir / el país

   _____

3. los consumidores / no distinguir / entre los dos productos

   _____

4. Ana / conseguir / la maestría en salud pública

   _____

5. unas empresas / reconstruir / los barrios bajos

   _____

6. ¿Ud. / oír / la noticia?

   _____

7. el soldado / caer / en la batalla

   _____

8. los usuarios / leer / las páginas Web

   _____

9. los habitantes oprimidos / huir / de la dictadura

   _____

10. ¿por qué / (Uds.) reñir / todo el día?

    _____

11. Uds. / seguir / por la autopista

    _____

12. los hombres de negocios / concluir / la negociación del contrato

    _____

13. la pastelera / heñir / la masa (*dough*)

    _____

14. todo el mundo / creer / sus relatos

    _____

Irregular Preterits

Irregular preterits in Spanish have two features: an irregular stem and a special set of endings. The endings for these verbs are **-e, -iste, -o, -imos, -isteis, -ieron**. Note that the **yo** and **él** forms are stressed on the stem, not on the ending.

Some of these irregular preterits have stems with the vowel **i**.

decir *to say, tell*		**hacer** *to do, make*	
dije	dijimos	hice	hicimos
dijiste	dijisteis	hiciste	hicisteis
dijo	dijeron	hizo	hicieron

querer *to want*		**venir** *to come*	
quise	quisimos	vine	vinimos
quisiste	quisisteis	viniste	vinisteis
quiso	quisieron	vino	vinieron

NOTES

There are two important irregularities in the verbs above.

1 · The **él/ella/Ud.** form of **hacer** is spelled with a **z**, not a **c** as in the other forms.

2 · The **ellos/ellas/Uds.** form of **decir** loses the **i** of the **-ieron** ending.

Other irregular preterits have stems with the vowel **u**.

andar *to walk, go*		**caber** *to fit*	
anduve	anduvimos	cupe	cupimos
anduviste	anduvisteis	cupiste	cupisteis
anduvo	anduvieron	cupo	cupieron

estar *to be*		**poder** *to be able to, can*	
estuve	estuvimos	pude	pudimos
estuviste	estuvisteis	pudiste	pudisteis
estuvo	estuvieron	pudo	pudieron

poner *to put*		**saber** *to know*	
puse	pusimos	supe	supimos
pusiste	pusisteis	supiste	supisteis
puso	pusieron	supo	supieron

tener *to have*	
tuve	tuvimos
tuviste	tuvisteis
tuvo	tuvieron

All verbs ending in **-ducir** have a preterit stem with the vowel **u**.

producir *to produce*	
produje	produjimos
produjiste	produjisteis
produjo	produjeron

The verb **traer** has **a** in the stem of the preterit.

traer *to bring*	
traje	trajimos
trajiste	trajisteis
trajo	trajeron

NOTES

1 · All preterit stems ending in **j** lose the **i** of the **-ieron** ending, as you saw in the preterit of the verb **decir: dijeron**.

2 · The verbs **conducir** *to drive* and **traducir** *to translate* are conjugated in the preterit like **producir**.

3 · Compounds of the verbs above show the same irregular stems in the preterit.

hacer

> **rehacer** *to do over, do again*: **rehice**
> **satisfacer** *to satisfy*: **satisfice**

poner

> **componer** *to fix, compose*: **compuse**
> **proponer** *to propose*: **propuse**

tener

> **detener** *to stop*: **detuve**
> **mantener** *to keep, support*: **mantuve**
> **sostener** *to support*: **sostuve**

traer

> **atraer** *to attract*: **atraje**
> **distraer** *to distract*: **distraje**

venir

> **convenir** *to be suitable*: **convine**
> **intervenir** *to intervene*: **intervine**
> **prevenir** *to notify, warn*: **previne**

4 · The preterit of **hay** is **hubo**.

There are several other irregular verbs in the preterit.

Dar takes the endings of regular **-er** and **-ir** verbs in the preterit.

dar *to give*	
di	dimos
diste	disteis
dio	dieron

Ser and **ir** have the same conjugation in the preterit. Context clarifies whether *to be* or *to go* is meant.

ser *to be* / **ir** *to go*	
fui	fuimos
fuiste	fuisteis
fue	fueron

Ver is regular in the preterit, but the **yo** and **él/ella/Ud.** forms are written without accent marks. Note that the **yo** and **él/ella/Ud.** forms of **ser/ir** and **dar** are also written without accent marks: **fui, fue, di, dio.** This is because they are forms of one syllable.

ver *to see*	
vi	vimos
viste	visteis
vio	vieron

F   *Identify the subject(s) of each verb in the preterit, and write the correct subject pronoun(s). Then write the infinitive of each verb on the line in parentheses.*

1. _____ hizo (_____)

2. _____ pudieron (_____)

3. _____ fue (_____)

4. _____ dijiste (_____)

5. _____ estuve (_____)

6. _____ supimos (_____)

7. _____ produjeron (_____)

8. _____ vi (_____)

9. _____ anduvisteis (_____)

10. _____ vine (_____)

11. _____ quisimos (_____)

12. _____ fui (_____)

13. _____ tuviste (_____)

14. _____ cupieron (_____)

15. _____ trajo (_____)

16. _____ di (_____)

G *Rewrite each sentence, changing the verb from present tense to preterit.*

MODELO Andan muy de prisa.
_Anduvieron muy de prisa._____

1. Pones fin a la discusión.

_____

2. Tienen mucho éxito con su compañía.

_____

3. Hago clic al botón.

_____

4. ¿Ud. viene en taxi?

_____

5. No decimos nada.

_____

6. ¿Cómo lo sabes?

_____

7. No puedo entender su actitud.

_____

8. Queremos salir a comer.

_____

9. Nos traen unos regalos.

_____

10. Soy la directora del equipo.

_____

11. Ve a Verónica en el cibercafé.

_____

12. Hay grandes ofertas en las tiendas.

_____

13. El compositor compone una canción.

_____

14. Me dan las gracias.

_____

15. Voy de compras.

_____

16. ¿Por qué intervienen en el conflicto?

_____

17. Conduzco a setenta millas por hora.

_____

18. ¿Qué les atrae?

_____

19. Traducimos los documentos al inglés.

_____

20. No cabe nadie más en el aula.

_____

Some Important Uses of the Preterit

■ The preterit is used to show that an event was completed in the past or that it happened once in the past.

Carla **salió** a las ocho.	*Carla left at eight.*
El mecánico **reparó** el coche.	*The mechanic repaired the car.*
Yo **terminé** mi trabajo.	*I finished my work.*
¿**Viste** la película?	*Did you see the movie?*

■ A series of preterits tells the events of a story.

Salí a comprar comida, **regresé** a casa, **preparé** la cena, **puse** la mesa, **comí**, **lavé** los platos y luego **fui** a casa de mi amigo para ver el partido de fútbol americano.	*I went out to buy food, came back home, prepared dinner, set the table, ate, washed the dishes, and then went to my friend's house to see the football game.*

■ Some verbs take on a different meaning when they are used in the preterit. The distinction in meaning will be especially important when you study the difference between the preterit tense and the imperfect tense, which are two aspects of (or ways of looking at) past time. When the verbs listed below are used in the preterit, the focus is on the beginning or completion of an action. For example, **conocí** means *I began to know someone,* that is, *I met someone.*

VERB	SPANISH	ENGLISH
saber *to know*	Supe la fecha hoy.	*I found out the date today.*
conocer *to know*	Conocimos a Carmen ayer.	*We met Carmen yesterday.*
tener *to have*	Tuvo una idea.	*He got an idea.*
poder *to be able to, can*	No pudieron salir.	*They didn't (manage to) go out.*
querer *to want*	No quisiste trotar.	*You refused to jog.*

H *Translation.* *Express the following sentences in Spanish.*

1. *Who set the table?*

_____

2. *I set it.*

_____

3. *What did you (Ud.) do yesterday?*

_____

4. *I played tennis and then took a walk.*

_____

5. *Where did you (tú) go last night?*

_____

6. *I went to the movies.*

_____

7. *Did you (tú) see our friends?*

_____

8. *No, I arrived late and I couldn't (didn't manage to) find them.*

_____

9. *Do you (Ud.) know Susana's e-mail address?*

_____

10. *Yes, I found it out last week.*

_____

BUILDING SENTENCES	**Sentences with indirect objects**

Remember that inanimate direct objects in Spanish are linked to the verb without a preposition.

| —¿María trajo **las flores**? | *"Did Maria bring the flowers?"* |
| —Sí, compró **un ramillete de tulipanes**. | *"Yes, she bought a bouquet of tulips."* |

However, when the direct object is a specific person (or an individualized animal), then the direct object is connected to the verb by personal **a**.

—¿Conociste **a Elena Sánchez**?	*"Did you meet Elena Sánchez?"*
—No, pero conocí **a su prima Marcia**.	*"No, but I met her cousin Marcia."*
—¿Paseaste **al perro** hoy?	*"Did you walk the dog today?"*
—Sí, llevé **al perro** al parque.	*"Yes, I took the dog to the park."*

Indirect objects are usually animate nouns, not things. They are connected to the verb by the preposition **a**. Indirect object nouns are usually accompanied by the corresponding third-person indirect object pronoun (**le** for singular nouns and **les** for plural nouns).

—Juan siempre **les** escribe **a sus padres.**	*"Juan always writes to his parents."*
—¿De veras? Yo prefiero llamar **a mi familia.**	*"Really? I prefer to call my family."*

Note that both object nouns in the sentences above are connected to the verb by **a**. However, **sus padres** is an indirect object because of the obligatory presence of **les**. The noun **mi familia** is a direct object because **le** cannot be used with it.

We can represent the underlying structure of the verbs **escribir** and **llamar** as follows. The word **uno** in these formulas represents any animate noun.

> **escribirle a uno** *to write to someone*
> **llamar a uno** *to call someone*

The presence of **le** in the above formula **escribirle a uno** tells you that **escribir** takes an indirect object of the person. The absence of **le** in **llamar a uno** indicates that **llamar** takes a direct object. The **a** of the two patterns is different. In **escribirle a uno**, the **a** is a preposition, roughly the equivalent of English *to*. In **llamar a uno**, the **a** is the personal **a**, the marker of an animate direct object.

Most verbs that take an indirect object of the person (an animate indirect object) also take an inanimate direct object. The verb **escribir** can be used both with or without an inanimate direct object.

—¿**Le** escriben Uds. mucho **a Paula**?	*"Do you write to Paula a lot?"*
—Sí, **le** escribimos **muchos mensajes electrónicos.**	*"Yes, we write many e-mails to her."*
—¿Qué **les** trajeron sus amigos?	*"What did your friends bring you?"*
—**Nos** regalaron **flores** y **bombones.**	*"They gave us flowers and candy."*
—¿Raúl **le** explicó **el problema a Carlos**?	*"Did Raúl explain the problem to Carlos?"*
—Sí, pero no **le** dijo **la verdad.**	*"Yes, but he didn't tell him the truth."*
—¿**Te** sirvieron **pescado**?	*"Did they serve you fish?"*
—Sí, y **me** ofrecieron **un bistec** también.	*"Yes, and they offered me steak too."*

Here is a table of all of the Spanish indirect object pronouns.

me	nos
te	os
le	les

Common Verbs Used with an Indirect Object of the Person and an Inanimate Direct Object

contarle algo a uno *to relate/recount something to someone*
darle algo a uno *to give something to someone*
decirle algo a uno *to tell/say something to someone*
devolverle algo a uno *to return something to someone*

enseñarle algo a uno *to show something to someone*
entregarle algo a uno *to hand over something to someone*
enviarle algo a uno *to send something to someone*
escribirle algo a uno *to write something to someone*
explicarle algo a uno *to explain something to someone*
mandarle algo a uno *to send something to someone*
mostrarle algo a uno *to show something to someone*
ofrecerle algo a uno *to offer something to someone*
pedirle algo a uno *to ask someone for something*
recetarle algo a uno *to prescribe something for someone*
recordarle algo a uno *to remind someone of something*
regalarle algo a uno *to give something to someone as a gift*
servirle algo a uno *to serve something to someone*
traerle algo a uno *to bring something to someone*
venderle algo a uno *to sell something to someone*

The indirect object is the equivalent of English *from* with verbs that mean *to take away, steal, remove,* etc.

arrancarle algo a uno *to snatch/grab something from someone*
arrebatarle algo a uno *to snatch/grab something from someone*
comprarle algo a uno *to buy something from someone*
esconderle algo a uno *to hide something from someone*
exigirle algo a uno *to demand something of someone*
ganarle algo a uno *to win something from someone*
ocultarle algo a uno *to hide something from someone*
pedirle algo a uno *to ask something of someone*
pedirle prestado algo a uno *to borrow something from someone*
quitarle algo a uno *to take something away from someone*
robarle algo a uno *to steal something from someone*
sacarle algo a uno *to get something out of someone*
solicitarle algo a uno *to ask/request something of someone*
suspenderle algo a uno *to revoke/cancel something of someone's*

—**Al extranjero le** exigieron **los documentos.**	*"They demanded the foreigner's papers from him."*
—Sí, y **le** quitaron **el pasaporte.**	*"Yes, and they took away his passport."*
—¿Quién **le** compró **el coche a Mónica?**	*"Who bought Mónica's car from her?"*
—Pablo. **Le** pidió prestado **dinero a su padre.**	*"Pablo. He borrowed the money from his father."*

Verbs That Can Take Both **le** and **lo** with a Difference in Meaning

Some verbs are used with both **le** and **lo** as direct objects. There is usually a slight difference in meaning. **Le** usually refers to a person, **lo** to a thing. Usage of **le** as a direct object referring to people is not limited to Spain, but is found in Spanish America too.

Nadie **le cree** porque miente mucho.	*No one believes him because he lies a lot.*
Eso es un cuento. Yo no **lo creo.**	*That's gossip (a lie). I don't believe it.*

Al hijo menor **le llaman Benjamín**.   *They call the youngest son Benjamín.*
Siempre **lo llamo** los domingos.   *I always call him (phone him) on Sundays.*

Al asesino **le pegaron**.   *They beat the murderer.*
Encontré los sellos y **los pegué** en el   *I found the stamps and pasted them on*
   sobre.   *the envelope.*

I Using the following strings of elements, write sentences that have a preterit tense verb
and an indirect object pronoun.

MODELO   Pedro / traer / un disco compacto / a ella
         Pedro le trajo un disco compacto.

1. tú / mostrar / tu iPod / a tus colegas

   _____

2. Uds. / enviar / un e-mail / a mí

   _____

3. Carolina / pedir / un favor / a él

   _____

4. yo / explicar / el concepto / a Uds.

   _____

5. ellos / hacer / una buena comida / a vosotros

   _____

6. nosotros / decir / el motivo / a Ud.

   _____

7. Ud. / leer / las instrucciones / a ellos

   _____

8. vosotros / vender / el coche / a nosotros

   _____

9. Carlos Manuel / recordar / la fecha de la conferencia / a ti

   _____

10. yo / entregar / los papeles / a ellas

    _____

11. Juan e Isabel / esconder / los regalos de cumpleaños / a su hijo

    _____

12. tú / ocultar / tu desilusión (*disappointment*) / a todos

    _____

J *Using the following strings of elements, write sentences that have a preterit verb, an indirect object noun, and a corresponding indirect object pronoun.*

MODELO   yo / enseñar / los carteles / a mi compañero de cuarto
          Yo le enseñé los carteles a mi compañero de cuarto.

1. tú / escribir / unos mensajes electrónicos / a los directores

   _____

2. él / contar / el argumento (*plot*) de la película / a su amigo

   _____

3. Uds. / enviar / unos paquetes / a los soldados

   _____

4. nosotros / comprar / el quitanieves / al vecino

   _____

5. la anfitriona / servir / comida italiana / a los invitados

   _____

6. Ud. / devolver / la calculadora de bolsillo / a su amiga

   _____

7. los jefes / ofrecer / el puesto / al programador

   _____

8. nuestro equipo / ganar / el partido / al equipo suyo

   _____

9. la niña / quitar / los cubos (*blocks*) / a los otros niños

   _____

10. yo / mostrar / mis maletas / al guardia de seguridad

    _____

K *Translation. Express the following sentences in English.*

1. Busqué a los programadores por todas partes.

   _____

2. Los Medias Rojas les ganaron la Serie Mundial a los Cardenales.

   _____

3. Le devolvimos los videos al empleado de la tienda.

   _____

4. La madre les contó un cuento de hadas (*fairy tale*) a sus hijitos.

   _____

5. ¿Le enviaste un mensaje electrónico a Pedro o lo llamaste?

_____

6. Martita paseó a su perro en el parque. Allí un perro grande le quitó los juguetes a su perro.

_____

_____

L *Translation.* *Express the following sentences in Spanish.*

1. *I handed the report in to my boss.*

_____

2. *My boss requested the other report from me.*

_____

3. *Adrián asked Jaime to borrow the car.*

_____

4. *Jaime said yes to him.*

_____

5. *The thief stole the man's gold watch from him.*

_____

6. *The man grabbed the watch from the thief.*

_____

7. *We brought the children apples and grapes.*

_____

8. *They thanked us.*

_____

9. *Did you (tú) show your new dress to Claudia?*

_____

10. *Yes, and I showed the dress to my other friends too.*

_____

11. *The waitress served the (male) customer the chocolate cake.*

_____

12. *The customer asked the waitress for a fork.*

_____

The Imperfect;
The Imperfect vs. the Preterit

The Imperfect Tense

The imperfect tense is used to describe background actions or situations in the past rather than events. Its formation is simple. Only three verbs are irregular. The endings of the imperfect tense for **-ar** verbs have **-aba-** in all forms. The endings for **-er** and **-ir** verbs have **-ía-** in all forms.

hablar *to speak*

habl**aba**	habl**ábamos**
hablabas	hablabais
hablaba	hablaban

vender *to sell*

vend**ía**	vend**íamos**
vendías	vendíais
vendía	vendían

abrir *to open*

abr**ía**	abr**íamos**
abrías	abríais
abría	abrían

NOTES

1 · The first- and third-person singular forms are identical for all verbs in the imperfect: **hablaba, vendía, abría.**

2 · In the imperfect of **-ar** verbs, the **nosotros** form is the only one with a written accent.

3 · In the imperfect of **-er** and **-ir** verbs, all forms have a written accent over the **i.**

4 · The imperfect of **hay** is **había** (*there was, there were*).

The verbs **ser, ir,** and **ver** are irregular in the imperfect.

ser *to be*

era	éramos
eras	erais
era	eran

ir *to go*

iba	íbamos
ibas	ibais
iba	iban

ver *to see*

veía	veíamos
veías	veíais
veía	veían

A *Identify the subject(s) of the following verbs in the imperfect, and write the correct subject pronoun(s).*

1. _____ hablaba
2. _____ creían
3. _____ empezábamos
4. _____ asistía
5. _____ compraban
6. _____ compartíamos
7. _____ preparabais
8. _____ eras
9. _____ seguíais

10. _____ iba
11. _____ merendabas
12. _____ cosías
13. _____ veían
14. _____ prendía
15. _____ éramos
16. _____ estaban
17. _____ atravesábamos
18. _____ ibais

B *Complete each sentence with the correct imperfect tense form of the verb in parentheses.*

1. (trabajar) Marcos y Eduardo _____ en una tienda de deportes.
2. (leer) Nosotros _____ la enciclopedia en línea.
3. (vivir) Los Lapesa _____ en las afueras.
4. (correr) Yo _____ a coger el tren.
5. (jugar) Uds. _____ al golf los sábados.
6. (subir) Los precios no _____.
7. (estar) Nosotros _____ muy contentos.
8. (decir) ¿Vosotros les _____ algo?
9. (poner) Tú nos _____ al día.
10. (esperar) Yo los _____ en el aeropuerto.
11. (rodar) El director _____ un film en Las Vegas.
12. (tener) Ud. _____ razón.
13. (abrir) Yo _____ las cajas.
14. (hacer) Uds. _____ investigaciones.
15. (tomar) Vosotros _____ clases de cinematografía.
16. (ser) Yo _____ el líder del grupo.
17. (aprender) Alejandra _____ a patinar sobre ruedas.
18. (escribir) Tú les _____ mensajes electrónicos a tus amigos.
19. (hablar) Se _____ italiano en casa.
20. (preferir) Uds. _____ invitarnos personalmente.
21. (beber) Vosotras _____ jugo de naranja.

22. (salir)   Nosotros _____ a las ocho de la mañana.
23. (ir)   Yo _____ de vacaciones.
24. (ver)   ¿Uds. _____ televisión?
25. (nevar)   _____ toda la noche.
26. (funcionar) La lavadora y la secadora no _____ .

C *Rewrite each sentence, changing the verbs from present tense to imperfect.*

1. Quiero acompañarlos.

   _____

2. Envuelven los paquetes.

   _____

3. ¿Qué dicen Uds.?

   _____

4. Suele nevar en enero.

   _____

5. Te diviertes muchísimo.

   _____

6. Algo huele mal.

   _____

7. Pide los billetes electrónicos por computadora.

   _____

8. Vamos a caballo en la hacienda.

   _____

9. Comienza a estudiar.

   _____

10. Vuelven para las diez de la noche.

    _____

11. Les doy la bienvenida.

    _____

12. Se despiertan tarde los fines de semana.

    _____

13. ¿Sirves carne o pescado?

    _____

14. Sueñan con ser millonarios.

    _____

15. Finjo no entender el chiste.

   _____

16. Cuenta con el apoyo de su familia.

   _____

17. No pueden tranquilizarse.

   _____

18. No entiendo el por qué.

   _____

19. Son muy serios.

   _____

20. Uds. se visten muy bien.

   _____

21. Concluyen la presentación.

   _____

22. Tiene mucho interés en el proyecto.

   _____

Uses of the Imperfect

The imperfect tense is used to describe conditions existing in the past or past actions seen as backgrounds rather than events, actions that help set the scene. Therefore, the imperfect is usually used for descriptions in the past. Here are some specific examples of how the imperfect is used.

Time

The imperfect is used in clauses that tell the time at which something happened in the past. This includes not only clock time, but also time words such as **tarde** and **temprano**.

Ya **eran** las diez cuando nos fuimos.	*It was already ten o'clock when we left.*
Era tarde cuando volví.	*It was late when I came back.*
Ya **era** de noche cuando terminó la reunión.	*It was already night when the meeting ended.*

Weather

The imperfect is usually (but not always) used to describe weather conditions existing in the past.

Llovía cuando salimos.	*It was raining when we went out.*
No hacía mucho sol cuando trotaba por el parque.	*It wasn't very sunny as I was jogging through the park.*

D **Time and weather.** *Rewrite each sentence, changing background verbs from the present tense to the imperfect and verbs telling what happened to the preterit.*

MODELO   Es la una cuando regresan.
          Era la una cuando regresaron.

1. Son las diez y media cuando llego a la oficina.

    _____

2. Hace sol cuando comienza la comida campestre.

    _____

3. Cuando vienen es mediodía ya.

    _____

4. Nieva cuando salgo para la pista de esquí.

    _____

5. Son las siete treinta cuando despega el avión.

    _____

6. Truena y hay relámpagos cuando aterrizamos.

    _____

7. Es la madrugada cuando suena mi teléfono celular.

    _____

8. Llueve a cántaros (*cats and dogs*) cuando los novios van a la iglesia.

    _____

9. Hace muy buen tiempo cuando los recién casados salen de la iglesia.

    _____

10. Hay montones de nieve en el parque cuando saco a mi perro a retozar (*romp, jump around*).

    _____

    _____

11. Hay tormenta cuando le devuelven el coche de alquiler al agente.

    _____

12. Cuando los jóvenes se duermen es ya tardísimo.

    _____

13. Está nublado y hace viento cuando llegamos a la cumbre de la montaña.

    _____

14. Son las dos en punto cuando empieza la función de la tarde (*matinee*).

    _____

Conditions

The imperfect is used to describe conditions in the past.

No fue fácil regresar a casa porque todos los autobuses **estaban** atestados.	*It wasn't easy to return home, because all the buses were crowded.*
Comimos en casa porque la mayor parte de los restaurantes **estaban** cerrados ese día.	*We ate at home because most restaurants were closed that day.*
Mis maletas **pesaban** tanto que tuve que llamar al cargador.	*My suitcases weighed so much that I had to call the porter.*
En esa época **venían** muchos inmigrantes al país. **Buscaban** la oportunidad de mejorar su vida. La población del país **subía** rápidamente.	*In that period, many immigrants were coming to the country. They were seeking the opportunity to improve their lives. The population of the country was rising rapidly.*

Description

The imperfect is used to describe in the past.

Su casa **era** muy grande. **Tenía** un jardín muy bonito.	*His house was very big. It had a very pretty garden.*
Los estudiantes **estaban** nerviosos porque sus cursos **eran** muy difíciles.	*The students were nervous because their courses were very difficult.*
Aquella señora **se llamaba** Laura Delgado. **Era** argentina, y **trabajaba** en el Ministerio de la Defensa.	*That woman's name was Laura Delgado. She was Argentine, and she was working in the Ministry of Defense.*
Mi abuela **era** una mujer sencilla que **se dedicaba** a su hogar y a sus cinco hijos. **Salía** poco porque **tenía** tantos quehaceres domésticos.	*My grandmother was a simple woman who devoted herself to her home and her five children. She didn't go out much, because she had so many household chores.*

Repeated Actions

The imperfect is used to label repeated actions in the past when the focus is on the actions themselves and not on when the actions began or ended. Adverbs and adverbial phrases such as **siempre, nunca, todos los veranos/días/domingos, cada vez, muchas veces, a menudo, generalmente, de costumbre**, etc. indicate repeated actions.

Cuando yo **era** joven, mi familia y yo **íbamos** al mar todos los veranos.	*When I was young, my family and I used to go to the seashore every summer.*
Él siempre me **telefoneaba** y me **hacía** preguntas.	*He would always call me and ask me questions.*
Ella nunca **recordaba** lo que yo le **decía**.	*She never used to remember what I would tell her.*
Cada vez que **venía** a mi casa, **se quedaba** a comer.	*Every time he would come to my house, he would stay for dinner.*

E *Repeated actions in the imperfect.* Rewrite each sentence in the imperfect, using the adverbs and adverbial phrases of frequency in parentheses.

MODELO   Lola me envía mensajes electrónicos. (todos los días)
Lola me enviaba mensajes electrónicos todos los días.

1. Les traigo bombones a los abuelos. (siempre)

   _____

2. Al terminar el trabajo los compañeros toman una copa. (de costumbre)

   _____

3. Daniela sale con Federico a bailar. (todos los sábados)

   _____

4. Paco le pide prestado el coche a su hermano. (a menudo)

   _____

5. Nadas en la piscina del gimnasio universitario. (cada semana)

   _____

6. Vamos a la sierra de Guadarrama para esquiar. (todos los inviernos)

   _____

7. Los chicos llegan hambrientos (*starved*) a la casa. (generalmente)

   _____

8. Pasamos un par de horas en el centro comercial. (muchas veces)

   _____

9. Ven a sus primos italianos. (todos los veranos)

   _____

10. ¿Hacéis un viaje de negocios? (todos los meses)

   _____

The Imperfect in Reported Speech

The imperfect usually replaces the present tense in reported speech (indirect speech) when the main verb of the sentence is in a past tense. English works similarly. Compare the following pairs of sentences.

Dice que lo **sabe.**	*He says that he knows (it).*
Dijo que lo **sabía.**	*He said that he knew (it).*
Me escribe que **no viene.**	*She writes to me that she isn't coming.*
Me escribió que **no venía.**	*She wrote to me that she wasn't coming.*
Siempre **insisten** en que **pueden** hacerlo.	*They always insist that they can do it.*
Siempre **insistían** en que **podían** hacerlo.	*They always insisted that they could do it.*

F *Rewrite each sentence, showing reported speech in the past by replacing the present tense verb in the first clause with the preterit and replacing the present tense verb in the second clause with the imperfect.*

MODELO   Ellos nos dicen que quieren visitarnos.
Ellos nos dijeron que querían visitarnos.

1. Ignacio les informa que busca trabajo.

2. Laura anuncia que va a casarse.

3. Ellos insisten en que saben hacerlo.

4. Les escribo que hago un viaje en mayo.

5. Nos avisan que no pueden llegar puntual a la cita.

6. Me advierten que el ordenador está descompuesto.

7. Los jefes notifican que despiden a muchos empleados.

8. Pedro y Consuelo me cuentan que son felices.

The Imperfect and Preterit Contrasted

The preterit and imperfect both refer to past time, but express different ways of looking at past actions and events. The imperfect tense denotes an action as going on in the past without any reference to its beginning or end. The preterit tense denotes an action that the speaker sees as completed in the past or as having happened once.

Cuando yo estaba en Panamá, **hablaba** español.	*When I was in Panama, **I spoke** Spanish.*
Ayer **hablé** español con Diego.	*Yesterday **I spoke** Spanish with Diego.*

Spanish speakers must select one of these two aspects of past time—imperfect or preterit—for every past action they refer to. English often does not distinguish between these two aspects of past time.

Completed Action

The preterit implies that an action was completed in the past. It also may imply that the action happened once.

Llamaron a la puerta.	*There was a knock at the door.*
De repente, **se abrió** la puerta.	*Suddenly, the door opened.*
El avión **llegó** tarde.	*The plane arrived late.*
Estalló la bomba.	*The bomb exploded.*

Continuous or Repeated Action

The imperfect is used for actions that the speaker sees as going on in the past without reference to the beginning or the end of the action. The imperfect may convey that the action happened repeatedly.

El barrio **se hacía** cada vez más ruidoso.	*The neighborhood was getting noisier and noisier.*
Los chicos **estudiaban** en la biblioteca.	*The kids used to study in the library.*
Tú siempre **te acostabas** temprano.	*You always went to bed early.*

Description in the Past

A series of imperfects may be used to describe what was going on in the past.

Eran las seis de la mañana. La gente **dormía**. En la calle **pasaban** pocos coches. Algunos transeúntes **caminaban** hacia la parada de autobús y **esperaban**. El sol **salía**. **Era** un día como cualquiera.	*It was six in the morning. People were asleep. In the street, few cars were going by. Some pedestrians were walking to the bus stop and were waiting. The sun was coming out. It was a day like any other.*

For a Spanish speaker, the logical question to ask after hearing the above paragraph is **¿Qué pasó?** because in the imperfect, nothing really happens—the narration is not advanced at all. To make the above paragraph part of a narration, a preterit has to be added.

Eran las seis de la mañana. La gente **dormía**. En la calle **pasaban** pocos coches. Algunos transeúntes **caminaban** hacia la parada de autobús y **esperaban**. El sol **salía**. **Era** un día como cualquiera. De repente **se oyó** el ruido fuerte de una explosión.	*It was six in the morning. People were asleep. In the street, few cars were going by. Some pedestrians were walking to the bus stop and were waiting. The sun was coming out. It was a day like any other. Suddenly the loud noise of an explosion was heard.*

Background for Past Actions or Events

The imperfect often provides the background for past actions or events that are expressed in the preterit.

Paula **leía** cuando **llegaron** sus amigos.	*Paula was reading when her friends arrived.*
Cuando yo **entré**, todos **trabajaban**.	*When I came in, everyone was working.*
Cerré las ventanas porque **llovía**.	*I closed the windows because it was raining.*

G Complete the following sentences, choosing either the imperfect or the preterit for each verb in parentheses. Each sentence has two verbs, one of which will be imperfect and the other preterit.

MODELO Mientras él _esperaba_ el autobús, _empezó_ a llover. (esperar, empezar)

1. _____ las once de la noche cuando ellos _____ para la discoteca. (ser, salir)

2. _____ tanta congestión en Internet que yo no _____ hacer la conexión. (hay, poder)

3. Elena _____ a Carlos mientras (ella) _____ arte en París. (conocer, estudiar)

4. Mientras tú _____ la película, nosotros _____ cinco millas. (ver, correr)

5. Felipe _____ mucho en el problema hasta que le _____ una solución. (pensar, venir)

6. Nosotros no _____ cuánto costaban los muebles hasta que el dependiente nos _____ el precio. (saber, decir)

7. _____ un fallo del sistema cuando tú _____ en línea. (hay, trabajar)

8. Vosotros _____ un paseo por el parque cuando alguien _____ un grito. (dar, dar)

9. El barrio donde Mercedes _____ _____ hermoso. (nacer, ser)

10. Nosotros los hinchas (fans) _____ muy entusiasmados hasta que el otro equipo _____ un gol. (estar, marcar)

11. El proyecto _____ difícil y complicado pero yo _____ realizarlo. (ser, lograr)

12. El gato _____ de la casa mientras Uds. _____. (huir, dormir)

13. Yo _____ en la facultad cuando se _____ la serie de conferencias. (enseñar, iniciar)

14. Su esposa _____ a luz (give birth) mientras Jorge _____. (dar, viajar)

15. El alumno no _____ atención hasta que la maestra lo _____. (prestar, reñir)

16. Yo _____ la cuenta aunque mis amigos todavía _____ su postre. (pagar, comer)

17. Hasta que Miriám y Alejandro _____ nosotros no _____ a nadie. (aparecer, conocer)

18. Roberto _____ el doctorado cuando _____ veinticinco años. (conseguir, tener)

19. Se _____ una gran oportunidad mientras ellos más la

_____. (presentar, necesitar)

20. Cuando _____ las visitas los anfitriones (*hosts*) todavía

_____ la comida. (llegar, preparar)

Continuing Past Action

Spanish uses the imperfect tense to refer to past actions that are seen as continuing at another point of time in the past. English uses a *had been doing something* construction for this function. The Spanish construction consists of the following elements.

- **¿cuánto tiempo hacía que** + verb in the imperfect?

  This construction is used to ask a question about how long something had been going on. The word **tiempo** can be omitted in the question.

¿Cuánto (tiempo) hacía que Ud. trabajaba en aquella oficina?	*How long had you been working in that office?*

- **hacía** + time expression + **que** + verb in the imperfect OR
  verb in the imperfect + **hacía** + time expression

  These constructions are used to tell how long something had been going on.

—**¿Cuánto tiempo hacía que asistías** a aquella universidad?	*"How long had you been attending that university?"*
—**Hacía un año que cursaba** informática allí.	*"I had been taking computer science there for a year."*
—**Cursaba** informática allí **hacía un año.**	*"I had been taking computer science there for a year."*

- **Desde** is added to specify the starting point of an action that began in the past and continues to another point in the past.

—**¿Desde cuándo vivías** al lado de los Paz?	*"Since when had you been living next door to the Pazes?"*
—**Éramos** vecinos **desde** septiembre.	*"We had been neighbors since September."*

- The imperfect of **llevar** (or, in Latin America, of **tener** as well) with expressions of time is commonly used to express *had been*.

—¿Cuánto tiempo **llevabas** en esa compañía?	*"How long **had you been** at that company?"*
—**Llevaba un año** allí.	*"I **had been** there **for one year.**"*
Llevábamos más de dos años en esta universidad.	*We **had been** at this university **for more than two years.***
¿Tenías mucho tiempo en esta oficina?	*Had you been at this office **for a long time?***

The imperfect in the constructions presented above frequently occurs in the same sentence with a preterit. The preterit expresses a point in past time up to which the action expressed by the imperfect had been continuing.

Tenía tres meses sin trabajar cuando por fin **le ofrecieron** un buen puesto.	*He hadn't worked in three months when finally he was offered a good position.*
Hacía un año que Luisa **estudiaba** informática cuando **decidió** inscribirse en la facultad de administración.	*Luisa had been studying computer science for a year when she decided to enroll in business school.*

End Point Specified for Past Action

Although the imperfect is usually used to express repeated actions in the past, when the end point of those actions is specified, the verb is in the preterit because the speaker's focus shifts to the completion of the actions. In the sentence below, no end point is specified.

Cuando yo **era** niño, **iba** al mar todos los veranos.	*When I was a child, I went to the seashore every summer.*

Notice the change in tense when an endpoint is specifically mentioned.

Hasta la edad de doce años, **fui** al mar todos los veranos.	*Until the age of twelve, I went to the seashore every summer.*

Differences in Meaning Between the Imperfect and the Preterit of Some Common Verbs

Sometimes English uses entirely different verbs to express the difference between the imperfect and the preterit of some Spanish verbs. For example, **tenía** means *I was in the process of having* or *I had;* **tuve** means *I began to have* or *I got, I received.*

Ella **tenía** muchas ideas.	*She **had** a lot of ideas. (They were in her head.)*
Ella **tuvo** una buena idea.	*She **had** a good idea. (It popped into her head.)*
Sabía su nombre.	*I **knew** his name.*
Supe su nombre.	*I **found out** his name.*
Conocíamos a Raquel.	*We **knew** Raquel.*
Conocimos a Raquel.	*We **met** Raquel.*
No podíamos salir por la nieve.	*We **couldn't** go out because of the snow. (It's not stated whether we went out or not, just that it was very difficult to go out.)*
No **pudimos** salir por la nieve.	*We **couldn't** go out because of the snow. (And we didn't go out.)*
Jaime **no quería** ir en taxi.	*Jaime **didn't want** to go by cab. (It leaves open whether he went or not.)*
Jaime **no quiso** ir en taxi.	*Jaime **didn't want** (= **refused**) to go by cab. (And he didn't go.)*

El cuadro **costaba** tanto que no lo compré.	*The painting **cost** so much that I didn't buy it.*
El cuadro **nos costó** 30 mil dólares.	*The painting **cost us** 30,000 dollars.*

Verbs of Perception

Verbs of mental activity and other verbs of perception can be used in either the preterit or the imperfect. However, the speaker's choice of tense determines the meaning of the sentence.

Pensé que él era colombiano.	*I thought that he was Colombian. (At that moment something made me think that he was Colombian.)*
Pensaba que él era colombiano.	*I thought that he was Colombian. (I used to think that he was Colombian.)*
Creí que no me entendían.	*I thought that they were not understanding me. (Something happened that made me think that.)*
Creía que no me entendían.	*I thought that they were not understanding me. (It was my ongoing impression.)*
Comprendió que yo no tenía interés.	*He understood that I had no interest. (He realized it at that moment.)*
Comprendía que yo no tenía interés.	*He understood that I had no interest. (He was under that impression because of what I was saying, doing, etc.)*
De repente **oímos** un ruido.	*Suddenly we heard a noise. (The noise began.)*
Oíamos mucho ruido.	*We heard a lot of noise. (There was a lot of noise going on.)*

Había/hubo and estaba/estuvo

The difference between **había** and **hubo** and between **estaba** and **estuvo** is especially difficult for English speakers.

Aquí **había** una fiesta.	*There was a party here. (It was going on here—the speaker may mention something that happened while the party was going on.)*
Aquí **hubo** una fiesta.	*There was a party here. (It took place and is finished.)*
En esa zona **había** muchas tormentas.	*In that region there were a lot of storms. (This describes the region in the past.)*
Hubo una tormenta ayer.	*There was a storm yesterday. (A completed event in the past.)*

En su casa casi no **había** muebles.   *There was almost no furniture in his house. (This describes the house in the past.)*

En su casa **hubo** un incendio.   *There was a fire in his house. (A completed event in the past.)*

¿Dónde **estabas** cuando llamé?   *Where were you when I called? (Where you were is a background to an event in the past.)*

Estuve diez horas en la oficina.   *I was in the office for ten hours. (The end of my time in the office is specified; my being there is seen as complete.)*

Estaban enfermos.   *They were sick. (A description in the past.)*

Estuvieron enfermos todo el mes.   *They were sick all month. (The endpoint of their illness is specified; their illness is seen as a completed event in the past.)*

H *Translation. Express the following sentences in Spanish.*

1. *How long had you (Uds.) been living in New York when you bought a condominium?*

   _____

   _____

2. *We had been living in the city for two years.*

   _____

3. *How long had you (tú) been studying Spanish in Madrid when you decided to return to your American (U.S.) university?*

   _____

   _____

4. *I had been there for six weeks.*

   _____

5. *How long had Julia been using her computer when she changed makes (brands)?*

   _____

   _____

6. *She had it for three years.*

   _____

7. *Since when had Jaime been working as a consultant?*

   _____

   _____

8. *Since last year when he got his MBA.*

_____

_____

_____

BUILDING SENTENCES	**Sentences with double object pronouns**

English doesn't allow a direct and an indirect object pronoun to occur together—the indirect object appears in a prepositional phrase beginning with *to* or *for* when a direct object is present.

*I gave it **to him**.*

In Spanish, however, double object pronouns are very common.

With Spanish double object pronouns, the indirect object always precedes the direct object. Thus, indirect object pronouns **me** (*to/for me*), **te** (*to/for you*, informal singular), **nos** (*to/for us*), **os** (*to/for you*, informal plural) precede direct object pronouns **lo, la, los, las.**

—¿No tienes el libro de física?	*"Don't you have the physics book?"*
—Sí, **me lo** prestó Juan Carlos.	*"Yes, Juan Carlos lent **it to me**."*
—Perdí la dirección de Consuelo.	*"I lost Consuelo's address."*
—Yo la tengo en casa. **Te la** mando por correo electrónico.	*"I have it at home. I'll send **it to you** by e-mail."*
—Tengo las fotos de mi viaje.	*"I have the photos of my trip."*
—¿**Me las** puedes mostrar?	*"Can you show **them to me**?"*
—No entiendo los problemas de matemáticas.	*"I don't understand the math problems."*
—A ver si el profe **nos los** explica.	*"Let's see whether the prof explains **them to us**."*

When one of the third-person indirect object pronouns, **le** (*to/for you* [formal singular], *to/for him/her*) or **les** (*to/for you* [formal plural], *to/for them*), precedes one of the direct object pronouns **lo, la, los, las,** it changes to **se.**

—Mis hijos quieren aquel videojuego.	*"My children want that video game."*
—¿**Se lo** vas a comprar? (**les + lo → se lo**)	*"Are you going to buy **it for them**?"*
—Éster y Julio quieren pedirte prestada tu maleta grande.	*"Éster and Julio want to borrow your big suitcase."*
—Yo **se la** presto con mucho gusto. (**les + la → se la**)	*"I'll gladly lend **it to them**."*
—José me dijo que le debías mil dólares.	*"José told me you owed him a thousand dollars."*
—Ya **se los** devolví. (**le + los → se los**)	*"I already returned **them to him**."*
—Luisa necesita sus tarjetas de crédito.	*"Luisa needs her credit cards."*
—Mañana **se las** doy. (**le + las → se las**)	*"I'll give **them to her** tomorrow."*

Here are the possible combinations of double object pronouns in Spanish.

me lo	me la	me los	me las
te lo	te la	te los	te las
se lo	se la	se los	se las
nos lo	nos la	nos los	nos las
os lo	os la	os los	os las
se lo	se la	se los	se las

Double object pronouns, like single object pronouns, appear before the conjugated verb. They may also follow an infinitive, and when thus placed they are attached to it in writing. When two object pronouns are added to an infinitive, a written accent must be placed over the **a**, **e**, or **i** preceding the **r** of the infinitive.

—¿Vas a enviár**selo**?	*"Are you going to send **it to him (to her, to them)**?"*
—Sí, **se lo** voy a enviar la semana que viene.	*"Yes, I'm going to send **it to him (to her, to them)** next week."*
—¿Quieres darles estas viejas sillas a los Aranda?	*"Do you want to give these old chairs to the Arandas?"*
—Cómo no. Debemos ofrecér**selas**.	*"Of course. We should offer **them to them**."*

To focus on the identity of the referent of **se**, Spanish uses a phrase consisting of **a** + noun or pronoun.

—¿**Le** mandaste los disquetes **a María**?	*"Did you send the diskettes **to María**?"*
—No, **a ella** no. **Se** los mandé **a Raquel**.	*"No, not **to her**. I sent them **to Raquel**."*
—Carlos y Rebeca querían ver tus fotos.	*"Carlos and Rebeca wanted to see your photos."*
—**Se** las mostré **a él**. **A ella se** las voy a mostrar hoy por la tarde.	*"I showed them **to him**. I'm going to show them **to her** this afternoon."*

The interrogatives **¿a quién?**, **¿a quiénes?** are also used with **se** when **se** is a replacement for **le** or **les** before a direct object pronoun.

—Tengo todos los apuntes de la clase de historia de los Estados Unidos.	*"I have all the notes from the United States history class."*
—¿**A quién se** los pediste?	*"Whom did you ask for them?"*

Since the subject often follows the verb in Spanish, the presence or absence of the preposition **a** is what clarifies the role of an animate noun at the end of a sentence when the verb is in the third person.

¿Las fotos? Se las mostró **David**.	*The photos? David showed them to her.*
¿Las fotos? Se las mostró **a David**.	*The photos? She showed them to David.*
¿El dinero? Se lo devolvió **Luisa**.	*The money? Luisa returned it to him.*
¿El dinero? Se lo devolvió **a Luisa**.	*The money? He returned it to Luisa.*

I *Rewrite each sentence, changing the direct object nouns to pronouns.*
¡Ojo! Be sure to make necessary changes and watch out for the placement
of object pronouns in the sentences.

MODELO   Les dejó el recado. *Se lo dejó.*

1. Les expliqué las estrategias. _____

2. Le pidió el helado de mango. _____

3. Nos enseñaban el apartamento. _____

4. Me devuelve la tarjeta telefónica. _____

5. ¿Te ofrecieron el puesto de analista? _____

6. Os sirven las chuletas de cordero. _____

7. Le regalamos los pendientes de oro. _____

8. Le envío el mensaje electrónico. _____

9. Les mandó la tarjeta de crédito. _____

10. Nos recomiendan esta marca. _____

11. Les vendimos el televisor plasma. _____

12. Me dijo la palabra clave. _____

13. Te prestamos el quemador CD. _____

14. ¿Nos demostráis vuestro sitio Web? _____

15. Le dio los libros de texto. _____

16. Os suben vuestro equipaje. _____

17. Le trajisteis las camisas. _____

18. Les hice esos platos vegetarianos. _____

19. Le comentaban lo ocurrido. _____

20. Me entregó las llaves. _____

J *Express the following sentences in English. ¡Ojo! Focus on the subject and indirect object*
in each pair of sentences.

1. a. Se los dio Ricardo.

   _____

   b. Se los dio a Ricardo.

   _____

2. a. Se lo describían los consultores.

   _____

   b. Se lo describían a los consultores.

   _____

3. a. Se las repitió Ofelia.

    _____

    b. Se las repitió a Ofelia.

    _____

4. a. Se la pide Ud.

    _____

    b. Se la pide a Ud.

    _____

5. a. Se los iba a mandar Sarita.

    _____

    b. Se los iba a mandar a Sarita.

    _____

6. a. Se la quieren mostrar nuestros colegas.

    _____

    b. Se la quieren mostrar a nuestros colegas.

    _____

7. a. No pudo explicárselo el profesor.

    _____

    b. No pudo explicárselo al profesor.

    _____

8. a. Acaban de pedírselas estas abogadas.

    _____

    b. Acaban de pedírselas a estas abogadas.

    _____

K *Translation.* *Express the following sentences in Spanish.*

1. *Can you (tú) lend me your digital camera?*

    _____

2. *I lent it to Esteban last week. You can ask him for it.*

    _____

3. *I bought this sweater to give to someone as a gift.*

    _____

4. *To whom do you want to give it?*

    _____

5. *We used to write them e-mails every day.*

   _____

6. *Do you still send them to them so often?*

   _____

7. *Did you (Uds.) make them dinner already?*

   _____

8. *We're going to make it for them soon.*

   _____

9. *Daniel wrote us that he was going to give his girlfriend a ring.*

   _____

10. *Did he say when he intended to give it to her?*

   _____

11. *Julia handed her thesis in to the professors the day before yesterday.*

   _____

   _____

12. *Didn't she have to hand it in to them last semester?*

   _____

13. *How long had they been working for the company when the boss gave them a raise (el aumento de sueldo)?*

   _____

   _____

14. *They had been doing programming for six months when he gave it to them.*

   _____

   _____

The Past Participle;
The Present Perfect;
The Pluperfect

Introduction to the Compound Tenses in Spanish

Compound tenses in Spanish consist of the appropriate form of the auxiliary verb **haber** plus the past participle. The past participle does not change for gender or number in the compound tenses.

The Past Participle

Most past participles are regular in Spanish. **-Ar** verbs change the **-ar** of the infinitive to **-ado**.

hablar	hablado	*spoken*
ganar	ganado	*earned, won*
ocupar	ocupado	*occupied*
enviar	enviado	*sent*

-Er verbs change the **-er** of the infinitive and **-ir** verbs change the **-ir** of the infinitive to **-ido**.

comer	comido	*eaten*
vender	vendido	*sold*
vivir	vivido	*lived*
dormir	dormido	*slept*

-Er and **-ir** verbs such as **caer**, **leer**, and **oír** whose stems end in a vowel add an accent mark over the **i** of the past participle ending **-ido**, just as they do over the **i** in the endings of the preterit.

caer	caído	*fallen*
creer	creído	*believed*
leer	leído	*read*
oír	oído	*heard*
poseer	poseído	*possessed*
traer	traído	*brought*

Some past participles are irregular. Most of them end in **-to**.

abrir	**abierto**	*opened*
cubrir	**cubierto**	*covered*
devolver	**devuelto**	*returned*
escribir	**escrito**	*written*
freír	**frito**	*fried*
imprimir	**impreso**	*printed*
morir	**muerto**	*dead*
poner	**puesto**	*put, placed*
resolver	**resuelto**	*resolved*
romper	**roto**	*broken, torn*
ver	**visto**	*seen*
volver	**vuelto**	*returned*

Two of the most common verbs have past participles ending in **-cho**.

decir	**dicho**	*said*
hacer	**hecho**	*done*

When a prefix is added to any of the verbs above, the past participle shows the same irregularities.

componer	**compuesto**	*composed*
descomponer	**descompuesto**	*broken, in disrepair*
describir	**descrito**	*described*
descubrir	**descubierto**	*discovered*
deshacer	**deshecho**	*undone*
imponer	**impuesto**	*imposed*
inscribir	**inscrito**	*registered, enrolled*
posponer	**pospuesto**	*postponed*
predecir	**predicho**	*predicted*
proponer	**propuesto**	*proposed, suggested*
prever	**previsto**	*foreseen*
rehacer	**rehecho**	*redone*
revolver	**revuelto**	*turned over*
satisfacer	**satisfecho**	*satisfied*

The past participles of **ser** and **ir** are **sido** and **ido**, respectively.

The Present Perfect Tense

The present tense of the auxiliary verb **haber** + the past participle forms the present perfect tense (English *I have done something.*)

Study the conjugation of the present perfect of **hablar**, **comer**, and **escribir**.

hablar *to speak*	
he hablado	hemos hablado
has hablado	habéis hablado
ha hablado	han hablado

comer *to eat*

he comido	hemos comido
has comido	habéis comido
ha comido	han comido

escribir *to write*

he escrito	hemos escrito
has escrito	habéis escrito
ha escrito	han escrito

The present perfect of **hay** is **ha habido** *there has/have been.*

In the compound tenses, no words are placed between the auxiliary verb and the past participle. Thus, object pronouns are placed before the forms of **haber** in these tenses. In questions, subject pronouns or noun subjects are placed after the past participle when the word order is inverted. In the equivalent English questions, the subject *does* come between the auxiliary and the participle.

Los hemos llamado.	*We've called them.*
Nos han mandado el paquete.	*They've sent us the package.*
Se lo he explicado.	*I've explained it to them.*
¿Por qué **ha salido Juan?**	*Why has Juan gone out?*
¿Qué **han comprado ellos?**	*What have they bought?*
¿Ha llegado el asesor?	*Has the consultant arrived?*
¿No los has visto tú?	*Haven't you seen them?*

Uses of the Present Perfect

- The Spanish present perfect corresponds to the English present perfect. Both languages use this compound tense to express a past action that has an effect on the present or some relationship to it.

Nadie ha llegado todavía.	*No one has arrived yet.*
¿Nunca has viajado por México?	*Have you ever traveled through Mexico?*
El mecánico ya ha reparado el carro.	*The mechanic has already fixed the car.*

- Many Spanish speakers, especially in Spain, use the present perfect for recent events—events that have happened earlier in the day. English often uses the simple past in these cases.

No he desayunado esta mañana.	*I didn't have breakfast this morning.*
Hoy por la tarde han cerrado a las cinco.	*This afternoon they closed at five.*
El cartero ha venido a mediodía.	*The mailman came at noon.*
Los chicos han salido hace cinco minutos.	*The children left five minutes ago.*

In most parts of Latin America, the preterit is used in these cases.

No desayuné esta mañana.	*I didn't have breakfast this morning.*
Hoy por la tarde cerraron a las cinco.	*This afternoon they closed at five.*

El cartero vino a mediodía.   *The mailman came at noon.*
Los chicos salieron hace cinco minutos.   *The children left five minutes ago.*

■ Many Spanish speakers use the present perfect to emphasize the relationship of a past action to the present. In most of these cases, English prefers the simple past. This category overlaps with the present perfect to express recent events.

¿Quién te ha dicho que yo no iba a venir?   *Who told you that I wasn't coming?*

¿Has visto las noticias? Ha habido un temblor.   *Did you see the news? There was an earthquake.*

A *Using the cue in parentheses, complete each verb phrase with either the missing form of the auxiliary verb **haber** or the past participle.*

1. _____ salido (nosotros)

2. han _____ (hablar)

3. _____ visto (Uds.)

4. habéis _____ (entender)

5. _____ vuelto (tú)

6. ha _____ (leer)

7. _____ aprendido (él)

8. ha _____ (decir)

9. _____ escogido (yo)

10. _____ hecho (Ud.)

11. han _____ (discutir)

12. has _____ (mirar)

13. ella ha _____ (llegar)

14. ellas han _____ (escribir)

15. ha _____ (haber)

B *Write sentences in the present perfect, using the following strings of elements.*

MODELO   Rita / tomar / un café
         Rita ha tomado un café.

1. tú / hablar / por teléfono móvil

   _____

2. nuestro equipo / ganar / el partido

   _____

3. ellos / poner / la mesa

   _____

4. Ud. / recibir / la correspondencia

   _____

5. Gerardo / hacer / un login

   _____

6. yo / leer / los titulares

   _____

7. nuestra familia / vivir / bien

   _____

8. Uds. / tener / mucha experiencia

   _____

9. tú / descargar / el fichero

   _____

10. vosotros / no comprender / el asunto

    _____

11. nosotros / ser / muy felices

    _____

12. nadie / decir / nada

    _____

13. ¿quién / romper / la ventana?

    _____

14. Nora y Daniela / ir / de compras

    _____

15. ¿Ud. / oír / esta orquesta?

    _____

16. yo / escribir / el informe

    _____

17. nosotros / resolver / el conflicto

    _____

18. ¿cómo / estar (Uds.)?

    _____

19. la cocinera / freír / el pescado

    _____

20. ellos / no querer molestar

   _____

21. vosotros / imprimir / los papeles

   _____

22. los electrodomésticos / funcionar / bien

   _____

C *Rewrite each sentence, changing the verb from the present tense to the present perfect.*

MODELO   Demuestra los resultados.
   Ha demostrado los resultados.

1. Almuerzan en la cafetería.

   _____

2. Llueve todo el día.

   _____

3. Hacen construir una casa.

   _____

4. Pierde el tren esta mañana.

   _____

5. Hay mucha congestión en Internet.

   _____

6. Este libro es un éxito de librería (*bestseller*).

   _____

7. Vuelven del viaje de negocios.

   _____

8. El director rueda la película en Texas.

   _____

9. Los niños quieren ver los dibujos animados.

   _____

10. Jorge consigue trabajar en la seguridad nacional y la ciberseguridad.

   _____

   _____

11. El armario huele mal.

   _____

12. Los despierta.

_____

13. Te lo digo.

_____

14. Se las devolvemos.

_____

15. Prefieren dársela.

_____

16. No se lo puedo recomendar.

_____

17. ¿Tratas de enviárnoslos?

_____

18. Te la piensan regalar.

_____

19. Vuelve a pedírmelas.

_____

20. ¿Por qué necesitáis recordárselo?

_____

D *Answer each question, writing the verb in the present perfect in your response. Change each direct object noun to a pronoun and make all necessary changes.*

MODELO ¿Actualizas los datos? *Ya los he actualizado.*

1. ¿Pruebas el guacamole? _____

2. ¿Empieza el programa de realidad? _____

3. ¿Uds. visitan esos sitios Web? _____

4. ¿Pedro rellena el formulario? _____

5. ¿La compañía lanza unos nuevos productos alimenticios?

   _____

6. ¿Repites el plato (*have a second helping*)? _____

7. ¿Ellos emprenden una campaña publicitaria? _____

8. ¿Vas a comer comida rápida hoy? _____

9. ¿Rafael piensa estudiar ingeniería del medio ambiente? _____

10. ¿Uds. pueden realizar su proyecto? _____

11. ¿Vosotros tenéis que hacer vuestras investigaciones? _____

12. ¿Te muestran su nueva computadora personal? _____

13. ¿Les contamos a Uds. los chismes? _____

14. ¿El vendedor de coches le va a entregar la llave a Leo? _____

15. ¿Van a serviros las enchiladas? _____

16. ¿Quieres leer ese blog? _____

The Pluperfect Tense

The pluperfect tense (also called the past perfect) consists of the imperfect of the auxiliary verb **haber** and the past participle. In formation and function it is very much like the English pluperfect: *had done something.*

Study the conjugation of the pluperfect of **hablar**, **comer**, and **escribir**.

hablar *to speak*

había hablado	habíamos hablado
habías hablado	habíais hablado
había hablado	habían hablado

comer *to eat*

había comido	habíamos comido
habías comido	habíais comido
había comido	habían comido

escribir *to write*

había escrito	habíamos escrito
habías escrito	habíais escrito
había escrito	habían escrito

The pluperfect of **hay** is **había habido** *there had been.*

The pluperfect labels a past event that was completed before another past event occurred.

Cuando yo llegué, ella ya **había salido.**	*When I arrived, she had already left.*
He venido a verte porque me **habían dicho** que estabas enfermo.	*I've come to see you because they had told me that you were sick.*
¡Qué bien! Yo no sabía que Uds. **habían resuelto** el problema.	*Terrific! I didn't know that you had solved the problem.*
A las cinco, todos los empleados **habían terminado** su trabajo.	*At five, all the employees had finished their work.*

E *Write sentences with the cues given, using verbs in the pluperfect tense to say that things happened before the past events asked about. Change each direct object noun to a pronoun and make all necessary changes.*

MODELO ¿Uds. llegaron de la costa el mes pasado? (hace un par de meses)
No, habíamos llegado de la costa hace un par de meses.

1. ¿Corriste en la carrera en julio? (abril)

    _____

2. ¿Uds. vieron al bebé por primera vez hace unos días? (hace un mes)

    _____

3. ¿Los Alonso hicieron la barbacoa el segundo fin de semana de mayo? (el primero)

    _____

4. ¿Abrieron la tienda de videos la semana pasada? (hace tres semanas)

    _____

5. ¿Ud. volvió de vacaciones ayer? (anteayer)

    _____

6. ¿Diana y Alberto compraron su casa este año? (el año pasado)

    _____

7. ¿El novio de Inés le pidió la mano el día de su cumpleaños? (el Día de los Enamorados)

    _____

8. ¿Plácido celebró su cumpleaños el nueve de marzo? (el primero del mes)

    _____

9. ¿Llamaste a Éster para invitarla a la fiesta el jueves? (martes)

    _____

10. ¿Le disteis el carro a Elías en diciembre? (noviembre)

    _____

F *Create sentences from the following strings of elements, using the preterit in the* **cuando** *clause and the pluperfect in the main clause.*

MODELO Marta / regresar del gimnasio / sus amigos / salir
Cuando Marta regresó del gimnasio, sus amigos ya habían salido.

1. tú / llamarnos / nosotros / ir de compras

    _____

2. yo / llegar al cine / Nicolás y Mari / ver la mitad de la película

    _____

    _____

3. los invitados / venir / Isabel / poner la mesa

_____

4. Paco / comenzar a trotar / los otros jugadores / correr cinco millas

_____

_____

5. Uds. / invitarme / yo / hacer planes para ese día

_____

6. nosotros / ir en lancha / haber tempestad

_____

7. vosotros / pasar la aspiradora / Susana / sacudir el polvo

_____

8. Toni / solucionar el problema / Ud. / resolverlo

_____

9. Vicente / pedirle la cuenta a la moza / Enrique / pagarla

_____

10. yo / volver a la tienda de antigüedades / alguien / comprar la estatua

_____

_____

BUILDING SENTENCES   **Uses of the past participle**

The Past Participle as an Adjective

Most past participles can be used as adjectives. They can modify nouns directly or serve as predicate adjectives. When a past participle is used as an adjective, it agrees in gender and number with the noun it modifies.

una novela mal **escrita**	*a poorly **written** novel*
unos edificios recién **construidos**	*recently **built** buildings*
un artículo muy **leído** y **comentado**	*a widely **read** and **commented upon** article*
el cielo **cubierto**	*the **overcast** sky*
cielos **despejados**	***clear** skies*
Trato **hecho.**	*It's a (**done**) deal.*
Luis tiene el brazo **roto.**	*Luis has a **broken** arm.*
Vimos unas aldeas **abandonadas.**	*We saw some **abandoned** villages.*
El contrato está **firmado.**	*The contract is **signed**.*
Sus padres estaban **preocupados.**	*His parents were **worried**.*
Mi computadora está **descompuesta.**	*My computer is **broken**.*
Las ventanas están **abiertas.**	*The windows are **open**.*

The Past Participle Used to Express Position

The past participle in Spanish is used to express position of the human body or of objects. English usually uses the -ing form for this function.

Estamos **sentados** en la primera fila.	*We're **sitting** in the first row.*
¿Por qué están Uds. **parados**?	*Why are you **standing**?*
Los feligreses estaban **arrodillados**.	*The congregants were **kneeling**.*
Lo vi **arrimado** a un árbol.	*I saw him **leaning** against a tree.*
¿Por qué estás **acostada**? ¿Estás enferma?	*Why are you **lying down**? Are you sick?*
Los chicos no están **levantados** todavía.	*The kids aren't **up** (= out of bed) yet.*

Absolute Use of the Participle

Past participles, especially in written Spanish, can be used as substitutes for clauses. This is possible in English too, but the English past participle is usually accompanied by the word *having*.

Aclarado el asunto, pudieron llegar a un acuerdo.	***The matter having been cleared up**, they were able to reach an agreement.*
Terminada la conferencia, los estudiantes se levantaron y se fueron.	***The lecture having ended**, the students got up and left.*
Entregado el informe de los asesores, los dirigentes empezaron a estudiarlo.	***The consultants' report having been submitted**, the directors began to study it.*

In everyday English, a clause in the pluperfect beginning with *once* is more common: *Once the matter had been cleared up, they were able to reach an agreement.*

Tener + Past Participle

Tener can be used with a past participle to emphasize the completion of an action, especially one that required considerable effort. In this construction, the past participle agrees in gender and number with the noun it refers to. This noun would be the direct object of the verb in the present perfect. Compare the following pairs of sentences.

He hecho la cena.	*I've made dinner.*
Tengo la cena **hecha**.	*I have dinner ready. (I have finished making dinner.)*
Hemos escrito todos nuestros informes.	*We have written all our reports.*
Tenemos escritos todos nuestros informes.	*We have completed the writing of all our reports.*
A ver si ya han reparado las computadoras.	*Let's see if they've already repaired the computers.*
A ver si ya **tienen reparadas** las computadoras.	*Let's see if they've already finished repairing the computers.*

G *Complete each phrase with an adjective derived from the past participle form of the verb in parentheses.*

MODELO   el coche <u>*descompuesto*</u> (descomponer)

1. a. la casa veraniega (*summer*) recientemente _____ (comprar)

   b. el apartamento recientemente _____ (alquilar)

   c. los condominios recientemente _____ (amueblar)

   d. las paredes recientemente _____ (pintar)

   e. el piso (*apartment,* Spain) recientemente _____ (vender)

   f. el centro comercial recientemente _____ (construir)

   g. las viviendas (*houses*) recientemente _____ (rehacer)

2. a. los datos electrónicamente _____ (entrar)

   b. la información electrónicamente _____ (introducir)

   c. las canciones electrónicamente _____ (bajar)

   d. el fichero electrónicamente _____ (cargar)

   e. los programas electrónicamente _____ (telecargar)

   f. los gráficos electrónicamente _____ (transmitir)

3. a. el pollo _____ (freír)

   b. los huevos _____ (cocer)

   c. el agua _____ (hervir)

   d. las hamburguesas _____ (asar)

   e. la carne muy _____ (hacer) (*too well done*)

   f. la carne poco _____ (hacer) (*underdone*)

4. a. un sitio Web frecuentemente _____ (ver)

   b. un sitio Web _____ (visitar) muy a menudo

   c. un sitio Web muy _____ (concurrir) (*visit*)

   d. un sitio Web fácilmente _____ (navegar)

   e. un sitio Web recientemente _____ (diseñar)

   f. un sitio Web inteligentemente _____ (crear)

5. a. las personas _____ (animar)

   b. las personas _____ (entusiasmar)

   c. las personas _____ (aburrir)

   d. las personas _____ (agradecer)

   e. las personas _____ (enfurecer)

   f. las personas _____ (casarse)

   g. las personas _____ (vestirse)

6. a. las palabras claramente _____ (decir)

   b. las palabras claramente _____ (escribir)

   c. las palabras claramente _____ (expresar)

   d. las palabras claramente _____ (pronunciar)

   e. las palabras claramente _____ (traducir)

   f. las palabras claramente _____ (oír)

H *Modismos (Idioms). Using the expressions given, complete each sentence with the correct form of **estar** in the present tense plus the adjective that derives from the present participle. ¡**Ojo!** Derive the adjective form from the verb if it is not already given.*

1. estar frito *to be done for, all washed up*

   Ella cree que _____ porque el jefe rechazó (*rejected*) todas sus ideas.

2. estar mojado hasta los huesos (*bones*) *to be soaking wet*

   Nosotros salimos sin paraguas y _____ hasta los huesos.

3. meterse en lo que no le importa *to meddle in things that don't concern someone*

   Como de costumbre él _____ en lo que no le importa.

4. dormirse en los laureles *to rest on one's laurels*

   Ellos han logrado mucho y ahora _____ en los laureles.

5. comerse de envidia *to be consumed by envy*

   Carolina _____ de envidia porque su ex-novio sale con otras chicas.

6. estar hecho una lástima *to be a sorry sight, in a sad state*

   Chicas, Uds. _____ una lástima. ¿Qué les pasa?

I *For each string of elements, write a sentence using the present perfect. Then write a sentence that shows the resulting condition of the sentence in the present perfect. ¡**Ojo!** Remember that the adjectives derive from past participles and therefore must show agreement with the subjects.*

MODELO   ellos / abrir / el puerto

   Han abierto el puerto.

   El puerto está abierto.

1. yo / escribir / los poemas

   _____

   _____

2. Marcia / teñir / la tela

   _____

   _____

3. nosotros / cubrir / los gastos

   _____

   _____

4. la abuela / acostar / a sus nietos

   _____

   _____

5. Patricio / fotocopiar / las cartas

   _____

   _____

6. tú / hacer / las galletas

   _____

   _____

7. Ud. / apagar / el fuego

   _____

   _____

8. vosotros / perder / la plata

   _____

   _____

9. Uds. / tirar / la basura

   _____

   _____

10. alguien / estacionar / el coche

    _____

    _____

11. Perla / enloquecer / a sus amigas

    _____

    _____

12. ellos / atravesar / el puente

    _____

    _____

13. los soldados / caer

_____

_____

14. yo / resolver / el problema

_____

_____

15. nosotros / imprimir / la tesis

_____

_____

16. Lorenzo / romper / sus pantalones

_____

_____

17. el arquitecto / rehacer / estas casas

_____

_____

18. la directora / posponer / la reunión

_____

_____

19. la cocinera / freír / las croquetas

_____

_____

20. el dramaturgo / terminar / el guión (_script_)

_____

_____

J _Translation._ _Express the following sentences in Spanish._

1. _We found out that you_ (tú) _had already returned from your business trip._

_____

2. _When the war broke out_ (estallar) _in their country, the Reyes had already fled to the United States._

_____

_____

3. The successful novel having been written, the (female) author began to write the second one.

_____

_____

4. I've said the most important thing.

_____

5. The video camera? Eva has lent it to them.

_____

6. The guests are sitting at the table. The food and wine are served.

_____

7. Have you (Uds.) heard the news on the radio? There's been a seaquake (el maremoto).

_____

8. The money? I've asked Andrés for it, but he hasn't wanted to give it to me.

_____

_____

9. Have you (Ud.) packed (the suitcases)?

_____

10. Yes, the suitcases are packed.

_____

11. Have you (tú) plugged in (enchufar) the computer?

_____

12. No, it's not plugged in, because it's working on batteries.

_____

The Imperative

The imperative, or command, forms in Spanish are used to tell someone to do something or not to do something.

There are imperative forms for **tú**, **Ud.**, **nosotros**, **vosotros**, and **Uds.** Most imperative forms involve a change in the vowel of the verb ending.

Formal Commands: Imperative Forms for **Ud.** and **Uds.**

Commands for **Ud.** and **Uds.** change the characteristic vowel of the conjugation. **-Ar** verbs change the endings of the present tense from **-a**, **-an** to **-e**, **-en** to form the commands. All stem changes occurring in statement forms appear in the command forms too.

STATEMENT FORM	COMMAND FORM
hablar	
(Ud.) habla	hable (Ud.)
(Uds.) hablan	hablen (Uds.)
pensar	
(Ud.) piensa	piense (Ud.)
(Uds.) piensan	piensen (Uds.)
regresar	
(Ud.) regresa	regrese (Ud.)
(Uds.) regresan	regresen (Uds.)
contar	
(Ud.) cuenta	cuente (Ud.)
(Uds.) cuentan	cuenten (Uds.)

For **Ud.** and **Uds.** commands, **-er** and **-ir** verbs change the endings of the present tense from **-e**, **-en** to **-a**, **-an**. All stem changes occurring in statement forms appear in the command forms too.

STATEMENT FORM	COMMAND FORM
comer	
(Ud.) come	coma (Ud.)
(Uds.) comen	coman (Uds.)
volver	
(Ud.) vuelve	vuelva (Ud.)
(Uds.) vuelven	vuelvan (Uds.)

STATEMENT FORM	COMMAND FORM
entender	
(Ud.) entiend**e**	entiend**a** (Ud.)
(Uds.) entiend**en**	entiend**an** (Uds.)
escribir	
(Ud.) escrib**e**	escrib**a** (Ud.)
(Uds.) escrib**en**	escrib**an** (Uds.)
advertir	
(Ud.) adviert**e**	adviert**a** (Ud.)
(Uds.) adviert**en**	adviert**an** (Uds.)
pedir	
(Ud.) pid**e**	pid**a** (Ud.)
(Uds.) pid**en**	pid**an** (Uds.)
dormir	
(Ud.) duerm**e**	duerm**a** (Ud.)
(Uds.) duerm**en**	duerm**an** (Uds.)

In command forms, the subject pronouns **Ud.** and **Uds.** may follow the verb to add a polite note to the imperative, rather like English *please*.

Terminen Uds. este proyecto para la semana que viene.	*Please finish this project by next week.*
Trate Ud. de ayudarnos, entonces.	*Then please try to help us.*
No entren Uds. por esta puerta.	*Don't go in through this door, please.*

The corresponding negative commands are formed by placing **no** before the verb.

No coma en la sala.	*Don't eat in the living room.*
No interrumpa Ud.	*Please don't interrupt.*
No hablen Uds. ahora.	*Please don't talk now.*
No griten.	*Don't shout.*
No insistan Uds. en ir.	*Please don't insist on going.*

Imperative Forms for **nosotros**

The command forms for **nosotros** are formed in the same way as those for **Ud.** and **Uds.** For **-ar** verbs, the present tense ending **-amos** changes to **-emos**, and for **-er** and **-ir** verbs, the present tense endings **-emos** and **-imos** change to **-amos**.

STATEMENT FORM	COMMAND FORM	MEANING
habl**amos**	habl**emos**	*let's speak*
pens**amos**	pens**emos**	*let's think*
com**emos**	com**amos**	*let's eat*
volv**emos**	volv**amos**	*let's return*
escrib**imos**	escrib**amos**	*let's write*
abr**imos**	abr**amos**	*let's open*

-Ir verbs that have a vowel change in the stem of the third-person singular of the preterit have that same stem vowel change in the **nosotros** form of the imperative.

STATEMENT FORM	3RD-PERSON SING. PRETERIT	COMMAND FORM	MEANING
pedimos	pidió	pidamos	*let's request*
advertimos	advirtió	advirtamos	*let's warn*
dormimos	durmió	durmamos	*let's sleep*

The negative **nosotros** command is formed by placing **no** before the command form of the verb.

no hablemos	*let's not speak*
no comamos	*let's not eat*
no pidamos	*let's not ask for*

—**Entremos** en este restaurante.	*"Let's go into this restaurant."*
—No, **no comamos** aquí. Dicen que es muy malo. **Busquemos** algo mejor.	*"No, let's not eat here. They say that it's very bad. Let's look for something better."*

-Ar verbs ending in **-car**, **-gar**, and **-zar** have the same spelling changes in the **Ud.**, **Uds.**, and **nosotros** imperative that they have in the **yo** form of the preterit. Here is a chart of the changes.

INFINITIVE	Ud. COMMAND	Uds. COMMAND	nosotros COMMAND
buscar	busque	busquen	busquemos
pagar	pague	paguen	paguemos
almorzar	almuerce	almuercen	almorcemos

-Er and **-ir** verbs ending in **-ger** or **-gir** change the final **g** of the stem to **j** before the imperative endings.

INFINITIVE	Ud. COMMAND	Uds. COMMAND	nosotros COMMAND
escoger	escoja	escojan	escojamos
corregir	corrija	corrijan	corrijamos

If the **yo** form of the present tense is irregular, that irregularity will show up in the **Ud.**, **Uds.**, and **nosotros** commands. The imperative endings are added to the stem of the **yo** form.

yo FORM	Ud. COMMAND	Uds. COMMAND	nosotros COMMAND
hago	haga	hagan	hagamos
pongo	ponga	pongan	pongamos
digo	diga	digan	digamos
ofrezco	ofrezca	ofrezcan	ofrezcamos
veo	vea	vean	veamos

Several verbs have irregular imperative stems.

INFINITIVE	Ud. COMMAND	Uds. COMMAND	nosotros COMMAND
ser	**sea**	**sean**	**seamos**
ir	**vaya**	**vayan**	**vayamos**
saber	**sepa**	**sepan**	**sepamos**

The **Ud.** command form of **dar** and the **Ud.** and **Uds.** command forms of **estar** have accent marks. These written accents serve to distinguish the imperative from unstressed words with the same spelling.

INFINITIVE	Ud. COMMAND	Uds. COMMAND	nosotros COMMAND
dar	**dé**	**den**	**demos**
estar	**esté**	**estén**	**estemos**

—**No hagamos** la cena todavía. Es temprano.	*"Let's not make dinner yet. It's early."*
—**Esperemos** a mamá. Ella llega a las siete.	*"Let's wait for Mom. She gets home at seven."*
—De acuerdo. Pero **pongamos** la mesa.	*"Okay. But let's set the table."*
—Sí, **comamos** todos juntos.	*"Yes, let's all eat together."*
—**Oiga**, necesitamos cajas de archivar.	*"Listen, we need file boxes."*
—**Vaya** a la tienda Staples y **compre** diez cajas.	*"Go to Staples and buy ten boxes."*
—No, **vaya** Ud. mientras yo archivo estos documentos.	*"No, you go while I file these papers."*

In everyday speech, the **vamos a** + infinitive construction replaces the **nosotros** command.

nosotros COMMAND (FORMAL)	nosotros COMMAND (EVERYDAY SPANISH)	MEANING
Regresemos a casa.	**Vamos a regresar** a casa.	*Let's go home.*
Seamos pacientes.	**Vamos a ser** pacientes.	*Let's be patient.*
Almorcemos aquí.	**Vamos a almorzar** aquí.	*Let's have lunch here.*
Demos una vuelta.	**Vamos a dar** una vuelta.	*Let's take a walk.*

Thus, sentences that use the everyday Spanish **nosotros** command have two meanings.

Vamos a almorzar aquí.	*Let's have lunch here.* OR *We are going to have lunch here.*

However, the **no vamos a** + infinitive construction can only mean *we are not going to do something*. Thus, to express a negative **nosotros** command, you must use **no** + the **nosotros** command form.

No paguemos con tarjeta de crédito.	*Let's not pay with a credit card.*
No pidamos otro trago.	*Let's not order another drink.*

Note that while **vamos** is used for *let's go*, you must use **no vayamos** to express *let's not go*.

A *Write both an affirmative and a negative* **Ud.** *command for each item.*

MODELO   mandar el correo electrónico

Mande el correo electrónico.

No mande el correo electrónico.

1. arreglar el cuarto

   _____

   _____

2. cerrar la puerta

   _____

   _____

3. correr en el maratón

   _____

   _____

4. leer el artículo

   _____

   _____

5. contar lo que pasó

   _____

   _____

6. compartir los gastos

   _____

   _____

7. reñir al chico

   _____

   _____

8. seguir por el río

   _____

   _____

9. probar la sopa

   _____

   _____

10. encender la luz

   _____

   _____

11. ir con nosotros

   _____

   _____

12. buscar al perro

   _____

   _____

13. imprimir el informe

   _____

   _____

14. beber el jugo

   _____

   _____

15. despertar al niño

   _____

   _____

16. pagar la cuenta

   _____

   _____

17. ver ese programa

   _____

   _____

18. jugar al tenis

   _____

   _____

19. descargar el fichero

   _____

   _____

20. dar un paseo

   _____

   _____

B *Write the affirmative or the negative* **Uds.** *command indicated for each item.*

    MODELOS tomar el autobús *Tomen el autobús.*

                  no tomar el autobús *No tomen el autobús.*

1. llevar los paquetes _____
2. aparcar en este parqueo _____
3. pedir el helado de coco _____
4. hacer una lista _____
5. organizar estos papeles _____
6. tocar jazz _____
7. no gastar tanto dinero _____
8. no decir tonterías _____
9. asistir al concierto _____
10. no rechazar su idea _____
11. no ser desagradables _____
12. empezar a programar _____
13. no volcar el florero _____
14. llegar a las ocho _____
15. sonreír _____
16. conseguir los billetes _____
17. no tener miedo _____
18. no caer por la casa sin llamar _____
19. venir lo antes posible _____
20. introducir los datos _____

C *Write affirmative or negative* **nosotros** *commands in response to each of the following questions, using the cues given. Write each affirmative command in two ways.*

    MODELOS ¿Quieres/Quiere nadar? (sí)

        Sí, nademos.

        Sí, vamos a nadar.

        ¿Quieres/Quiere nadar? (no)

        No, no nademos.

1. ¿Quieres alquilar un video? (sí)

    _____

    _____

2. ¿Quiere navegar en la Red? (sí)

    _____

    _____

3. ¿Quieres comer algo? (sí)

    _____

    _____

4. ¿Quiere volver a ese balneario? (no)

    _____

5. ¿Quieres comenzar el proyecto? (sí)

    _____

    _____

6. ¿Quieres jugar al béisbol? (sí)

    _____

    _____

7. ¿Quiere oír música? (sí)

    _____

    _____

8. ¿Quieres salir al cine? (sí)

    _____

    _____

9. ¿Quiere hacer planes? (no)

    _____

10. ¿Quieres escoger un postre? (sí)

    _____

    _____

11. ¿Quieres ir al centro comercial? (no)

    _____

12. ¿Quiere dar una vuelta? (sí)

    _____

    _____

13. ¿Quieres reducir nuestros gastos? (sí)

    _____

    _____

14. ¿Quiere envolver el regalo? (no)

   _____

15. ¿Quiere subir en el telesquí? (no)

   _____

16. ¿Quieres traer una botella de vino? (sí)

   _____

   _____

17. ¿Quieres servir arroz con pollo? (no)

   _____

18. ¿Quieres mecer al bebé? (no)

   _____

19. ¿Quiere seguir por esta calle? (sí)

   _____

   _____

20. ¿Quieres conocer al nuevo asesor? (sí)

   _____

   _____

Informal Commands: Imperative Forms for **tú** and **vosotros**

For most verbs, the affirmative **tú** command is formed by dropping the **-s** ending of the present tense.

STATEMENT FORM	**tú** COMMAND FORM
regres**as**	regresa
cierr**as**	cierra
com**es**	come
vuelv**es**	vuelve
abr**es**	abre
pid**es**	pide
duerm**es**	duerme

Eight verbs have irregular affirmative **tú** command forms, all of which are one-syllable forms.

INFINITIVE	**tú** COMMAND
decir	**di**
hacer	**haz**

INFINITIVE	**tú** COMMAND
ir	**ve**
poner	**pon**
salir	**sal**
ser	**sé**
tener	**ten**
venir	**ven**

—**Sal** y **cierra** la puerta con llave. *"Go out and lock the door."*
—**Ve** y **busca** la llave entonces. *"Then go and look for the key."*

—**Pasa** la aspiradora y **saca** la basura. *"Vacuum the house and take out the garbage."*

—Y tú, **pon** la ropa limpia en la cómoda. *"And you, put the clean clothes in the chest of drawers."*

Note that the affirmative **tú** command forms for the verbs **ver** and **ir** are identical: **ve**. Context clarifies which one is meant.

Compounds of the above eight verbs have the same irregularity in their affirmative **tú** command forms. Note the use of accent marks on compound command forms ending in **n**.

INFINITIVE	**tú** COMMAND
rehacer	**rehaz**
suponer	**supón**
mantener	**mantén**

Negative **tú** command forms are not the same as the corresponding affirmative command forms. To form the negative **tú** command, add **-s** to the corresponding **Ud.** command and place **no** before the verb.

NEGATIVE **Ud.** COMMAND	NEGATIVE **tú** COMMAND	AFFIRMATIVE **tú** COMMAND
no hable	no hables	habla
no cierre	no cierres	cierra
no coma	no comas	come
no escriba	no escribas	escribe
no pida	no pidas	pide
no duerma	no duermas	duerme
no haga	no hagas	**haz**
no **vaya**	no **vayas**	ve
no **sea**	no **seas**	**sé**
no **esté**	no **estés**	**está**

No hables así con tu profesor. *Don't speak like that to your teacher.*
No seas arrogante. *Don't be arrogant.*
No estés inquieta. *Don't be nervous.*

D *Write both affirmative and negative* **tú** *commands for each item.*

MODELO   preparar los tacos

Prepara los tacos.

No prepares los tacos.

1. escribir en el disquete

_____

_____

2. leer los cuentos

_____

_____

3. repetir el plato

_____

_____

4. hacer un clic en el icono

_____

_____

5. enviar un fax

_____

_____

6. colgar el cartel en esta pared

_____

_____

7. exigir más de ellos

_____

_____

8. poner un anuncio en el periódico

_____

_____

9. pedir un aumento de sueldo

_____

_____

10. decir que sí

_____

_____

11. ver el sitio Web

_____

_____

12. ser interesado

_____

_____

13. analizar la información

_____

_____

14. salir a pasear

_____

_____

15. ir a caballo

_____

_____

16. llegar temprano

_____

_____

17. venir al cibercafé

_____

_____

18. teñir la camisa

_____

_____

19. crear una base de datos

_____

_____

20. tener confianza en ellos

_____

_____

NEOLOGISMS   computer terms

The need to create terms for the computer has influenced the Spanish language. As Spanish-speaking societies adopted the technology, many English words were brought into Spanish unchanged, while others were borrowed and completely or partially adapted to Spanish spelling.

Here are some commonly used verbs borrowed from English and adapted to the Spanish language with their synonyms in parentheses: **formatear**, **escanear**, **cliquear**, **linkear** (**enlazar**), **chatear** (**conversar**, **charlar**, **platicar**), **hackear** or **jaquear** (**piratear**), and **crashear** (**chocar**, **colgar**, **quebrar**, **romper**, **estrellar**, **congelar**). These new verbs created in Spanish are integrated into the **-ar** conjugation, with the **-ear** suffix.

Another way of creating new verbs is to use the verb **hacer** + an English noun: **hacer (un) clic**, **hacer un login/logon/logoff/download/backup/link**, etc. Spanish verbs such as **bajar**, **descargar**, and **subir** take on new meanings to accommodate the new functions: **bajar** and **descargar** *to download*, **subir** *to upload*.

For all verbs, the affirmative **vosotros** command is formed by replacing the **-r** ending of the infinitive with **-d**. All **vosotros** commands are regular.

INFINITIVE	**vosotros** COMMAND
habla**r**	habla**d**
pensa**r**	pensa**d**
come**r**	come**d**
volve**r**	volve**d**
escribi**r**	escribi**d**
pedi**r**	pedi**d**
dormi**r**	dormi**d**

To form the negative **vosotros** command, replace the ending **-emos** of **nosotros** command forms with **-éis**, and replace the ending **-amos** of **nosotros** command forms with the ending **-áis**. The word **no** stands before the verb form.

NEGATIVE **nosotros** COMMAND	NEGATIVE **vosotros** COMMAND
no habl**emos**	no habl**éis**
no pens**emos**	no pens**éis**
no est**emos**	no est**éis**
no com**amos**	no com**áis**
no volv**amos**	no volv**áis**
no escrib**amos**	no escrib**áis**
no pid**amos**	no pid**áis**
no advirt**amos**	no advirt**áis**
no durm**amos**	no durm**áis**
no busqu**emos**	no busqu**éis**
no pagu**emos**	no pagu**éis**
no corrij**amos**	no corrij**áis**
no hag**amos**	no hag**áis**

NEGATIVE **nosotros** COMMAND	NEGATIVE **vosotros** COMMAND
no ofrez**camos**	no ofrez**cáis**
no vay**amos**	no vay**áis**
no se**amos**	no se**áis**

—Mamá, queremos ir al parque.

—Chicos, **no seáis** impacientes. **Tened** un poco de paciencia y **no hagáis** tanto ruido.

"Mom, we want to go to the park."
"Children, don't be impatient. Be a little patient and don't make so much noise."

E *Write both affirmative and negative* **vosotros** *commands for each item.*

> MODELO   trotar hoy
>
> *Trotad hoy.*
>
> *No trotéis hoy.*

1. estudiar mercadeo

   _____

   _____

2. vender vuestro coche

   _____

   _____

3. abrir el baúl

   _____

   _____

4. recoger las uvas

   _____

   _____

5. ser agresivos

   _____

   _____

6. seguir nuestros consejos

   _____

   _____

7. hacer cola

   _____

   _____

8. venir en taxi

   _____

   _____

9. dormir la siesta

   _____

   _____

10. publicar vuestras memorias

    _____

    _____

11. ir al dentista

    _____

    _____

12. tragar rápidamente

    _____

    _____

13. salir a bailar

    _____

    _____

14. aplazar la reunión

    _____

    _____

15. medir las cortinas

    _____

    _____

16. oír las noticias

    _____

    _____

17. traer el cheque

    _____

    _____

18. buscar el cajero automático (*ATM*)

    _____

    _____

19. decir la clave personal (*PIN*)

_____

_____

20. invertir en esta industria

_____

_____

Indirect Commands

Indirect commands are commands about the third person: *he, she, it,* and *they.* In English, indirect commands are formed with the verbs *let* or *have*: *Let him do it, Have them come in.*

Spanish indirect commands consist of **Que** + the **Ud.** or **Uds.** command form of the verb. Remember that **Ud.** and **Uds.** forms are third-person forms.

Que Juan te **ayude**.	*Let Juan help you.*
Que los programadores **terminen** el proyecto esta semana.	*Have the programmers finish the project this week.*
Que nadie **entre** antes de las ocho.	*Don't let anyone in before eight.*
Que los clientes **esperen** abajo.	*Have the customers wait downstairs.*
Que se lo **hagan** (a Ud.).	*Have them do it for you.*

F   *Write indirect commands in which Jaime says* let *or* have *others do the things people want him to do.*

MODELO   Juan dice que debes sacar la basura.
Yo no quiero. Que saque la basura él.

1. Anita dice que debes hacer los quehaceres.

_____

2. Paco y Javier dicen que debes comprar la cerveza.

_____

3. Consuelo dice que debes aprender a bailar salsa.

_____

4. Tu hermana dice que debes llevar a tu novia al cine más a menudo.

_____

5. Tu entrenador de baloncesto dice que debes practicar todos los días.

_____

6. Tus amigos dicen que debes buscar trabajo.

_____

7. Lorenzo dice que debes llamar a Pedro.

_____

8. Mario dice que debes ir a ver el partido de tenis.

_____

G **Translation.** *Express the following sentences in English.*

1. Disfruten Uds. esta estupenda exposición de arte.

_____

2. Que vean todos esta estupenda exposición de arte.

_____

3. Que vaya él por los cartuchos de tinta.

_____

4. Que envíe la secretaria los mensajes electrónicos ahora mismo.

_____

5. Que los clientes hagan cola en la taquilla.

_____

6. Que nadie interrumpa la reunión de los jefes de Estado.

_____

7. Que participen los demás en el evento.

_____

8. Que alguien nos advierta lo antes posible.

_____

Other Ways of Giving Commands

The infinitive of the verb, rather than the command form, is often used as an imperative in newspaper ads, recipes, instructions, and notices.

Interesados **mandar** curriculum vitae.	*Interested persons send your curriculum vitae.*
Enviar historial a esta dirección electrónica.	*Send résumé to this e-mail address.*
Pasar las chuletas por harina y **freírlas** en aceite hirviendo.	*Dip the chops in flour and fry them in boiling oil.*
Doblar a la derecha y **pasar** bajo el puente.	*Turn right and go under the bridge.*
Arrastrar y **soltar**.	*Drag and drop.*

> **Agregar** compra, **ver** carrito, **pasar** a la caja.
>
> *Add purchase, see cart, go to checkout.*
>
> **Destornillar** los tornillos.
>
> *Unscrew the screws.*

The infinitive rather than the command form is used with the following expressions that convey formality and politeness.

> **Favor de esperar** aquí.
>
> *Please wait here.*
>
> **Haga el favor de entregar** el informe.
>
> *Please hand in the report.*
>
> **Tengan la bondad de registrarse.**
>
> *Please register.*

H *Rewrite each sentence, changing the command forms to infinitives that will serve as imperatives.*

MODELO   Vengan a la apertura (*opening*) de la nueva tienda.

Venir a la apertura de la nueva tienda.

1. Sigan derecho.

   _____

2. No pisen el césped.

   _____

3. Utilicen nuestra banca electrónica (*online banking*).

   _____

4. Reserven sus billetes en línea.

   _____

5. Agreguen una cucharadita de canela (*teaspoonful of cinnamon*).

   _____

6. Abran una cuenta corriente (*checking account*).

   _____

7. Guarden las recetas en su PDA (*personal digital assistant*).

   _____

8. Para más información llamen al teléfono 182329.

   _____

9. Para mayores informes envíen un e-mail a esta dirección.

   _____

10. Calienten el guisado (*stew*) a fuego lento.

   _____

11. Abróchense el cinturón de seguridad.

    _____

12. No toquen los cables de electricidad.

    _____

13. Interesados pónganse en contacto con el director.

    _____

14. Alójense en el Hotel Caribe.

    _____

I *Rewrite each formal* **Ud.** *or* **Uds.** *command as an infinitive, using the expressions in parentheses. You are giving commands to people with whom you have a formal relationship.*

MODELO   Archive los documentos. (Favor de)
          Favor de archivar los documentos.

1. Vuelva más tarde. (Haga el favor de)

    _____

2. Espérenos en la oficina. (Favor de)

    _____

3. Siéntense en la sala. (Tengan la bondad de)

    _____

4. Hágame un copia de seguridad. (Favor de)

    _____

5. Pulse el botón. (Tenga la bondad de)

    _____

6. Explíquenmelo. (Hagan el favor de)

    _____

7. Reúnanse la semana próxima. (Favor de)

    _____

8. No se meta en este asunto. (Haga el favor de)

    _____

9. No se oponga al plan. (Favor de)

    _____

10. No se lo digan a nadie. (Tengan la bondad de)

    _____

| BUILDING SENTENCES | **Imperative sentences with object pronouns** |

The rules for the placement of object pronouns are different with imperatives than with other verb forms.

In negative commands, object pronouns are placed before the verb, just as they are with statement forms. This applies to both single and double object pronouns.

—Este libro no me interesa.	*"I'm not interested in this book."*
—**No lo lea**, entonces.	*"Then don't read it."*
—Estas acciones no nos parecen muy buenas.	*"We don't think these stocks are very good."*
—Entonces, **no las compren**.	*"Then don't buy them."*
—¿Te traigo la revista?	*"Shall I bring you the magazine?"*
—No, gracias, **no me la traigas**.	*"No, thanks. Don't bring it to me."*
—Este reloj no le va a gustar a Pablo.	*"Pablo won't like this watch."*
—En ese caso, **no se lo regalemos**.	*"In that case, let's not give it (as a gift) to him."*
—¿Les envío los documentos mañana?	*"Shall I send you the documents tomorrow?"*
—No, **no nos los envíe**.	*"No, don't send them to us."*
—Roberto no quiere prestarle su bicicleta a Memo.	*"Roberto doesn't want to lend his bicycle to Memo."*
—Bueno, **que no se la preste** entonces.	*"Okay, then don't have him lend it to him."*

J   *Answer each question with a negative command. Change direct object nouns to pronouns and make all necessary changes in your answers. ¡Ojo! Make sure to use the correct command forms for **tú**, **Ud.**, **Uds.**, **nosotros**, or **vosotros**. Some items will have more than one answer.*

MODELOS   ¿Compro la mochila?

     No, no la compres/compre.

¿Te llevo al centro?

     No, no me lleves al centro.

¿Le entregamos el informe a José?

     No, no se lo entreguen (Uds.)/entreguéis (vosotros)/

     entreguemos (nosotros).

1. ¿Pulso el botón?

2. ¿Pisamos el césped?

3. ¿Hago la lista?

   _____

4. ¿Comemos las ensaladas?

   _____

5. ¿Te llamo mañana?

   _____

6. ¿Los ayudo (a Uds.) con los cajones?

   _____

7. ¿Traemos el café?

   _____

8. ¿Le regalamos la videocámara a José?

   _____

9. ¿Les mandamos los contratos a Uds.?

   _____

10. ¿Paseamos al perro?

    _____

11. ¿La buscamos (a Ud.) esta noche?

    _____

12. ¿Les enseño las fotos a nuestros amigos?

    _____

13. ¿Os cuento el secreto?

    _____

14. ¿Le solicito la beca a mi profesor?

    _____

15. ¿Os explicamos las ideas?

    _____

16. ¿Te doy tu regalo de cumpleaños ahora?

    _____

In affirmative commands, object pronouns follow the verb form and are attached to it in writing. A written accent is added on the vowel of the stressed syllable of the verb.

—¿Debo servir el pollo?   *"Shall I serve the chicken?"*
—Sí, **sírvelo.**   *"Yes, serve it."*

—¿Qué hago con esta ropa, señora?   *"What shall I do with this clothing, ma'am?"*
—**Lávela** y **plánchela**, por favor.   *"Please wash it and iron it."*

—¿Usted necesita estos informes, señor?   *"Do you need these reports, sir?"*
—Sí, **entréguemelos** en seguida.   *"Yes, submit them to me immediately."*

—¿Uds. saben lo que le pasó a Julia?   *"Do you know what happened to Julia?"*
—No, **cuéntanoslo.**   *"No, tell (it to) us."*

When the pronoun **se** is added to an affirmative **nosotros** command, the resulting double **s** is reduced to a single **s** in writing.

> **Mandemos + selo → Mandémoselo.**

When the pronoun **nos** is added to an affirmative **ustedes** command, a double **n** is written (and often pronounced in deliberate speech), thus distinguishing the **ustedes** command from the **usted** command. Compare the two forms below.

> **Enseñe + nos → Enséñenos Ud.**
> **Enseñen + nos → Enséñennos Uds.**

The imperative of **dar**, **dé**, often keeps its written accent when a single pronoun is attached, in spite of the fact that two-syllable words ending in a vowel and stressed on the first syllable don't have written accent marks: **Déme ese libro.** It must have the written accent when double object pronouns are attached to it in writing: **Démelo.**

K   *Answer each question with an affirmative command. Change nouns to direct object pronouns and make all necessary changes in your answers. ¡Ojo! Make sure to use the correct command forms for tú, Ud., Uds., nosotros, or vosotros. Some items will have more than one answer.*

    MODELOS   ¿Descargo el archivo?

         Sí, descárgalo/descárguelo.

         ¿Te llevo al centro?

         Sí, llévame al centro.

         ¿Le entregamos el informe a José?

         Sí, entréguenselo/entregádselo/entreguémoselo.

1. ¿Escribo el mensaje electrónico?

2. ¿Cierro la cuenta?

3. ¿Alquilamos los apartamentos?

4. ¿Dirigimos la orquesta?

5. ¿Las recojo (a Uds.) en el museo?

_____

6. ¿Les pagamos la cena a ellos?

_____

7. ¿Te decimos qué pasó?

_____

8. ¿Le hago el sándwich a Isabel?

_____

9. ¿Les devolvemos los libros a Uds.?

_____

10. ¿Vestimos a los niños?

_____

11. ¿Te recordamos la fecha?

_____

12. ¿Le mostramos las pinturas a Ud.?

_____

13. ¿Les sirvo los aperitivos a las visitas?

_____

14. ¿Le pedimos un préstamo al banco?

_____

15. ¿Os espero en el bar?

_____

16. ¿Te vendo el quemador de CD?

_____

L *Translation. Express the following commands in English. Then write the infinitive and the subject of the command form. Some items will have more than one answer.*

MODELO   Démelo. _Give it to me. (dar, Ud.)_

1. Ve y velo. _____

2. Muéstreselo. _____

3. Envíenselas. _____

4. Subídnoslos. _____

5. Dásela. _____

6. Tráigannosla. _____

7. No se los ocultes. _____

8. No me la diga. _____

9. Pidámoselos. _____

10. Hágaselo. _____

M ***Translation.*** *Express the following sentences in Spanish, using the cues given.*

1. *The cell phone? Give it to me.* (tú)

   _____

2. *The computer? Show it to us.* (Uds.)

   _____

3. *The packages? Wrap them up for me.* (Ud.)

   _____

4. *Your questions? Ask him them.* (vosotros)

   _____

5. *The (piece of) news? Let's write it to her.*

   _____

6. *That brand? Let's not ask them for it.*

   _____

7. *If the meal is made, serve it to us.* (tú)

   _____

8. *If the report is printed, read it to them.* (Ud.)

   _____

9. *The tennis racket? Offer it to him.* (Ud.)

   _____

10. *Be patient. Don't go yet.* (tú)

   _____

The Future and the Conditional; The Future Perfect and the Conditional Perfect

The Future Tense

The future tense in Spanish is formed by adding a specific set of endings to the infinitive of the verb. The endings are the same for all verbs.

Hablaré.	*I will speak.*
Comeré.	*I will eat.*
Escribiré.	*I will write.*

hablar *to speak*

hablar**é**	hablar**emos**
hablar**ás**	hablar**éis**
hablar**á**	hablar**án**

comer *to eat*

comer**é**	comer**emos**
comer**ás**	comer**éis**
comer**á**	comer**án**

escribir *to write*

escribir**é**	escribir**emos**
escribir**ás**	escribir**éis**
escribir**á**	escribir**án**

Several verbs have modified infinitive forms in the future. These verbs have the same endings as the verbs in the charts above. The **yo** form is given as a model for the entire conjugation.

Some verbs replace the infinitive vowel **e** or **i** with **d**.

INFINITIVE	FUTURE
poner	**pondré**
salir	**saldré**
tener	**tendré**
valer	**valdré**
venir	**vendré**

Some verbs lose the infinitive vowel **e**.

INFINITIVE	FUTURE
caber	**cabré**
haber	**habré**
poder	**podré**
querer	**querré**
saber	**sabré**

Note that the future of **hay**—a modified form from **haber**—is **habrá** (*there will be*).

Some verbs shorten the infinitive.

INFINITIVE	FUTURE
decir	**diré**
hacer	**haré**

-Ir verbs that have an accent mark in the infinitive—**oír**, **reír**, **sonreír**—lose that accent mark in the future tense form.

INFINITIVE	FUTURE
oír	**oiré**
reír	**reiré**
sonreír	**sonreiré**

Compounds of verbs that have modified infinitives in the future show the same shortened infinitives in the future.

INFINITIVE	FUTURE
componer	**compondré**
retener	**retendré**
prevenir	**prevendré**
contradecir	**contradiré**
satisfacer	**satisfaré**

A   *Rewrite each sentence, changing the verb from present tense to future tense in order to tell what will happen.*

MODELO   Paso el día en la biblioteca.

Pasaré el día en la biblioteca.

1. Compramos muchas cosas en una tienda virtual.

   _____

2. Cuentan con nosotros para llevarlo a cabo.

   _____

3. Aprendes los lenguajes de programación.

   _____

4. Nieva pasado mañana.

_____

5. ¿A qué hora vienen?

_____

6. Gabriela estudia enfermería pediátrica.

_____

7. No les digo nada.

_____

8. Tenéis mucho que hacer.

_____

9. Hay millones de navegantes en línea.

_____

10. Marcos efectúa grandes cambios.

_____

11. No pueden vernos hasta la semana entrante.

_____

12. Jaime hace el papel del protagonista.

_____

13. Están muy emocionados por la noticia.

_____

14. Oyes la música mejor desde esta fila.

_____

15. La situación va de mal en peor.

_____

16. Nos ponemos los zapatos.

_____

17. Caben quinientas personas en el salón de actos.

_____

18. Queremos pintar unos paisajes.

_____

19. Persiguen al culpable.

_____

20. Empezáis a acostumbraros al horario.

_____

LA LENGUA ESPAÑOLA   the future

The endings of the future tense in Spanish look very much like the forms of the auxiliary verb **haber** for good reason. In late spoken Latin, the original Latin future was replaced by a verb + infinitive construction consisting of the auxiliary verb **habere** + the infinitive. The meaning shifted from *I have to go/ I am to go* to *I will go*. As late as the seventeenth century, the ending could still be separated from the verb and an object pronoun could be inserted between them: **ver lo he** *I will see him*. In the modern language, this separation is impossible, and in modern Spanish you can only say **lo veré**.

The future tense is used to express future events, although in spoken Spanish the **ir a** + infinitive construction and the present tense compete with it and are probably more common.

Mañana **iré** al centro.	*Tomorrow I'll go downtown.*
Mañana **voy a ir** al centro.	*Tomorrow I'm going to go downtown.*
Mañana **voy** al centro.	*Tomorrow I'm going downtown.*

In English we often use the future tense to ask for instructions. Spanish also uses the present tense for this function.

¿**Estaciono** aquí?	*Shall I park here?*
¿Te **ayudo**?	*Shall I help you?*
¿**Salimos** por aquella puerta?	*Shall we go out through that door over there?*
¿**Preparamos** la cena?	*Shall we prepare dinner?*

Both English and Spanish use the future tense in the main clause of sentences that express possible hypotheses. These sentences consist of a **si**-clause (*if*-clause) and a main clause. Notice that the **si**-clause and the main clause can be inverted.

Vendremos si tenemos tiempo.	*We'll come if we have time.*
Si recibo el software hoy, te lo **prestaré**.	*If I get the software today, I'll lend it to you.*

B *Rewrite each sentence, changing the infinitive of the **ir a** + infinitive construction to a future tense verb to tell what will happen.*

MODELO   Jorge va a necesitar un nuevo módem.

    Jorge necesitará un nuevo módem.

1. Virginia va a cumplir veintitrés años el lunes.

   _____

2. Ellos van a ponernos al día.

   _____

3. Vamos a profundizar el tema.

   _____

4. Voy a hacer un login.

_____

5. Van a formatear el documento.

_____

6. ¿No va a caber más memoria en el ordenador?

_____

7. La boda va a ser en un hotel céntrico.

_____

8. Estos jóvenes van a tener mucho éxito.

_____

9. Va a llover toda la temporada.

_____

10. Va a haber un simulacro de incendio (*fire drill*) esta tarde.

_____

11. Su cumpleaños va a caer en un miércoles.

_____

12. Sus esfuerzos van a valer la pena.

_____

13. Van a salir ganando como siempre.

_____

14. Los cursos van a satisfacer los requisitos.

_____

15. ¿Nos los vais a traer?

_____

16. Vamos a querer dársela.

_____

17. Voy a poder informarte mañana.

_____

18. Van a venir lo antes posible.

_____

19. Voy a saberlo pronto.

_____

20. La vas a oír cantar en la comedia musical.

_____

The Future Perfect Tense

The future perfect tense in Spanish consists of the future of the auxiliary verb **haber** + the past participle. The future perfect expresses the idea *will have spoken, will have eaten, will have written.*

hablar *to speak*

habré hablado	habremos hablado
habrás hablado	habréis hablado
habrá hablado	habrán hablado

comer *to eat*

habré comido	habremos comido
habrás comido	habréis comido
habrá comido	habrán comido

escribir *to write*

habré escrito	habremos escrito
habrás escrito	habréis escrito
habrá escrito	habrán escrito

Note that the past participle does not change for gender or number in the compound tenses.

In both Spanish and English, the future perfect tense indicates an event that will be completed in the future before another event occurs or that will be completed before some point in the future.

Si Uds. llegan a las diez, la reunión ya **habrá empezado**.	*If you arrive at ten, the meeting will have already begun.*
¿**Habrá terminado** Ud. el proyecto para el jueves de la semana entrante?	*Will you have finished the project by Thursday of next week?*
Habremos vuelto antes del quince.	*We will have returned before the fifteenth.*

C *Write sentences using the following strings of elements. Use verbs in the future perfect to tell what will have happened by some point in the future.*

MODELO   ellos / abrir la tienda de ropa / para principios del año

Ellos habrán abierto la tienda de ropa para principios del año.

1. los empleados / salir de la oficina / para la hora de la cena

   _____

2. Diana y yo / volver del museo / a eso de las cuatro

   _____

3. Rogelio / conseguir la maestría en comunicaciones / para fines del semestre

_____

_____

4. yo / hacérselo / para la semana que viene

_____

5. Uds. / reservar los billetes electrónicos / antes de las vacaciones de verano

_____

_____

6. Ud. / enviarles el correo / después de verlos

_____

7. tú / resolver el problema / antes de la reunión

_____

8. vosotros / dárnoslas / para mediados de enero

_____

9. nosotros / verlos / para el Día de la Independencia

_____

10. ellos / mandar los impuestos (_taxes_) / para el quince de abril

_____

The Conditional Tense

The conditional tense in Spanish is formed by adding the imperfect endings of **-er** and **-ir** verbs to the infinitive. These **-ía** endings are used for all verbs.

Hablaría.   _I would speak._
Comería.   _I would eat._
Escribiría.   _I would write._

hablar _to speak_

hablar**ía**	hablar**íamos**
hablar**ías**	hablar**íais**
hablar**ía**	hablar**ían**

comer _to eat_

comer**ía**	comer**íamos**
comer**ías**	comer**íais**
comer**ía**	comer**ían**

escribir *to write*

escribiría	escribiríamos
escribirías	escribiríais
escribiría	escribirían

Those verbs that have modified infinitive forms in the future also form the conditional from those shortened infinitives.

Some verbs replace the infinitive vowel **e** or **i** with **d**.

INFINITIVE	CONDITIONAL
poner	**pondría**
salir	**saldría**
tener	**tendría**
valer	**valdría**
venir	**vendría**

Some verbs lose the infinitive vowel **e**.

INFINITIVE	CONDITIONAL
caber	**cabría**
haber	**habría**
poder	**podría**
querer	**querría**
saber	**sabría**

Note that the conditional of **hay**—modified from **haber**—is **habría** (*there would be*).

Some verbs shorten the infinitive.

INFINITIVE	CONDITIONAL
decir	**diría**
hacer	**haría**

-Ir verbs that have an accent mark in the infinitive lose that accent mark in the conditional tense form.

INFINITIVE	CONDITIONAL
oír	**oiría**
reír	**reiría**
sonreír	**sonreiría**

Compounds of verbs that have modified infinitives in the conditional form the conditional with the shortened infinitive as well.

INFINITIVE	CONDITIONAL
componer	**compondría**
retener	**retendría**
prevenir	**prevendría**
contradecir	**contradiría**
satisfacer	**satisfaría**

D *Complete each sentence with the correct conditional form of the verb in parentheses to tell what would happen. The sentences in parentheses explain why these things would happen.*

MODELO   (Tardan en llegar al aeropuerto.) Ellos _*correrían*_ a la puerta (*gate*). (correr)

1. (No has comido ni bebido en todo el día.) Tú _____ hambre y sed. (tener)

2. (Vemos a la recién nacida.) Nosotros la _____ en brazos. (tomar)

3. (Un excelente restaurante acaba de abrir.) Yo _____ probar la comida. (querer)

4. (La reunión es mañana pero nadie sabe a qué hora.) Ellos _____ de averiguarla. (tratar)

5. (Uds. están inquietos y agotados de mucho trabajar.) Uds. _____ música para relajarse. (oír)

6. (Hay que comprar muchas cosas.) Ud. _____ una lista. (hacer)

7. (Su novia está enojada.) Diego le _____ tres ramilletes de flores y dos cajas de bombones. (traer)

8. (La carne está sosa [*tasteless*].) La cocinera _____ sal. (añadir)

9. (Se niegan a devolverle su dinero.) Ella _____. (exigírselo)

10. (Vosotros sabéis algo importante que desconoce vuestro amigo.) Vosotros _____. (decírselo)

As in English, the conditional in Spanish is used in hypotheses, or statements about what would happen.

¿Qué **harías** tú en ese caso?	*What would you do in that case?*
Yo no **diría** eso.	*I wouldn't say that.*
Con un jefe como el tuyo, yo **buscaría** otro trabajo.	*With a boss like yours, I would look for another job.*

In most sentences where the conditional is used to express a hypothesis, there are two clauses. The main clause has a verb in the conditional, and the **si**-clause (*if*-clause) has a verb in the imperfect subjunctive. This type of conditional sentence expresses a *contrary-to-fact* condition. (This pattern is studied in greater depth in Chapter 12. See "Building Sentences: Conditional sentences," p. 222.)

Si Uds. me **explicaran** el problema que tienen, a lo mejor les **podría** ayudar.	*If you would explain the problem that you have to me, maybe I would be able to help you.*

The conditional appears frequently in subordinate (dependent) clauses after main verbs of communication (e.g., **decir**, **escribir**) and knowledge or belief (**saber**, **creer**), when the main verb is in one of the past tenses. There is a correspondence of tenses in Spanish and English in such situations: *main clause in present/subordinate clause in future; main clause in past/subordinate clause in conditional.*

El profesor **dice** que mañana **habrá** examen.	*The teacher says there will be an exam tomorrow.*
El profesor **dijo** que mañana **habría** examen.	*The teacher said there would be an exam tomorrow.*
Carla **escribe** que **llegará** el domingo.	*Carla writes that she will arrive on Sunday.*
Carla **escribió** que **llegaría** el domingo.	*Carla wrote that she would arrive on Sunday.*
No **sabemos** si **aceptarán** la invitación.	*We don't know if they will accept the invitation.*
No **sabíamos** si **aceptarían** la invitación.	*We didn't know if they would accept the invitation.*
Creo que **vendrán**.	*I think they will come.*
Creía que **vendrían**.	*I thought they would come.*
Estoy seguro de que te lo **dirán**.	*I'm sure that they will tell you.*
Estaba seguro de que te lo **dirían**.	*I was sure that they would tell you.*

Note that English often uses the auxiliary verb *would* to express habitual or repeated action in the past. In this function, Spanish uses the imperfect tense, not the conditional.

Ella siempre me **mandaba** e-mails.	*She would always send me e-mails.*
Los sábados **íbamos** al cine.	*On Saturdays we would go to the movies.*

The conditional of some verbs is used to express polite requests, suggestions, or refusals. The English conditional is often used in the same way.

¿Me **podría** Ud. ayudar?	*Could you help me?*
¿Le **gustaría** salir un poco?	*Would you like to go out for a while?*
Lo siento, pero no le **sabría** decir.	*I'm sorry, but I don't know (the information you asked for).*

E Complete each sentence with the correct form of the verb in parentheses. Select the future or the conditional, depending on the tense of the verb that appears in the main clause.

MODELOS (llamar) Él dice que nos _llamará_ .

(llamar) Él dijo que nos _llamaría_ .

1. (venir) Me escribieron que (ellos) _____ a pasar el fin de semana.

2. (caber) ¿Sabes si _____ diez más en el autobús?

3. (hay) Pensaba que _____ lugar para todos.

4. (aceptar) Pedro les informó que (él) _____ el puesto de analista.

5. (saber) Creíamos que Ud. _____ el código.

6. (comprar) Estáis seguros que nosotros _____ el condominio.

7. (poder)   Dijiste que (tú) _____ entregármelo, ¿verdad?

8. (estar)   Les expliqué que nadie _____ para atenderlos.

9. (hacer)   El programador nos dice que (él) _____ el trabajo mañana.

10. (aterrizar)   No sabían si el avión _____ a la hora fijada (*scheduled*).

11. (interesarle) Gabriela nos dijo que _____ ver la película.

12. (encantarles) Creen que a los chicos _____ los regalos de Navidad.

The Conditional Perfect Tense

The conditional perfect tense in Spanish consists of the conditional of the auxiliary verb **haber** + the past participle. The conditional perfect expresses the idea *would have spoken, would have eaten, would have written.*

hablar *to speak*

habría hablado	habríamos hablado
habrías hablado	habríais hablado
habría hablado	habrían hablado

comer *to eat*

habría comido	habríamos comido
habrías comido	habríais comido
habría comido	habrían comido

escribir *to write*

habría escrito	habríamos escrito
habrías escrito	habríais escrito
habría escrito	habrían escrito

The conditional perfect is used to designate an action or event that would have been completed in the past, given an expressed or implied condition.

Yo no lo **habría hecho** eso.	*I wouldn't have done that.*
Nadie le **habría entendido**.	*Nobody would have understood him.*
¿Le **habrías dicho** tú la verdad?	*Would you have told her the truth?*

In most sentences in which the conditional perfect is used to express a hypothesis about the past, there are two clauses. The main clause has a verb in the conditional perfect, and the **si**-clause (*if*-clause) has a verb in the pluperfect subjunctive. This type of conditional sentence expresses a *contrary-to-fact* condition. (This pattern is studied in greater depth in Chapter 12. See "Building Sentences: Conditional sentences," p. 222.)

Si Uds. me **hubieran explicado** el problema que tenían, a lo mejor les **habría podido** ayudar.	*If you had explained the problem that you had to me, maybe I would have been able to help you.*

F *Write sentences that express that people (the subjects in parentheses) would not have done things that others did do.*

MODELO   Edita contó chismes. (Ud.)

       Ud. no habría contado chismes.

1. Inés mintió. (tú)

   _____

2. Yo los invité a comer en un restaurante caro. (Ud.)

   _____

3. Cristóbal cayó en una trampa. (nosotros)

   _____

4. Tú dijiste algo sin querer. (ellos)

   _____

5. Uds. comieron comida basura (*junk food*). (yo)

   _____

6. Mari y Sofi pusieron al cantante por las nubes. (Uds.)

   _____

7. Nosotros repetimos el plato de carne. (vosotros)

   _____

8. Vosotros visteis el programa de realidad. (Isaac)

   _____

9. Yo les regalé a los novios esa cámara digital. (Daniela y Alfredo)

   _____

10. Maximiliano utilizó una chuleta (*cheat sheet*) en el examen. (tú)

    _____

BUILDING SENTENCES   **Sentences expressing probability**

The four tenses studied in this lesson—the future, the future perfect, the conditional, and the conditional perfect—can all be used to express probability or conjecture.

The Future of Probability

The future tense expresses probability or conjecture about the present. The future of probability is used in both statements and questions. Notice the various English translations it may have.

Tus padres **estarán** cansados después de su viaje.

Your parents must be tired after their trip.

Será demasiado tarde ya.

It is probably too late already.

Juan **querrá** estudiar hoy.

I guess Juan wants to study today.

Tendrás hambre.

You must be hungry.

Laura **sacará** buenas notas.

Laura probably gets good grades.

¿Qué hora **será**?

I wonder what time it could be.

¿**Nevará** mañana?

Do you think it may snow tomorrow?

¿Qué **pensarán** de nosotros?

I wonder what they think of us.

¿Cómo **estará** Juana?

I wonder how Juana is.

¿Quién **ganará**?

Who do you think will win?

The construction using **deber de** in the present tense + the infinitive may be used to express probability or conjecture in present time. The preposition **de** may be omitted.

Deben (de) ser las dos. = **Serán las dos.**   *It's probably two o'clock.*
Debe (de) tener suerte. = **Tendrá suerte.**   *She must be lucky.*

G *Rewrite each sentence to express probability or conjecture about the present. Remove the words or phrases that indicate probability or conjecture, and write the verbs in the future tense.*

MODELO   Probablemente son las diez.
          Serán las diez.

1. Probablemente hay celos entre las cuñadas (*sisters-in-law*).

   _____

2. Me imagino que la noche cae pronto.

   _____

3. Supongo que los gemelos tienen veintiún años.

   _____

4. Probablemente quieren bailar el tango.

   _____

5. Me imagino que los aficionados están entusiasmados.

   _____

6. Supongo que su sortija de diamantes vale mucho.

   _____

7. ¿Probablemente llueve mañana?

   _____

8. Me imagino que es la una y media.

   _____

H   *Translation.* *Write questions using the future tense to express probability in the present.*

1. *I wonder when they're arriving.*

   _____

2. *I wonder what time it could be.*

   _____

3. *Who do you think might know their telephone number?*

   _____

4. *I wonder where the meeting might be.*

   _____

5. *What do you think the weather might be like this week?*

   _____

6. *I wonder how they are.*

   _____

The conditional expresses probability or conjecture about the past. The conditional of probability is most commonly used about past conditions that would appear in the imperfect in statement form.

—¿Por qué no vino el señor Galíndez?	*"Why didn't Mr. Galíndez come?"*
—No sé. **Estaría** enfermo.	*"I don't know. Maybe he was sick."*

(Statement would be: El señor Galíndez no vino porque **estaba** enfermo.)

—¿A qué edad se mudó Javier a la capital?	*"At what age did Javier move to the capital?"*
—No estoy seguro. Él **tendría** unos quince años cuando se fue con su familia a Ciudad de México.	*"I'm not sure. He was probably about fifteen years old when he left with his family for Mexico City."*

(Statement would be: Javier **tenía** unos quince años cuando se mudó a la capital.)

—¿Los chicos regresaron muy tarde anoche?	*"Did the kids get back very late last night?"*
—Ya lo creo. **Serían** las dos y media o las tres cuando oí la puerta.	*"I should say so. It must have been two thirty or three when I heard the door."*

(Statement would be: **Eran** las dos y media o las tres cuando oí la puerta.)

—¿Por qué crees que no compraron aquel carro que tanto les gustaba?	*"Why do you think they didn't buy that car that they liked so much?"*
—¿Quién sabe? **Costaría** un dineral.	*"Who knows? It probably cost a fortune."*

(Statement would be: No compraron aquel carro porque **costaba** un dineral.)

The construction using **deber de** in the imperfect tense + the infinitive may be used to express probability or conjecture in past time. The preposition **de** may be omitted.

Debían (de) ser las diez. = Serían las diez.   *It was probably ten o'clock.*
Debía (de) tener razón. = Tendría razón.   *He was probably right.*

I *Rewrite each sentence to express probability or conjecture about the past.*
Remove the words or phrases that indicate probability or conjecture,
and write the verbs in the conditional tense.

MODELO   Probablemente eran las diez.

> *Serían las diez.*

1. Probablemente había treinta invitados en la fiesta.

2. Supongo que era un verano muy caluroso.

3. Probablemente tenía veintinueve años.

4. Me imagino que las joyas costaban un ojo de la cara.

5. Probablemente estaban de viaje.

6. Supongo que hacía mucho frío.

7. ¿Probablemente nevaba mucho en la sierra?

8. Me imagino que él estaba contentísimo.

J *Translation.* *Express the following sentences in Spanish, using the conditional tense*
to express probability in the past.

1. *I wonder what time it was when they called us.*

2. *It was probably nine thirty.*

3. *Why do you think she was so tired?*

4. *It was probably because of the long and difficult flight.*

5. *I think there was probably a problem with his car.*

6. *Maybe it (the car) was broken.*

The Future Perfect of Probability

The future perfect is used to express probability or conjecture about the past. It is very common in this function, and is used about actions or conditions that would appear in the preterit or present perfect in statement form.

—¿Quién le **habrá prohibido** ir?	*"I wonder who could have forbidden him to go."*
—**Habrá sido** su padre.	*"It was probably his father."*
—Parece que el perro no tiene mucha hambre.	*"It seems that the dog is not very hungry."*
—Le **habrán dado** de comer.	*"They must have fed him."*
—Mira, las calles están mojadas.	*"Look, the streets are wet."*
—**Habrá llovido** mientras estábamos en el cine.	*"I guess it must have rained while we were in the movie theater."*
—Mi computadora está funcionando.	*"My computer is working."*
—Raúl la **habrá arreglado**.	*"Raúl probably fixed it."*
—¿Por qué **habrá contestado** así?	*"Why do you think he answered like that?"*
—No **habrá entendido** lo que le preguntaron.	*"I guess he didn't understand what they asked him."*
—¡Qué contentos están esos hinchas!	*"How happy those fans are!"*
—Su equipo **habrá ganado** el partido.	*"I suppose their team won the game."*

The construction using **deber de** + the perfect infinitive (**haber** + past participle) can be used instead of the future perfect tense to express probability in past time. The preposition **de** may be omitted.

Carolina debe (de) haber salido.	*Carolina must have (probably) gone out.*
Deben (de) haberlo hecho.	*They must have (probably) done it.*

K *Rewrite each sentence to express probability or conjecture about the past. Remove the word **probablemente** and write the verbs in the future perfect tense. The sentences in parentheses explain why these things would have happened.*

MODELO   (Todos están inquietos.) Probablemente ocurrió algo desagradable.

      Habrá ocurrido algo desagradable.

1. (Los amigos están reñidos.) Probablemente riñeron por una tontería.

---

2. (¡Qué linda capa de nieve!) Probablemente nevó toda la noche.

---

3. (El perro vomita.) Probablemente el perro tragó la pelota.

_____

4. (El incendio no ha hecho mucho daño.) Probablemente los bomberos llegaron muy rápidamente para apagar el incendio.

_____

5. (La cocina huele mal.) Probablemente no sacaron la basura.

_____

6. (¡Qué montón de periódicos!) Probablemente Emilio no recicló los periódicos en seis meses.

_____

The Conditional Perfect of Probability

The conditional perfect may also be used to express probability or conjecture about the past. It may add a note of astonishment or bewilderment to the conjecture, especially in questions.

¿Y le **habrían creído**?	_And could they possibly have believed him?_
¿Tú **habrías dicho** tal cosa?	_Would you possibly have said such a thing?_
¿Quién lo **habría hecho**?	_Who could possibly have done it?_

L   _Translation._ _Express the following sentences of probability or conjecture in Spanish._ **¡Ojo!** _Pay special attention to the tenses of the verbs and to English cues such as the words_ I wonder, probably, _and_ possibly. _There may be more than one way to express these sentences._

1. _I wonder when they'll come to see us._

_____

2. _It was probably eleven o'clock when I arrived at the train station._

_____

3. _You (Uds.) must have (probably) seen them at the party._

_____

4. _The Ferrari probably cost them a fortune._

_____

5. _Unbelievable! He could not possibly have said such a terrible thing._

_____

6. _When we met Irene, she was probably about twenty-two years old._

_____

7. *I guess you (tú) must have sent me an e-mail while you were at the Internet café.*

   _____

8. *I wonder what time it could be.*

   _____

9. *I wonder why Carlos might have left without letting us know.*

   _____

10. *I guess something unexpected* (algo imprevisto) *must have happened.*

    _____

11. *I guess everyone read* The Da Vinci Code.

    _____

12. *You* (Uds.) *probably feel like going to the movies.*

    _____

13. *I suppose it's too late already.*

    _____

14. *There are probably no more shows* (la función).

    _____

The Subjunctive (Part I): The Present Subjunctive

BUILDING SENTENCES

Compound and complex sentences

The subjunctive is largely a mood used in subordinate clauses, clauses introduced by **que** that are part of a larger sentence. The subjunctive is used after main clauses expressing volition (the imposition of will to get someone to do something), emotion and value judgment (personal reaction to an event or condition), doubt and denial, and wishes, and is used to form most commands.

Regular Verbs in the Present Subjunctive

The present subjunctive is formed by changing the ending vowel **a** (and the **-o** of the **yo** form) of the present indicative to **e** in **-ar** verbs, and changing the ending vowels **e** and **i** (and the **-o** of the **yo** form) of the present indicative to **a** in **-er** and **-ir** verbs. **-Er** and **-ir** verbs have the same set of endings in the subjunctive. The verbs in the main clause of the examples below express volition: **querer** *to want*, **esperar** *to hope*, **preferir** *to prefer*. Note that in the present subjunctive, the **yo** form and the **él/ella/Ud.** form are identical.

firmar *to sign*

Quiere que firm**e** el contrato.	*He wants me to sign the contract.*
Quiere que firm**es** el contrato.	*He wants you to sign the contract.*
Quiere que firm**e** el contrato.	*He wants her to sign the contract.*
Quiere que firm**emos** el contrato.	*He wants us to sign the contract.*
Quiere que firm**éis** el contrato.	*He wants you to sign the contract.*
Quiere que firm**en** el contrato.	*He wants them to sign the contract.*

vender *to sell*

Espera que vend**a** la casa.	*She hopes I'll sell the house.*
Espera que vend**as** la casa.	*She hopes you'll sell the house.*
Espera que vend**a** la casa.	*She hopes he'll sell the house.*
Espera que vend**amos** la casa.	*She hopes we'll sell the house.*
Espera que vend**áis** la casa.	*She hopes you'll sell the house.*
Espera que vend**an** la casa.	*She hopes they'll sell the house.*

abrir *to open*

Prefieren que no abra las ventanas.	*They prefer me not to open the windows.*
Prefieren que no abras las ventanas.	*They prefer you not to open the windows.*
Prefieren que no abra las ventanas.	*They prefer her not to open the windows.*
Prefieren que no abramos las ventanas.	*They prefer us not to open the windows.*
Prefieren que no abráis las ventanas.	*They prefer you not to open the windows.*
Prefieren que no abran las ventanas.	*They prefer them not to open the windows.*

-Ar and **-er** verbs that have changes in the vowel of the stem in the present indicative have these same stem changes in the present subjunctive. The changes take place in those forms of the present subjunctive where the stem is stressed.

Queremos que lo **pienses** con calma.	*We want you to think it over at your leisure.*
No quiero que Uds. **vuelvan** tarde.	*I don't want you to return late.*
Espero que **podamos** ir.	*I hope we will be able to go.*
No quieren que **cerréis** la cuenta bancaria.	*They don't want you to close the bank account.*

-Ir verbs that have changes in the vowel of the stem in the present indicative have additional changes in the stem vowel of the present subjunctive. They have the same changes as in the present indicative but, in addition, show a change in the **nosotros** and **vosotros** forms of the present subjunctive. Verbs that have the stem change **e** > **ie** or **e** > **i** change their stem vowel from **e** to **i** in the **nosotros** and **vosotros** forms. The verbs **dormir** and **morir**, in addition to the stem change **o** > **ue** in those forms where the stem is stressed, also change their stem vowel from **o** to **u** in the **nosotros** and **vosotros** forms.

In the following charts, the subjunctive forms appear in clauses beginning with **que** as they do in Spanish speech and writing.

invertir *to invest*

PRESENT INDICATIVE		PRESENT SUBJUNCTIVE	
invierto	invertimos	que invierta	que invirtamos
inviertes	invertís	que inviertas	que invirtáis
invierte	invierten	que invierta	que inviertan

pedir *to ask for*

PRESENT INDICATIVE		PRESENT SUBJUNCTIVE	
pido	pedimos	que pida	que pidamos
pides	pedís	que pidas	que pidáis
pide	piden	que pida	que pidan

dormir *to sleep*

PRESENT INDICATIVE		PRESENT SUBJUNCTIVE	
duermo	dormimos	que duerma	que durmamos
duermes	dormís	que duermas	que durmáis
duerme	duermen	que duerma	que duerman

Irregular Verbs in the Present Subjunctive

Verbs that have an irregularity such as **g** or **zc** in the **yo** form of the present indicative have that same irregularity in all persons of the present subjunctive. These irregularities occur only in **-er** and **-ir** verbs, and therefore all the present subjunctive forms have the expected vowel ending **-a-**.

yo	tú	él/ella/Ud.	nosotros	vosotros	ellos/ellas/Uds.
caer (caigo)					
que caiga	que caigas	que caiga	que caigamos	que caigáis	que caigan
decir (digo)					
que diga	que digas	que diga	que digamos	que digáis	que digan
hacer (hago)					
que haga	que hagas	que haga	que hagamos	que hagáis	que hagan
oír (oigo)					
que oiga	que oigas	que oiga	que oigamos	que oigáis	que oigan
poner (pongo)					
que ponga	que pongas	que ponga	que pongamos	que pongáis	que pongan
salir (salgo)					
que salga	que salgas	que salga	que salgamos	que salgáis	que salgan
tener (tengo)					
que tenga	que tengas	que tenga	que tengamos	que tengáis	que tengan
traer (traigo)					
que traiga	que traigas	que traiga	que traigamos	que traigáis	que traigan
venir (vengo)					
que venga	que vengas	que venga	que vengamos	que vengáis	que vengan

The present subjunctive forms of other verbs that are irregular in the **yo** form are shown in the chart that follows. The **que** has been omitted to save space.

yo	tú	él/ella/Ud.	nosotros	vosotros	ellos/ellas/Uds.
caber (quepo)					
quepa	quepas	quepa	quepamos	quepáis	quepan
conocer (conozco)					
conozca	conozcas	conozca	conozcamos	conozcáis	conozcan
nacer (nazco)					
nazca	nazcas	nazca	nazcamos	nazcáis	nazcan
ofrecer (ofrezco)					
ofrezca	ofrezcas	ofrezca	ofrezcamos	ofrezcáis	ofrezcan
parecer (parezco)					
parezca	parezcas	parezca	parezcamos	parezcáis	parezcan

	yo	tú	él/ella/Ud.	nosotros	vosotros	ellos/ellas/Uds.
construir (construyo)	construya	construyas	construya	construyamos	construyáis	construyan
destruir (destruyo)	destruya	destruyas	destruya	destruyamos	destruyáis	destruyan
ver (veo)	vea	veas	vea	veamos	veáis	vean

The verbs **haber**, **ir**, **saber**, and **ser** have irregular stems in the present subjunctive. However, they follow the pattern of regular **-er** and **-ir** verbs in the subjunctive and thus have the expected endings with **-a-**.

	yo	tú	él/ella/Ud.	nosotros	vosotros	ellos/ellas/Uds.
haber	haya	hayas	haya	hayamos	hayáis	hayan
ir	vaya	vayas	vaya	vayamos	vayáis	vayan
saber	sepa	sepas	sepa	sepamos	sepáis	sepan
ser	sea	seas	sea	seamos	seáis	sean

Spelling Changes in the Present Subjunctive

Many verbs that are regular in the present subjunctive in speech have spelling changes according to the rules of Spanish orthography.

-Ar verbs whose stem ends in **c**, **g**, or **z** have the same spelling change in all forms of the present subjunctive that they do in the **yo** form of the preterit. (See Chapter 6, p. 93.)

c > qu
g > gu
z > c

	yo	tú	él/ella/Ud.	nosotros	vosotros	ellos/ellas/Uds.
buscar (busqué)	busque	busques	busque	busquemos	busquéis	busquen
pagar (pagué)	pague	pagues	pague	paguemos	paguéis	paguen
cruzar (crucé)	cruce	cruces	cruce	crucemos	crucéis	crucen

-**Er** and -**ir** verbs whose stems end in **g, gu**, or **c** have the same spelling change in all forms of the present subjunctive that they do in the **yo** form of the present indicative. (See Chapters 1 and 3.)

g > **j**
gu > **g**
c > **z**

yo	tú	él/ella/Ud.	nosotros	vosotros	ellos/ellas/Uds.
escoger (escojo)					
escoja	escojas	escoja	escojamos	escojáis	escojan
seguir (sigo)					
siga	sigas	siga	sigamos	sigáis	sigan
convencer (convenzo)					
convenza	convenzas	convenza	convenzamos	convenzáis	convenzan

NOTE

-**Ar** verbs whose stems end in **j** do not change **j** to **g** before **e**.

Trabajo los domingos.
Quieren que trabaje los domingos.

Note the use of accent marks in the present subjunctive forms of **dar** and **estar**.

yo	tú	él/ella/Ud.	nosotros	vosotros	ellos/ellas/Uds.
dar (doy)					
dé	des	dé	demos	deis	den
estar (estoy)					
esté	estés	esté	estemos	estéis	estén

Uses of the Subjunctive in Noun Clauses

A *noun clause* is a subordinate clause that functions as a noun, that is, it can serve as either the subject or the object of a verb. Noun clauses are introduced in Spanish by the conjunction **que**.

All the Spanish tenses studied so far belong to the *indicative mood*. Verbs in the *indicative mood* express events or states that are considered factual, definite, or part of the speaker's experience or of reality as perceived by the speaker. The following examples have dependent noun clauses in the indicative. They show events perceived as part of reality because they are the objects of verbs such as **saber, parecer, oír**, and **ver**.

Sé que Juan **vive** por aquí.	*I know that Juan lives around here.*
Me parece que la reunión **es** arriba.	*I think that the meeting is upstairs.*
Hemos oído que la empresa **tiene** problemas.	*We have heard that the firm has problems.*
Veo que los resultados **son** buenos.	*I see that the results are good.*

The subjunctive is used after main clauses expressing volition, emotion and value judgment, doubt and denial, and wishes.

Volition (Imposition of Will)

The present subjunctive is used in subordinate clauses appearing after main clauses that imply that someone wants someone to do something or that someone wants something to happen that is not yet part of reality or that person's experience. Verbs of wanting, hoping, insisting, demanding, needing, and advising are representative of this type of main clause.

Quiero que me ayudes.	*I want you to help me.*
	She hopes that she gets the job.
	They insist that we leave now.
	I demand that they pay immediately.
	We need for you to call us.
	They advise you to look for another job.

In [...] object [...] the two clauses. When the verbs of both cla[...]use appears as an infinitive.

	I want to help my neighbors.
	She hopes to get the job.
	They insist on going out now.
	We need to call you.

NO[...]

[...] receded by the indirect object pronoun [...] nate clause.

	I demand that they pay immediately.
	They advise you to look for another job.

Ot[...] **proponer**, **recomendar**, **rogar**, **sugerir**, and **suplicar**. They, too, are often preceded by the indirect object pronoun corresponding to the subject of the subordinate clause.

¿Por qué **les** dices que no vengan?	*Why are you telling them not to come?*
Él siempre **nos** pide que le prestemos el carro.	*He always asks us to lend him the car.*
Te recomiendo que veas esa película.	*I recommend that you see that film.*
Les ruego que no fumen.	*I request that you do not smoke.*
Me proponen que trabajemos juntos.	*They're proposing that we work together.*

Note the difference in meaning between the indicative and the subjunctive after **decir** in the examples that follow.

Les digo que **van** mañana. (INDICATIVE)	*I'm telling them **that they're going** tomorrow.*
Les digo que **vayan** mañana. (SUBJUNCTIVE)	*I'm telling them **to go** tomorrow.*

Several words of related meaning (influencing the actions of others) are more commonly constructed with the infinitive than with the subjunctive. Here are the most common of these verbs.

dejar a uno hacer algo *to let someone do something*
hacer a uno hacer algo *to make someone do something*
impedirle a uno hacer algo *to prevent/keep someone from doing something*
mandarle a uno hacer algo *to order someone to do something*
ordenarle a uno hacer algo *to order someone to do something*
permitirle a uno hacer algo *to permit/allow someone to do something*
prohibirle a uno hacer algo *to forbid someone to do something*

Note that **dejar** and **hacer** take direct objects; the other verbs take indirect objects.

Sus padres no **lo dejan salir**.	*His parents don't let him go out.*
Mi trabajo **me impide aceptar** tu invitación.	*My work keeps me from accepting your invitation.*
Le mandé poner la mesa.	*I ordered her to set the table.*
¿Por qué no **les permite colaborar** con Ud.?	*Why don't you allow them to work with you?*
Te **prohíbo hablarme** así.	*I forbid you to talk to me like that.*

However, the subjunctive may also be found with these verbs. Compare the following pairs of sentences. Note that when a subjunctive clause is used, the direct or indirect object pronoun may be omitted.

Sus padres no **lo dejan salir**. Sus padres no **dejan que él salga**. }	*His parents don't let him go out.*
Nunca **lo hacen hacer** la tarea. Nunca **hacen que haga** la tarea. }	*They never make him do his homework.*
Te **prohíbo hablarme** así. **Prohíbo que me hables** así. }	*I forbid you to talk to me like that.*

Some impersonal expressions (expressions beginning with **es** or expressions with no personal subject) also express influence and volition and are followed by the subjunctive.

Es necesario/preciso que *It's necessary that*
Es esencial que *It's essential that*
Es imprescindible que *It's crucial that*
Es obligatorio que *It's mandatory that*
Es importante que *It's important that*
Es urgente que *It's urgent that*
Hace falta que *It's necessary that*
Urge que *It's urgent that*

Es necesario que entreguemos el informe.	*It's necessary for us to submit the report.*
Es importante que lo **sepas**.	*It's important for you to know that.*
Es obligatorio que estudien física.	*It's mandatory for them to study physics.*
Hace falta que Ud. **responda** por e-mail.	*You must answer by e-mail.*

These expressions can be followed by the infinitive when no subject is specified for the second verb.

Es preciso estudiar mucho.	*It's necessary to study hard.*
Es importante tomarlo todo con calma.	*It's important to take things calmly.*
Urge llamar al médico.	*It's urgent that someone call the doctor.*

Emotion and Value Judgment

The subjunctive is used in subordinate clauses that are dependent on main clauses expressing an emotional reaction to the action of the subordinate clause or a value judgment about it. The main clause may consist of a conjugated verb, a third-person verb with an indirect object, or an impersonal expression.

Me alegro de que puedan venir.	*I'm glad you can come.*
Sienten que su equipo **pierda** el partido.	*They're sorry their team is losing the game.*
Nos da rabia que nunca **quieran** ayudar.	*It makes us angry that they never want to help.*
Estoy furioso que no me **hagan** caso.	*I'm furious that they don't pay attention to me.*
Tengo miedo de que no **vengan**.	*I'm afraid they won't come.*
Temo que no me **ofrezcan** el puesto.	*I fear they won't offer me the job.*
Me sorprende que no **sepas** su nombre.	*I'm surprised that you don't know his name.*
Me asusta que viva tan sola.	*It frightens me that she's living so alone.*
No nos gusta que se **ofendan**.	*We don't like them to get insulted.*
Es triste que tenga esa enfermedad.	*It's sad that he has that illness.*
Es bueno que llegues temprano.	*It's good that you arrive early.*
Es malo que nadie **coopere**.	*It's bad that nobody is cooperating.*
Es útil que repasemos nuestros apuntes.	*It's useful for us to review our notes.*
Está mal que no te lo **digan**.	*It's bad that they won't tell it to you.*
Es una lástima que se **muden**.	*It's a pity that you're moving away.*
¡Qué lástima que la guerra **continúe**!	*What a pity the war goes on!*
Más vale que lleguemos todos a la misma hora.	*It's better that we all arrive at the same time.*

Note that **sorprender, asustar,** and **gustar** are usually used with an indirect object pronoun.

Main clause verbs expressing emotion or value judgment may be followed by the infinitive when the subject of the verbs of both clauses is the same. Impersonal expressions may be followed by the infinitive when no subject is specified for the second verb.

Me alegro de verte.	*I'm glad to see you.*
Le da rabia tener que hacer esto.	*He's furious that he has to do this.*
Tienen miedo de resfriarse.	*They're afraid to catch cold.*
Me sorprende oír eso.	*I'm surprised to hear that.*
Es útil repasar los apuntes.	*Reviewing one's notes is useful.*
Está mal decírselo.	*It's bad to tell him.*

Doubt and Denial

The subjunctive is used in subordinate clauses that are dependent on main clauses expressing doubt or uncertainty about the action of the subordinate clause, or that deny its existence.

Dudo que le **den** el ascenso.	*I doubt that they'll give him the promotion.*
Es dudoso que se venda este producto.	*It's doubtful that this product will sell.*
No creo que el jefe **acepte** eso.	*I don't think the boss will accept that.*
No piensa que tengas razón.	*She doesn't think that you're right.*
No me parece que lo **sepa.**	*I don't think she knows it.*
Niego que él **sea** mejor contable que ella.	*I deny that he is a better accountant than she is.*
No he dicho que él **sea** perezoso.	*I didn't say that he is lazy.*
No estamos seguros que haya reunión hoy.	*We are not sure that there is a meeting today.*
Es posible que ya **estén.**	*It's possible that they're here already.*
Es poco probable que se vayan hoy.	*It's improbable that they'll leave today.*
No es cierto que ese empleado **entienda** chino.	*It's not true that that employee understands Chinese.*
Tal vez / Quizás tenga lugar el viernes.	*Perhaps it will take place on Friday.*
No es que suban los precios.	*It's not that prices are rising.*

The opposite of expressions of doubt or denial are followed by the indicative.

No dudo que lo **van** a ascender.	*I don't doubt that they'll promote him.*
No es dudoso que se venderá este producto.	*It's not doubtful that this product will sell.*
Creo que el jefe **acepta** eso.	*I think the boss will accept that.*
Me parece que lo **sabe.**	*I think she knows it.*
No niego que él **es** un buen contable.	*I don't deny that he is a good accountant.*
He dicho que él **es** perezoso.	*I said that he is lazy.*
Estamos seguros que hay reunión hoy.	*We are sure that there is a meeting today.*
Es cierto que ese empleado **entiende** chino.	*It's true that that employee understands Chinese.*
Es que los precios **suben.**	*The fact is that prices are rising.*

However, **es probable que** and **es imposible que** are followed by the subjunctive.

Sometimes the indicative is used after **no creer que, no pensar que, tal vez,** and **quizás.** By choosing the indicative rather than the subjunctive, the speaker signals a greater degree of certainty about the action.

No creo que captes la idea.	*I don't think you get the idea.*
No creo que captas la idea.	*I **really** don't think you get the idea.*
Tal vez se queden.	*Maybe they will stay. (The speaker is uncertain.)*
Tal vez se quedan (OR **se quedarán**).	*Maybe they will stay. (The speaker thinks they probably will stay.)*

Wishes

The present subjunctive is used after **ojalá (que)** to express a wish.

Ojalá que consigamos pasajes en ese vuelo.	*I hope we get tickets on that flight.*
Ojalá tengamos éxito con este negocio.	*I hope we're successful with this business deal.*

LA LENGUA ESPAÑOLA　borrowings from Arabic

The Spanish word **ojalá** is one of the most striking borrowings from Arabic in Spanish. It derives from the Arabic phrase *inshallah,* meaning *would to Allah.* It has become a word in Spanish that expresses hopes and wishes.

The Arabs (**los musulmanes**) began their invasion of Spain from North Africa in 711. Their domination of a large part of the country decreased steadily due to the efforts of the Christian kingdoms to take back their land. This reconquest, **la Reconquista**, began with the Battle of Covadonga in 718 and ended with the taking of Granada and the definitive expulsion of the Arabs in 1492.

The Spanish lexicon has approximately 4,000 words borrowed from Arabic. Many words referred to facets of medieval life and have fallen out of use, but others form part of the basic vocabulary of the language, such as **el azúcar, la tarea, la zanahoria, el álgebra, el alcohol, el cero, el café**, and **hasta**.

A clause beginning with **Que** followed by a verb in the subjunctive can also be used to express wishes.

¡Que tengas mucha suerte!	*Best of luck to you!*
Que te vaya bien.	*All the best to you.*
Que duermas bien.	*Sleep well.*

A　*Complete each dependent noun clause with either the present indicative or the present subjunctive of the verb in parentheses. ¡Ojo! Think about the meaning of the verb in the main clause to determine the tense or mood you will use in the dependent clause.*

　　MODELOS　(poder)　Creo que Jorge no __*puede*__ venir hoy.

　　　　　　　(poder)　Dudo que Jorge __*pueda*__ venir hoy.

1. (tener)　Comprenden que nosotros _____ prisa hoy.

2. (hacer)　Quieren que Uds. _____ construir la casa.

3. (estar)　Sé que su coche _____ descompuesto.

4. (encargar)　Prefieren que yo me _____ del proyecto.

5. (conocer)　Tememos que tú no _____ a nadie en la ciudad.

6. (ser)　Nos parece que Sol _____ muy comprensiva.

7. (venir)　Han oído que Ud. _____ el jueves.

8. (salir)   Prohíben que el público _____ por esa puerta.

9. (discutir)   ¿Deseáis que nosotros _____ el tema?

10. (utilizar) Vemos que vosotros _____ un nuevo ordenador.

11. (decir)   No permiten que Carlos _____ palabrotas (*swear*).

12. (ir)   Pienso que _____ a hacer mal tiempo mañana.

13. (llegar)   ¿Necesitas que ellos _____ para principios del mes?

14. (ocupar)   Entienden que yo me _____ de los planes.

15. (rechazar) Aconsejan que tú no _____ la oferta.

B *Complete each sentence with the correct form of the present subjunctive of the verb in parentheses.*

   MODELO   (tener)   Te suplico que _*tengas*_ cuidado.

1. (impedir)   Esperamos que él no _____ su progreso.

2. (ver)   Insisten en que tú los _____ lo antes posible.

3. (almorzar)   Siente que Uds. no _____ con ella hoy.

4. (ser)   Me alegro de que ellos _____ tan responsables y serios.

5. (traer)   ¿No te sorprende que ellos no nos _____ una botella de vino?

6. (poner)   Le exijo que me _____ al día.

7. (hay)   Dudan que _____ cartuchos de tinta.

8. (pagar)   Te recomiendan que _____ la cuenta inmediatamente.

9. (estar)   Niegan que Jaime _____ metido en el asunto.

10. (aparecer) No creemos que él _____ por aquí hoy.

11. (ir)   Nos piden que _____ de compras con ellos.

12. (criticar) Te digo que no lo _____ más.

13. (jugar)   ¿Le proponéis que _____ al baloncesto en vuestro equipo?

14. (salir)   No dejan que María Elena _____ con ese tipo (*guy*).

15. (invertir) Quieren que nosotros _____ más dinero en su empresa.

16. (saber)   Me extraña que Memo no _____ ni jota del lenguaje de computadora.

17. (dar)   Nos gusta que nuestro hotel _____ a la playa.

18. (oír)   Les ruego que _____ la música de este compositor.

19. (volver)   No pienso que ellas _____ antes del anochecer.

20. (seguir)   Sugieren que nosotros _____ la autopista.

C   *Rewrite the following impersonal expressions, using the subjects in parentheses.*
        ¡Ojo! *Be sure to conjugate the verbs using the present subjunctive.*

    MODELO   Es necesario salir para el aeropuerto ahora mismo. (nosotros)

        Es necesario que salgamos para el aeropuerto ahora mismo.

1. Es importante seguir una dieta equilibrada. (ellos)

    _____

2. Es útil tener palanca (*pull, influence*). (Ud.)

    _____

3. Es mejor esperar un par de días. (yo)

    _____

4. Es preciso hacer clic en el enlace. (Uds.)

    _____

5. Es imprescindible entender la política exterior (*foreign policy*). (tú)

    _____

    _____

6. Urge enviar el correo electrónico. (él)

    _____

7. Es obligatorio asistir a la reunión. (nosotros)

    _____

8. Más vale ir a pie. (Uds.)

    _____

9. Hace falta descargar los documentos. (vosotros)

    _____

10. Es bueno vivir cómodamente. (nuestra familia)

    _____

11. Es inútil buscar su billetera. (Anita)

    _____

12. Es malo no devolver el dinero prestado. (Pedro)

    _____

D *Rewrite each sentence, using the cues in parentheses. Choose either the present subjunctive or the present indicative tense for the verb.*

MODELOS   Viven en Barcelona. (es verdad)

Es verdad que viven en Barcelona.

Viven en Barcelona. (no es verdad)

No es verdad que vivan en Barcelona.

1. Hay tantos adelantos (*advances*) tecnológicos. (es bueno)

   _____

2. Yo trabajo para una compañía de alta tecnología. (es cierto)

   _____

3. Tienen interés en el proyecto. (no es evidente)

   _____

4. El dueño de la empresa abre otras sucursales. (no es dudoso)

   _____

5. No conocemos bien el interior del país. (es que)

   _____

6. Los novios están enamorados. (es obvio)

   _____

7. Sois de origen irlandés. (no es seguro)

   _____

8. Nadie quiere ayudarlos. (es una lástima)

   _____

9. La cosa no sale bien. (está mal)

   _____

10. El huracán hace tanto daño. (es triste)

    _____

E *Write sentences using the following strings of elements. Choose either the present subjunctive or the present indicative tense for the verb. ¡**Ojo!** Make sure you know how many subjects there are.*

MODELOS   yo / esperar / visitar el museo

Espero visitar el museo.

yo / esperar / Patricia / visitar el museo

Espero que Patricia visite el museo.

1. nosotros / querer / nuestros hijos / ser felices

   _____

2. el programador / necesitar / bajar el programa

   _____

3. yo / alegrarse / hacer el patinaje sobre hielo

   _____

4. tú / aconsejarle / Francisca / servir entremeses

   _____

5. ellos / temer / hay piratas informáticos (*hackers*) en Internet

   _____

6. Ud. / duda / ellos / saber utilizar la hoja de cálculo (*spreadsheet*) electrónica

   _____

7. a Uds. / gustarles / Paco / estudiar urbanización

   _____

8. vosotros / desear / practicar deportes acuáticos

   _____

9. yo / no creer / Ramón / tener don de gentes (*charm, getting on well with people*)

   _____

10. ellos / no pensar / hacer pintar la casa este año

    _____

11. Uds. / tener miedo / un virus / infectar su computadora

    _____

12. tú / pedirle / la agencia virtual / mandarte dos billetes electrónicos de ida y vuelta

    _____

    _____

13. ella / no dejar / hablar

    _____

14. ellas / sentir / nosotros / no verlas

    _____

15. Ud. / insistir en / llegar antes que nadie

    _____

F *Translation. Express the following sentences in Spanish.*

1. *We hope you* (Uds.) *will be able to attend the lecture tonight.*

   _____

2. *The report? It's crucial that you* (Ud.) *give it to them right now.*

   _____

3. *I'm glad that they are going on vacation with us.*

   _____

4. *It's necessary that we pack the suitcases the night before.*

   _____

5. *They advise him to ask his boss for a raise.*

   _____

6. *They've suggested that we look for that brand in department stores.*

   _____

7. *Isn't he afraid you're* (tú) *deleting all the files?*

   _____

8. *At the online store they tell us to put our purchases in the cart and go to the cashier* (la caja).

   _____

   _____

9. *It's important to enjoy life. Enjoy* (Uds.) *life!* [Use a clause beginning with **Que**.]

   _____

10. *I hope you* (tú) *succeed in life.*

   _____

Uses of the Subjunctive in Adjective Clauses

An adjective clause is a subordinate clause that describes a noun much as an adjective does. Adjective clauses are also called *relative clauses*.

Most adjective clauses appear in the indicative.

Él tiene un trabajo **que le gusta.**	*He's got a job that he likes.*
Tenemos una oficina **que es cómoda.**	*We have an office that's comfortable.*
Utilizo una computadora **que tiene mucha memoria.**	*I use a computer that has a lot of memory.*
Hay empresas aquí **que comercian con México.**	*There are firms here that trade with Mexico.*

However, if the noun of the main clause is not identified or is negated, then the verb of the adjective clause appears in the subjunctive.

Él quiere un trabajo **que le guste**.	*He wants a job that he will like.*
Necesitamos una oficina **que sea cómoda**.	*We need an office that's comfortable.*
Busco una computadora **que tenga mucha memoria**.	*I'm looking for a computer that has a lot of memory.*
No hay empresas aquí **que comercien con México**.	*There are no firms here that trade with Mexico.*

The subjunctive is therefore used after **no hay nada que**, **no hay nadie que**, and **no hay ningún/ninguna X que**.

No hay nada que me **interese**.	*There's nothing that interests me.*
No hay nadie aquí **que sepa** programar.	*There's no one here who knows how to program.*
No hay ningún banco que abra hoy.	*There's no bank that's open today.*

but

Hay algo que me **interesa**.	*There's something that interests me.*
Hay alguien aquí **que sabe** programar.	*There's someone here who knows how to program.*
Hay algún banco que abre hoy.	*There's some bank that's open today.*

However, the subjunctive is usually used after **hay algo/alguien/algún/alguna** in questions because the antecedent is not identified.

¿Hay algo que te **guste**?	*Is there something you like?*
¿Hay alguien aquí **que sepa** programar?	*Is there someone here who knows how to program?*
¿Hay algún banco que abra hoy?	*Is there any bank that's open today?*

G *Complete each sentence with the correct form of the verb in parentheses. Choose either the present indicative or the present subjunctive for the adjective clauses.*

1. (interesar)   Roberto tiene un puesto que le _____.

2. (esforzar)   No conozco a nadie que se _____ más.

3. (saber)   ¿Hay alguien en la oficina que _____ reparar la máquina?

4. (tener)   Necesitan unos analistas que _____ varios años de experiencia.

5. (ser)   Quiere amigos que _____ leales y sensibles.

6. (dar)   Viven en un apartamento que _____ al jardín público.

7. (crear)   Quieren contratar al administrador de Web que _____ sitios muy eficaces.

8. (atraer)   ¿No hay nada que te _____?

9. (gustar)   No hay ningún plato en la carta que me _____.

10. (hacer)   Queremos ver una película que nos _____ reír.

11. (estar)   Buscan una casa que _____ cerca del centro.

12. (tener)   Tengo una videocámara digital que _____ muchos píxeles.

Uses of the Subjunctive in Adverb Clauses

An adverb clause is a subordinate clause that modifies a verb much as an adverb does.

Certain adverbial conjunctions (conjunctions that introduce an adverb clause) are always followed by the subjunctive.

a condición de que *on the condition that*
a fin de que *so that, in order that*
a menos de que *unless*
antes de que *before*
con tal de que *provided that, as long as*
en caso de que *in case*
para que *so that, in order that*
sin que *without*

The **de** that appears in several of the conjunctions listed above is often omitted in Latin America.

Te diré lo que pasó **con tal (de) que** no **se lo cuentes** a nadie.
I'll tell you what happened as long as you don't tell it to anyone.

Vamos a discutir el proyecto **antes (de) que lleguen** los asesores.
Let's discuss the project before the consultants arrive.

Voy a prender mi computadora **para que** Ud. **consulte** la hoja de cálculo.
I'm going to turn on my computer in order for you to consult the spreadsheet.

No vale la pena reunirnos **a menos que** todo el mundo **lea** los artículos del folletín electrónico.
It doesn't pay to have a meeting unless everyone reads the articles in the e-zine.

Tu computadora no va a servir **sin que** le **pongas** este nuevo sistema operativo.
Your computer won't be of any use without your installing this new operating system on it.

En caso de que Ud. **tenga** que ponerse en contacto conmigo, te doy mi casilla electrónica.
In case you have to contact me, I'll give you my e-mail address.

If the subjects of both clauses are the same, the subordinate clause is usually replaced by an infinitive.

No puedo empezar a trabajar **sin depurar** este programa.
I can't begin working without debugging this program.

¿Qué hago **para bajar** la base de datos?
What do I do to download the database?

No se vaya **antes de suprimir** todos esos archivos.	*Don't leave without deleting all those files.*
No podrás hacerte asesor **a menos de tener** un buen ordenador portátil.	*You won't be able to become a consultant unless you have a good laptop computer.*

Adverbial Clauses of Time Followed by Indicative or Subjunctive

Adverbial clauses of time are introduced by the following conjunctions.

después (de) que *after*
cuando *when*
hasta que *until*
tan pronto (como) *as soon as*
en cuanto *as soon as*
luego que *as soon as*

When the verb of the main clause is in one of the past tenses or the present tense, these conjunctions are followed by the indicative. The past tense signals actions that have taken place and are part of the speaker's experience. The present tense signals habitual actions that are part of reality.

Esperé **hasta que llamaron**.	*I waited until they called.*
Empezamos **tan pronto como llegó** el jefe.	*We began as soon as the boss arrived.*
Siempre leo mi correo electrónico **cuando estoy** de viaje.	*I always read my e-mail when I am traveling.*

However, when the verb of the main clause is in the future or is a command, these conjunctions are followed by the subjunctive, because the action of the subordinate clause is neither part of reality nor part of the speaker's experience.

Avíseme **en cuanto lleguen** los contables.	*Let me know as soon as the accountants arrive.*
Iré a comprarme un traje **cuando haya** rebajas.	*I'll go buy a suit when there are sales.*
Me quedaré **hasta que descargues** el programa.	*I'll stay until you download the program.*
Ud. se podrá ir **después de que yo vuelva**.	*You'll be able to leave after I get back.*

When the subjects of both clauses are the same, the infinitive is used after **hasta** and **después de**.

Me quedaré **hasta terminar**.	*I'll stay until I finish.*
Trabajaré **después de volver**.	*I'll work after returning.*

After **cuando**, **en cuanto**, and **tan pronto como**, a subordinate clause in the subjunctive may be used even when the subjects of both clauses are the same.

Te avisaré **en cuanto llegue**.	*I'll notify you as soon as I arrive.*
Saldré **cuando termine**.	*I'll go out when I finish.*

The **al** + infinitive construction can replace the subjunctive clause when the subjects of the two clauses are the same. **Al** + the infinitive is interpreted as having the same subject as the main verb of the sentence.

Te avisaré **al llegar**.	*I'll notify you **when I arrive**.*
Saldré **al terminar**.	*I'll go out **when I finish**.*

Other Adverbial Clauses in Which Indicative and Subjunctive Contrast

There are other conjunctions besides adverbial conjunctions of time that may introduce clauses in the indicative as well as the subjunctive. Such conjunctions are followed by the indicative when the action of the subordinate clause is considered a known or established fact, but they are followed by the subjunctive when the action of the subordinate clause is considered uncertain or indefinite.

These conjunctions include **como** *how,* **aunque** *although, even though,* **según** *according to,* **donde** *where,* **mientras** *while,* **de manera que** *so that,* and **de modo que** *so that.* When these dependent clauses are used with a subjunctive verb, the conjunction often has the English equivalent of *ever* attached to it, as in *whenever, however,* or *wherever.*

Hazlo **como** ella **dice**.	*Do it **how (the way)** she says.* *(I know the way she says.)*
Hazlo **como** ella **diga**.	*Do it **however** she says.* *(I don't know the way she says.)*
Aunque va Jorge, nosotros no vamos.	***Even though Jorge is going**, we're not going. (I know Jorge is going.)*
Aunque vaya Jorge, nosotros no vamos.	***Even though Jorge may go**, we're not going. (I don't know whether Jorge is going or not.)*
Pintaré la casa **según me mandan**.	*I'll paint the house **the way they tell me to**. (I know how they want me to paint it.)*
Pintaré la casa **según me manden**.	*I'll paint the house **however they tell me to**. (I don't yet know how they want me to paint it.)*
Iré **donde** Uds. **quieren**.	*I'll go **where** you want to go. (I know where you want to go.)*
Iré **donde** Uds. **quieran**.	*I'll go **wherever** you want to go. (I don't know yet where you want to go.)*
Te lo expliqué **de modo que lo comprendiste**.	*I explained it to you **so that you understood it**. (Your understanding is the result of the action.)*
Te lo explicaré **de modo que lo comprendas**.	*I'll explain it to you **so that you will understand it**. (Your understanding is the purpose of the action.)*

H *Complete each sentence with the correct form of the verb in parentheses. Choose either the present indicative or the present subjunctive for the adverbial clauses.*

1. Te voy a dar mi contraseña (*password*) para que me _____ el correo electrónico. (hojear *to glance at*)

2. Compraré el libro antes de que Ud. lo _____ de la biblioteca. (sacar)

3. No les daré más información hasta que me la _____. (pedir)

4. Siempre me reúno con mis amigos tan pronto como nosotros _____ de la oficina. (salir)

5. Irán a la estación de invierno (*ski resort*) para esquiar a menos que no _____ nieve. (hay)

6. Se servirá la comida después que yo _____ el vino. (traer)

7. No saliste hasta que _____ a despejar. (comenzar)

8. Siempre como perros calientes y palomitas de maíz (*popcorn*) cuando nosotros _____ a los partidos de béisbol. (asistir)

9. En caso de que tú _____ a Esteban, dile que me llame. (ver)

10. Les prestaré mi videocámara con tal que me la _____ para el sábado. (devolver)

11. No podrás seguir con tu trabajo sin que yo _____ este programa para hacer gráficos. (instalar)

12. Visitaremos con nuestros amigos ingleses cuando ellos _____ a los Estados Unidos en mayo. (venir)

I *Translation. Express the following sentences in Spanish.*

1. *I don't think you (tú) want to see this film.*

   _____

2. *It's necessary that he send them an e-mail.*

   _____

3. *It's useful that we do our research on the Internet.*

   _____

4. *I'm glad that they're coming to see us this weekend.*

   _____

5. *We're looking for a house that has six bedrooms.*

   _____

6. *They need a director who knows the company very well.*

   _____

7. *I hope our team will win the game on Sunday.*

   _____

8. *Have* (tú) *a good time!* [Use a clause beginning with **Que**.]

   _____

9. *There's no sandwich on the menu that I like.*

   _____

10. *Let's get the e-tickets as soon as I log in.*

   _____

11. *I'll show you* (tú) *the travel Web site so that you can choose a tourist package.*

   _____

   _____

12. *Do you* (Uds.) *want to eat something before the play starts?*

   _____

13. *We'll buy you* (tú) *a souvenir* (recuerdo) *when we get to Granada.* [Write in two ways.]

   _____

   _____

14. *It doesn't pay to organize the get-together unless all our friends can come.*

   _____

   _____

BUILDING SENTENCES   **Compound and complex sentences**

There are two types of conjunctions that join sentences together.

Coordinating conjunctions create compound sentences, sentences in which neither clause is subordinate to the other. Typical coordinating conjunctions are **y**, **pero**, and **o**.

Fui a su oficina **y** pedí una entrevista.	*I went to his office and asked for an interview.*
Nosotros salimos, **pero** ella se quedó en casa.	*We went out, but she stayed home.*

Compound sentences joined by **o** usually have an additional **o** before the first sentence.

O aprenderás a trabajar con los demás, **o** tendrás que renunciar.	*Either you will learn to work with the others or you will have to quit.*

If there is a negative in the first clause of a compound sentence, then **pero** changes to **sino que**.

No sólo sabe francés, **sino que** también
   habla español.

*He not only knows French, but speaks
   Spanish too.*

Él no miente, **sino que** dice disparates.

*He doesn't lie, but (rather) says silly
   things.*

Subordinating conjunctions embed a sentence within a larger sentence, and that embedded sentence is then dependent on or subordinate to the main clause. This is called a complex sentence. The most common subordinating conjunction in Spanish is **que**.

Que is followed by the indicative after verbs that emphasize the truth value of the subordinate clause, like **saber**, **afirmar**, **confirmar**, and **jurar**.

Sabemos que les gusta España.

We know they like Spain.

Confirmo que vendí mi casa.

I am confirming that I sold my house.

Juro que se lo devolví.

I swear that I returned it to him.

Subordinating conjunctions that express cause and result also introduce clauses in the indicative. One of the most common is **porque** *because*.

No podemos salir **porque** llueve.

We can't go out because it's raining.

Subordinating conjunctions that express result only—**así que**, **conque**, **de tal modo que**, **de tal manera que**, and **de tal forma que**—are followed by the indicative.

Me llamaron desde la oficina, **así que**
   me tuve que ir.

*They called me from the office, so I had
   to leave.*

Conque no se pusieron en contacto
   contigo.

So they didn't get in touch with you.

Most other subordinating conjunctions take the subjunctive in certain situations. The conjunctions **de modo que**, **de manera que**, and **de forma que** take the subjunctive when they express purpose, but the indicative when they express results. Notice that **tal** is dropped in these conjunctions when they express purpose.

Arregla la sala **de modo que podamos**
   recibir a nuestros invitados.

*Straighten up the living room so that we
   can receive our company. (A purpose
   is stated; subjunctive is used.)*

Arreglamos la sala **de (tal) modo que**
   pudimos recibir a nuestros invitados.

*We straightened up the living room so that
   we could receive our company. (A result
   is stated; indicative is used.)*

J *Join the following pairs of sentences with a conjunction to create a new sentence,
choosing one of the coordinating or subordinating conjunctions that appear in
parentheses.*

MODELO   Me llamaron. Fui a verlos. (sino que | y)

   Me llamaron y fui a verlos.

1. Yo la invité al concierto. Ella no pudo ir. (pero | que)

   _____

2. No puede tomar el seminario de ciencias políticas a las once. Cursa literatura mundial a la misma hora. (y | porque)

_____

_____

3. Llegas puntualmente. No te dejan entrar. (o | así que)

_____

4. Terminó de mandar el correo electrónico. Hizo el logoff. (porque | y)

_____

5. No lo encontramos ni en casa ni en la oficina. Lo llamamos por teléfono móvil. (así que | que)

_____

_____

6. Él no sólo se ocupa de los quehaceres domésticos. Hace la jardinería también. (pero | sino que)

_____

_____

7. Te afirmo. Son dignos de confianza. (que | de forma que)

_____

8. Ellos fueron corriendo. Ud. no consiguió alcanzarlos. (porque | de tal modo que)

_____

9. Pasaron por mí a las seis. Logramos llegar al aeropuerto con tiempo de sobra (*time to spare*). (de manera que | porque)

_____

_____

10. El avión iba a despegar. Los pasajeros se abrocharon el cinturón de seguridad (*seat belt*). (o | conque)

_____

_____

K *Translation.* *Express the following sentences in Spanish.*

1. *She doesn't only sing, but she dances also.*

_____

2. *Either we will call them on the phone today or we will talk to them when we see them.*

_____

_____

3. *Are you (Ud.) confirming that you've received the e-tickets?*

   _____

4. *I swear that I am not guilty.*

   _____

5. *He's going to spend his vacation in San Francisco because his parents live there.*

   _____

   _____

6. *Turn on (tú) the computer so that I can see your Web site.*

   _____

7. *So nobody was there when they arrived.*

   _____

8. *They went to the movies, but we decided to rent a film.*

   _____

9. *We went to the department store so that we could buy them a housewarming gift (inaugurar la casa).*

   _____

   _____

10. *She logged on and went to her Web site first.*

    _____

11. *I know those files are formatted and stored already.*

    _____

12. *They want us to travel with them, but we find them very boring.*

    _____

The Subjunctive (Part II): The Present Perfect Subjunctive; The Imperfect Subjunctive; The Pluperfect Subjunctive

BUILDING SENTENCES

Conditional sentences

The Present Perfect Subjunctive

The present perfect subjunctive consists of the present subjunctive of the auxiliary verb **haber** + the past participle. Remember that **haber** has an irregular subjunctive stem: **hay-**.

hablar *to speak*

que haya hablado	que hayamos hablado
que hayas hablado	que hayáis hablado
que haya hablado	que hayan hablado

comer *to eat*

que haya comido	que hayamos comido
que hayas comido	que hayáis comido
que haya comido	que hayan comido

vivir *to live*

que haya vivido	que hayamos vivido
que hayas vivido	que hayáis vivido
que haya vivido	que hayan vivido

hacer *to do, make*

que haya hecho	que hayamos hecho
que hayas hecho	que hayáis hecho
que haya hecho	que hayan hecho

The present perfect subjunctive is used in the same kinds of dependent clauses as the present subjunctive. It is used to indicate that the action of the dependent clause happens before the action of the main clause. Study the following contrasting pairs of sentences.

210

Espero que **llegue** para la una.	*I hope that he arrives by one o'clock.*
Espero que **haya llegado** para la una.	*I hope that he arrived by one o'clock.*
Es triste que **no puedas** ir.	*It's sad that you can't go.*
Es triste que **no hayas podido** ir.	*It's sad that you couldn't go.*
No creo que **vengan**.	*I don't think they'll come.*
No creo que **hayan venido**.	*I don't think they came.*
Dudamos que el equipo **gane**.	*We doubt that the team will win.*
Dudamos que el equipo **haya ganado**.	*We doubt that the team won.*

The present subjunctive can be translated as a present or future tense. The present perfect subjunctive can be translated by a variety of past tenses. Subordinate clauses in the subjunctive have fewer tense distinctions than main clauses.

A   *Rewrite each sentence, using the cue in parentheses. Use the present perfect subjunctive tense for the verb in the dependent clause.*

MODELO   Imprimió los papeles. (no creo)

    No creo que haya impreso los papeles.

1. Se divirtieron mucho. (es probable)

2. Antonio y Nora fueron novios. (dudo)

3. Yo se lo expliqué. (es útil)

4. Él mintió. (estamos furiosos)

5. No tuvieron una vida privada. (es una lástima)

6. Ud. no la vio. (me sorprende)

7. El avión despegó. (es posible)

8. Los rescatadores (*rescue workers*) los encontraron sanos y salvos. (es bueno)

9. Me dijeron eso. (niego)

10. Llegaron a casa achispados (*tipsy*). (no es cierto)

11. Hubo un fallo del sistema (*crash*). (es malo)

_____

12. Su gato murió. (sienten)

_____

13. Hicimos algo interesante. (espera)

_____

14. Tecleaste correctamente la palabra clave. (es importante)

_____

15. No contribuyó nada a la caridad. (no nos gusta)

_____

B   *Translation. Express the following sentences in Spanish.*

1. *I doubt that Rebeca found her gold earring.*

_____

2. *It's good that you (Uds.) solved your problem.*

_____

3. *We don't like that they dropped by without calling.*

_____

4. *It's useful that you (tú) downloaded the files.*

_____

5. *Are you (Ud.) surprised that they didn't offer Carlos a raise?*

_____

6. *I'm glad it turned out well for you (tú).*

_____

7. *It's not true that Isabel quit her job.*

_____

8. *He's furious that the dog tore the rug to pieces.*

_____

9. *They're sorry that things went from bad to worse.*

_____

10. *It's probable that you (vosotros) already returned the umbrella to her.*

_____

The Imperfect Subjunctive

The imperfect subjunctive in Spanish serves as the past of the present subjunctive. It is formed the same way for all verbs: drop the **-ron** ending of the **ellos/ellas/Uds.** form of the preterit, and replace it with a series of endings in **-ra**.

hablar (3RD-PERSON PLURAL PRETERIT **hablaron**)

que habla**ra**	que hablá**ramos**
que habla**ras**	que habla**rais**
que habla**ra**	que habla**ran**

comer (3RD-PERSON PLURAL PRETERIT **comieron**)

que comie**ra**	que comié**ramos**
que comie**ras**	que comie**rais**
que comie**ra**	que comie**ran**

vivir (3RD-PERSON PLURAL PRETERIT **vivieron**)

que vivie**ra**	que vivié**ramos**
que vivie**ras**	que vivie**rais**
que vivie**ra**	que vivie**ran**

Any irregularity or vowel change in the stem of the third-person plural of the preterit occurs in all persons of the imperfect subjunctive, as in the following examples.

3RD-PERSON PLURAL PRETERIT	1ST-PERSON SINGULAR IMPERFECT SUBJUNCTIVE
pidieron	que yo **pidiera**
mintieron	que yo **mintiera**
durmieron	que yo **durmiera**
hicieron	que yo **hiciera**
pudieron	que yo **pudiera**
fueron	que yo **fuera**
dieron	que yo **diera**
trajeron	que yo **trajera**
riñeron	que yo **riñera**

An alternate set of endings in **-se** exists in the imperfect subjunctive. The **-se** endings are less frequent in speech and can convey a formal tone. They have the same functions as the **-ra** endings, with the exception that the **-se** form never replaces the conditional in conditional sentences.

hablar (3RD-PERSON PLURAL PRETERIT **hablaron**)

que habla**se**	que hablá**semos**
que habla**ses**	que habla**seis**
que habla**se**	que habla**sen**

---

comer (3RD-PERSON PLURAL PRETERIT **comieron**)

que comie**se**	que comié**semos**
que comie**ses**	que comie**seis**
que comie**se**	que comie**sen**

---

vivir (3RD-PERSON PLURAL PRETERIT **vivieron**)

que vivie**se**	que vivié**semos**
que vivie**ses**	que vivie**seis**
que vivie**se**	que vivie**sen**

The **yo** and **él/ella/Ud.** forms are identical in the imperfect subjunctive, as they are in the present subjunctive, and all the **nosotros** forms have a written accent mark on the vowel before the **-ramos** or **-semos** ending.

> **habláramos, comiéramos, viviéramos**
> **hablásemos, comiésemos, viviésemos**

The use of the imperfect subjunctive in subordinate clauses in Spanish is determined by the *sequence of tenses*. You have learned that the present subjunctive is used in subordinate clauses when the verb in the main clause is in the present, future, present perfect, or imperative. The imperfect subjunctive is used in subordinate clauses when the verb in the main clause is in the imperfect, preterit, past perfect, or conditional.

The types of main clauses that trigger the subjunctive are the same. Compare the following pairs of sentences.

Noun Clauses

No **quiero** que **salgas**.	*I don't want you to go out.*
No **quería** que **salieras**.	*I didn't want you to go out.*
Es importante que se lo **dé**.	*It's important for you to give it to him.*
Fue importante que se lo **diera**.	*It was important for you to give it to him.*
Aconséjele que **busque** otro puesto.	*Advise her to look for another job.*
Ud. le aconsejó que **buscara** otro puesto.	*You advised her to look for another job.*
Le **pediré** que me **pague**.	*I will ask him to pay me.*
Le **pedí** que me **pagara**.	*I asked him to pay me.*
Insiste en que Ud. se lo **diga**.	*She insists that you tell her.*
Insistió en que Ud. se lo **dijera**.	*She insisted that you tell her.*
No **cree** que lo **hagamos**.	*He doesn't think we'll do it.*
No **creía** que lo **hiciéramos**.	*He didn't think we'd do it.*
He dudado que lo **sepan**.	*I have doubted that they know it.*
Dudaba que lo **supieran**.	*I doubted that they knew it.*
Nos alegramos de que Uds. **se diviertan**.	*We're happy that you are having a good time.*
Nos alegrábamos de que Uds. **se divirtieran**.	*We were happy that you were having a good time.*

Note that the English equivalents of the verb in many Spanish subjunctive noun clauses are infinitives and therefore do not show the tense distinctions that are seen in Spanish.

Adjective Clauses

Buscan un condominio que **sea** céntrico.	*They're looking for a condominium that is centrally located.*
Buscaban un condominio que **fuera** céntrico.	*They were looking for a condominium that was centrally located.*
He buscado una cámara digital que **tenga** muchos píxeles.	*I've looked for a digital camera that has a lot of pixels.*
Había buscado una cámara digital que **tuviera** muchos píxeles.	*I had looked for a digital camera that had a lot of pixels.*
No hay ningún postre que le **apetezca**.	*There's no dessert that she feels like eating (that tempts her, appeals to her).*
No había ningún postre que le **apeteciera**.	*There was no dessert that she felt like eating (that tempted her, appealed to her).*
Necesitamos asesores que **conozcan** muy bien estas industrias.	*We need consultants who are very familiar with these industries.*
Necesitábamos asesores que **conocieran** muy bien estas industrias.	*We needed consultants who were very familiar with these industries.*

Adverb Clauses

No **darán** un paseo **a menos que deje** de llover.	*They won't go for a walk unless it stops raining.*
No **daban** un paseo **a menos que dejara** de llover.	*They weren't going for a walk unless it stopped raining.*
Los **veremos antes de que se vayan**.	*We'll see them before they leave.*
Los **vimos antes de que se fueran**.	*We saw them before they left.*
Le **he prestado** mi computadora portátil **para que pueda** enviar el e-mail.	*I've lent him my laptop so that he can send e-mail.*
Le **había prestado** mi computadora portátil **para que pudiera** enviar el e-mail.	*I had lent him my laptop so that he could send e-mail.*
Compra carne **en caso de que queramos** hacer hamburguesas.	*Buy meat in case we want to make hamburgers.*
Comprarías carne **en caso de que quisiéramos** hacer hamburguesas.	*You would buy meat in case we'd want to make hamburgers.*

In Spanish, the infinitive is usually used instead of the subjunctive when the subject of both verbs is the same, whether the sentence is in the present or a past tense.

Queremos verte.	*We want to see you.*
Queríamos verte.	*We wanted to see you.*

Compare the use of the subjunctive when the subjects of the verbs of both clauses are different.

Queremos que **ella te vea.**   *We want her to see you.*
Queríamos que **ella te viera.**   *We wanted her to see you.*

Special Uses of the Imperfect Subjunctive

The imperfect subjunctive is used after **ojalá (que)** to express a wish for something that will probably not happen (English *I wish that*).

Ojalá que pudieran comprender esto.   *I wish they could understand this.*
Ojalá discutieran menos.   *I wish they would argue less.*
Ojalá no trataras de persuadirlo.   *I wish you wouldn't try to convince him.*

The imperfect subjunctive of a few verbs (mostly **poder, querer,** and **deber**) is used in main clauses to make polite requests and to soften suggestions.

¿Pudieran Uds. volver mañana?   *Could you come back tomorrow?*
Quisiera ir con Ud.   *I'd like to go with you.*
Debieras tratarlo mejor.   *You ought to treat him better.*

The imperfect subjunctive is used after **como si** *as if* to express an action that happens at the same time as the action of the main clause.

Él actúa **como si fuera** abogado.   *He acts **as if he were** a lawyer.*
Hablan **como si** realmente **supieran** algo   *They talk **as if they** actually **knew***
   de lo ocurrido.   *something about what happened.*
Salió furtivamente **como si tuviera** miedo.   *She sneaked out **as if she were** afraid.*

C   *Complete each sentence, using the correct imperfect subjunctive form of the verb in parentheses. Write each verb, using both imperfect subjunctive endings, **-ra** and **-se**.*

MODELO   Queríamos que ellos ___*fueran/fuesen*___ al cine con nosotros. (ir)

1. Yo esperaba que tú _____ tus sueños. (realizar)

2. Le aconsejé que no _____ en los asuntos ajenos (*other people's*). (meterse)

3. Era probable que _____ buen tiempo toda la semana de nuestras vacaciones. (hacer)

4. Preferirían que Aurora _____ en informática. (especializarse)

5. Les dijimos que _____ con cuidado por aquel barrio. (andar)

6. Había dudado que treinta mil personas _____ en el estadio. (caber)

7. Nos gustaría que Uds. _____ el manual del usuario. (leer)

8. Me alegré que vosotros lo _____ tan bien en el desfile. (pasar)

9. No fue posible que nosotros _____ antes de las once. (estar)

10. Era bueno que nosotros _____ los gastos. (reducir)

11. Era importante que yo _____ los datos actualizados. (entrar)

12. No creían que tú _____ tantos regalos. (traer)

13. Buscaba un puesto que le _____ mucha oportunidad. (dar)

14. Necesitaban un gerente de ventas que _____ el mercado. (conocer)

15. No había nadie que _____ más a su profesión. (dedicarse)

16. ¿No habías visto ningún traje que te _____? (gustar)

17. Le entregaría el informe para que él lo _____. (corregir)

18. Yo te acompañaría al centro comercial con tal de que nosotros no

    _____ antes de las dos. (ir)

19. Le habíamos traído los disquetes sin que nos los _____. (pedir)

20. Tenían el celular en caso de que yo _____ ponerme en contacto con ellos. (querer)

D *Translation. Express the following sentences in Spanish.*

1. *We hoped you (tú) would bring your digital camera to the party.*

    _____

2. *I advised her to buy the white silk blouse.*

    _____

3. *There was nothing that excited them.*

    _____

4. *Mariana asked them to set the table.*

    _____

5. *They had sent us the videos without our paying for them.*

    _____

6. *We would prefer that you (Ud.) not tell it to them.*

    _____

7. *They wanted a computer that would work well.*

    _____

8. *I carried my mobile phone everywhere so that my children could call me at any time.*

   _____

   _____

9. *I wish they were arriving today.*

   _____

10. *She would like us to give (as a gift) her an iPod.*

    _____

11. *I wish they would calm down.*

    _____

12. *I wish you* (tú) *were staying.*

    _____

The Pluperfect Subjunctive

The pluperfect subjunctive (or past perfect subjunctive) consists of the imperfect subjunctive of **haber** and the past participle. The imperfect subjunctive of **haber**, like that of all verbs, derives from the third-person plural form of the preterit: **hubieron**.

hablar *to speak*

que hubiera hablado	que hubiéramos hablado
que hubieras hablado	que hubierais hablado
que hubiera hablado	que hubieran hablado

comer *to eat*

que hubiera comido	que hubiéramos comido
que hubieras comido	que hubierais comido
que hubiera comido	que hubieran comido

vivir *to live*

que hubiera vivido	que hubiéramos vivido
que hubieras vivido	que hubierais vivido
que hubiera vivido	que hubieran vivido

hacer *to do, make*

que hubiera hecho	que hubiéramos hecho
que hubieras hecho	que hubierais hecho
que hubiera hecho	que hubieran hecho

The **-se** form of the imperfect subjunctive of **haber** can also be used to form the pluperfect subjunctive, but it is used less frequently, especially in speech.

hablar *to speak*	
que hubiese hablado	que hubiésemos hablado
que hubieses hablado	que hubieseis hablado
que hubiese hablado	que hubiesen hablado

comer *to eat*	
que hubiese comido	que hubiésemos comido
que hubieses comido	que hubieseis comido
que hubiese comido	que hubiesen comido

vivir *to live*	
que hubiese vivido	que hubiésemos vivido
que hubieses vivido	que hubieseis vivido
que hubiese vivido	que hubiesen vivido

hacer *to do, make*	
que hubiese hecho	que hubiésemos hecho
que hubieses hecho	que hubieseis hecho
que hubiese hecho	que hubiesen hecho

The primary function of the pluperfect subjunctive is parallel to that of the present perfect subjunctive: It indicates that the action of the subordinate clause happened before that of the main clause. Study the following contrasting pairs of sentences.

Esperábamos **que ellos vinieran**.	*We hoped that they were coming.*
Esperábamos **que ellos hubieran venido**.	*We hoped that they had come.*
Me alegré **de que lo supieras**.	*I was glad that you knew it.*
Me alegré **de que lo hubieras sabido**.	*I was glad that you had found it out.*
Me sorprendió **que la conocieras**.	*I was surprised that you knew her.*
Me sorprendió **que la hubieras conocido**.	*I was surprised that you had met her.*

The pluperfect subjunctive is used after **ojalá (que)** to express a contrary-to-fact wish in the past (English *I wish that had happened*). **Ojalá que** + the pluperfect subjunctive expresses a wish for something that can't happen.

Ojalá me lo **hubieras dicho**.	*I wish you had told me.*
Ojalá que no se hubieran divorciado.	*I wish they hadn't gotten divorced.*
Ojalá nuestra casa **hubiera tenido** una piscina.	*I wish our house had had a pool.*

The Present and Imperfect Subjunctives vs. the Perfect Subjunctives

It is important to understand the contrasts between the present and imperfect subjunctives, which express actions simultaneous with or subsequent to the action of the main clause, and the perfect subjunctives (present perfect and pluperfect subjunctives), which express actions happening before the action of the main clause.

No creo **que salgan**.	*I don't think they are going out.*
No creo **que hayan salido**.	*I don't think they went out.*
No creía **que salieran**.	*I didn't think they were going out.*
No creía **que hubieran salido**.	*I didn't think they had gone out.*

The pluperfect subjunctive is used after **como si** to express an action that hypothetically occurred prior to the action of the main clause.

Comes **como si no hubieras comido** en un mes.	*You're eating **as if you hadn't eaten** in a month.*
Cantó **como si hubiera cantado** toda su vida.	*She sang **as if she had sung** her whole life.*
Actuaban **como si** nada **hubiera pasado**.	*They acted **as if** nothing **had happened**.*

E *Rewrite each sentence, using the cue in parentheses. Use the pluperfect subjunctive tense for the verb in the dependent clause.*

MODELO   Ellos habían llamado. (dudaba)

  Dudaba que ellos hubieran llamado.

1. Habíamos hecho un viaje a Santa Fe. (me alegré)

   _____

2. Nos habían puesto al día. (era importante)

   _____

3. Ella había hecho la comida. (esperábamos)

   _____

4. No se lo habías dicho a nadie. (nos extrañó)

   _____

5. Había pasado una cosa así. (fue imposible)

   _____

6. Habíais leído tantos libros. (nos gustó)

   _____

7. Ellos habían impreso los documentos. (fue probable)

_____

8. Lo habíamos sabido lo antes posible. (ojalá)

_____

9. La computadora había tenido un gusano (*worm*). (temían)

_____

10. Yo había conseguido unos billetes electrónicos tan baratos. (les sorprendió)

_____

_____

F **Translation.** *Express the following sentences in Spanish.*

1. *It wasn't true that Angélica had broken up with her boyfriend.*

_____

2. *He denied that they had said swear words.*

_____

3. *She was glad that we had heard the CDs.*

_____

4. *He answered as if he hadn't understood the question.*

_____

5. *I wish you* (Uds.) *could have spent the whole summer with us.*

_____

6. *We were surprised that you* (tú) *hadn't attended the meeting.*

_____

7. *It was bad that it had rained before the race.*

_____

8. *It was possible they had tried to telephone us.*

_____

9. *Did they doubt that I had told them the truth?*

_____

10. *I didn't think that you* (Ud.) *had written to them yet.*

_____

BUILDING SENTENCES	**Conditional sentences**

One of the most frequent uses of the imperfect subjunctive and pluperfect subjunctive is to express conditions. There are two main types of conditions: *possible conditions* and *contrary-to-fact conditions.*

Possible Conditions

Sentences expressing possible conditions tell what will happen if something else happens. Both Spanish and English use the present in the **si**-clause (*if*-clause) and the future in the main clause to express possible conditions.

si-CLAUSE	MAIN CLAUSE	MEANING
Si sales, (present)	**yo saldré** también. (future)	*If you go out, I'll go out too.*

Contrary-to-fact Conditions

To express a condition that is contrary to a fact or to a situation in *present* time, Spanish uses the imperfect subjunctive in the **si**-clause and the conditional in the main clause.

si-CLAUSE	MAIN CLAUSE	MEANING
Si salieras, (imperfect subjunctive)	**yo saldría** también. (conditional)	*If you were going out, I'd go out too.*

The sentence **Si salieras, yo saldría también** expresses a condition that is *contrary to fact.* The fact is that **tú no sales** and the result is that **yo no salgo.** The meaning is **(pero) si salieras** (*but if you were going out, which you're not*), **yo saldría** también (*I'd go out too.*)

Spanish expresses a condition that is contrary to a fact or situation in *past* time by using the past perfect subjunctive in the **si**-clause and the conditional perfect or the past perfect subjunctive in the main clause.

si-CLAUSE	MAIN CLAUSE	MEANING
Si hubieras salido, (past perfect subjunctive)	**yo habría salido** también. (conditional perfect)	*If you had gone out, I would have gone out too.*
Si hubieras salido, (past perfect subjunctive)	**yo hubiera salido** también. (past perfect subjunctive)	*If you had gone out, I would have gone out too.*

Additional examples of conditional sentences follow.

Sentences expressing possible conditions use the present and future tenses.

Si le **pides** ayuda, él te **ayudará.**	*If you ask him for help, he will help you.*
Les **contestaremos** si **se ponen** en contacto con nuestra empresa.	*We'll answer them if they contact our firm.*

Sentences expressing conditions that are contrary to present fact use the imperfect subjunctive and conditional tenses.

Si la empresa **mejorara** la calidad de
sus productos, **vendería** mucho más
en Europa.
La gente **viviría** mejor si el gobierno
bajara los impuestos.

*If the firm improved the quality of its
products, it would sell a lot more
in Europe.*
*People would live better if the government
would lower taxes.*

Sentences expressing conditions that are contrary to past fact use the past perfect subjunctive tense with either the conditional perfect or the past perfect subjunctive tense.

Si le **hubiera visto** la cara, la **habría
reconocido**.
La empresa mexicana nos **habría
concedido** el contrato si nuestro
representante **hubiera hablado**
español.

*If I had seen her face, I would have
recognized her.*
*The Mexican firm would have given us
the contract if our representative had
spoken Spanish.*

G **Possible conditions.** *Complete each sentence with the correct forms of the verbs
in parentheses, using present indicative and future tense forms. ¡Ojo! Choose the
appropriate tense for the **si**-clause and for the main clause.*

MODELO   Si yo _tengo_ tiempo más tarde, _iré_ al cibercafé. (tener, ir)

1. Si yo _____ a Costa Rica, _____ ecoturismo.
   (ir, hacer)

2. Nosotros _____ esta noche si no _____ mucho.
   (salir, nevar)

3. Si Ud. me _____ el problema, _____ resolvérselo.
   (explicar, procurar)

4. Laura me _____ al concierto si _____ ir en carro.
   (llevar, decidir)

5. Si _____ posible, Ignacio nos _____ en contacto con ellos.
   (ser, poner)

6. Elena se _____ en el curso si no _____ cupo (*limited
   enrollment*). (matricular, hay)

7. Si Uds. _____ a eso de las cuatro, _____ a toda la familia.
   (venir, ver)

8. Si tú _____ ahora, no _____ hambre a la hora de la cena.
   (merendar, tener)

9. Yo _____ ayudarte si _____ las plantas. (querer, regar)

10. Si Uds. _____ por comprar la casa con piscina, _____
    nadar todos los días. (optar, poder)

H *Contrary-to-fact conditions in present time.* *Complete each sentence with the correct forms of the verbs in parentheses, using imperfect subjunctive and conditional tense forms.* **¡Ojo!** *Choose the appropriate tense for the* **si**-*clause and for the main clause.*

MODELO　Si Paquita _obedeciera_ a sus papás, ellos no la _reñirían_.
　　　　(obedecer, reñir)

1. Si tú _____ al cine, yo _____ contigo. (ir, ir)

2. ¿Nosotros _____ hacer más operaciones si _____ ese software? (poder, tener)

3. Si _____ más tiempo, ellos se _____ un mes entero en Sicilia. (hay, quedar)

4. Si Uds. no se _____ por toda cosita, _____ más felices. (preocupar, ser)

5. Ud. _____ más salidas (*openings*) si _____ bilingüe. (tener, ser)

6. Nosotros _____ el día en la playa si _____ calor y sol. (pasar, hacer)

7. Si ellos _____ la dieta, _____ peso. (seguir, perder)

8. Si tú les _____ disculpas (*apologize*), ellos te _____. (pedir, perdonar)

9. Guillermo no se _____ si _____ mucho café. (dormir, tomar)

10. Si tú me _____ flores, yo te _____ un beso. (traer, dar)

I *Contrary-to-fact conditions in past time.* *Complete each sentence with the correct forms of the verbs in parentheses, using past perfect subjunctive and conditional perfect forms.* **¡Ojo!** *Choose the appropriate tense for the* **si**-*clause and for the main clause.* *Write the verbs in the main clause in two ways.*

MODELO　Si él _hubiera hecho_ el viaje a la Suiza, _habría/hubiera hecho_ alpinismo. (hacer, hacer)

1. Si tú _____ por la Red,

　_____ el sitio Web de mi compañia.
　(navegar, ver)

2. Ud. _____ empleo al graduarse

　si _____ informática. (conseguir, estudiar)

3. Si ellos no _____ el amor y el apoyo de su familia,

　¿_____ tanto éxito? (recibir, tener)

4. Ese chico _____ buenas notas

　si no _____ videojuegos todo el día. (sacar, jugar)

5. Si nosotros _____ nuestro correo electrónico,

_____ lo de Julia. (leer, saber)

6. Si Uds. _____ en el extranjero,

_____ de menos (*miss*) a su familia.

(vivir, echar)

7. Yo te _____

si tú _____ más puntualmente. (ver, volver)

8. Si vosotros _____ las rebajas de enero,

_____ mucho dinero. (aprovechar, ahorrar)

9. Leo y Olivia no se _____

si no _____ al baile. (conocer, ir)

10. Si no _____ un fallo del sistema, tú no

_____ tu trabajo. (haber, perder)

11. Ellos _____ menos calor

si _____ el aire acondicionado. (tener, prender)

12. Si tú no _____ de la arroba (@) en el e-mail,

yo lo _____. (olvidarse, recibir)

J *Translation. Express the following sentences in Spanish.*

1. *If we see him at the game, we'll say hello to him for you* (tú).

_____

2. *They would share the expenses if they could.*

_____

3. *The company would have hired her if she had had five years of experience.*

_____

_____

4. *If it weren't raining, we'd take a walk.*

_____

5. *If you* (Ud.) *had given me the contract, I would have signed it.*

_____

6. *I'd wait for them if I didn't have to catch the six o'clock train.*

_____

7. *They'll ski this weekend if the weather is good.*

_____

8. *If our colleagues were more hardworking, we wouldn't have so much to do.*

    _____

    _____

9. *If you (tú) wanted to use the car, we'd lend it to you.*

    _____

10. *If she had asked them for an iPod, they would have given it (as a gift) to her.*

    _____

    _____

11. *I would have taken the red-eye* (el vuelo de medianoche) *from San Diego to New York
    if I had had to attend a meeting at 9:00 A.M.*

    _____

    _____

12. *If you (Uds.) shop online, you'll save time and money.*

    _____

Reflexive Verbs

Reflexive verbs constitute a large verb class in Spanish. Spanish reflexive verbs always appear with an object pronoun that refers to the subject. English reflexive verbs, a relatively small category, usually imply that the subject is doing something to himself, for example, *to hurt oneself, to cut oneself.*

The function of reflexive verbs is different in the two languages. Most Spanish reflexive verbs correspond to English intransitive verbs (verbs that do not have a direct object) or English verb phrases consisting of *to be* or *to get* + an adjective or past participle.

In verb lists and vocabulary, Spanish reflexive verbs appear with the reflexive pronoun **se** attached to the infinitive.

> **levantarse** *to get up*
> **peinarse** *to comb one's hair*
> **quemarse** *to get burned*
> **vestirse (e > i)** *to get dressed*

Formation of Reflexive Verbs

Study the conjugation of reflexive verbs in the different tenses. Note that the reflexive pronoun **se** changes to agree with the subject of the verb. The reflexive pronoun precedes the conjugated verb in the simple tenses; it precedes the auxiliary verb **haber** in the compound tenses; it precedes the verb **estar** or is attached to the present participle in writing in the progressive tenses (see Chapter 14, p. 249).

Present Tense

acostarse (o > ue) *to go to bed*

me acuest**o**	**nos** acost**amos**
te acuest**as**	**os** acost**áis**
se acuest**a**	**se** acuest**an**

Preterit

vestirse (e > i) *to get dressed*

me vest**í**	**nos** vest**imos**
te vest**iste**	**os** vest**isteis**
se vist**ió**	**se** vist**ieron**

Imperfect

levantarse *to get up*

me levant**aba**	**nos** levant**ábamos**
te levant**abas**	**os** levant**abais**
se levant**aba**	**se** levant**aban**

Future

alegrarse *to be glad/happy*

me alegrar**é**	**nos** alegrar**emos**
te alegrar**ás**	**os** alegrar**éis**
se alegrar**á**	**se** alegrar**án**

Conditional

entusiasmarse *to get excited*

me entusiasmar**ía**	**nos** entusiasmar**íamos**
te entusiasmar**ías**	**os** entusiasmar**íais**
se entusiasmar**ía**	**se** entusiasmar**ían**

Present Perfect

caerse *to fall down*

me he caído	**nos hemos** caído
te has caído	**os habéis** caído
se ha caído	**se han** caído

The agreement of the reflexive pronoun with the subject of the sentence takes place both when the pronoun is attached to the infinitive and when it precedes the conjugated verb. This is shown in the examples that follow, which include verb + infinitive constructions and verb + connector + infinitive constructions.

No quiero levantar**me**. No **me** quiero levantar.	*I don't want to get up.*
V**as** a alegrar**te**. **Te** v**as** a alegrar.	*You're going to be glad.*
Empezab**an** a entusiasmar**se**. **Se** empezab**an** a entusiasmar.	*They were beginning to get excited.*

Study the following chart to see the changes of the reflexive pronouns in all persons and in both possible positions.

sentarse *to sit down*

Quiero sentar**me**.	Queremos sentar**nos**.	**Me** quiero sentar.	**Nos** queremos sentar.
Quieres sentar**te**.	Queréis sentar**os**.	**Te** quieres sentar.	**Os** queréis sentar.
Quiere sentar**se**.	Quieren sentar**se**.	**Se** quiere sentar.	**Se** quieren sentar.

Reflexive and Nonreflexive Verb Pairs

Most reflexive verbs can also be used nonreflexively. When they are used without the reflexive pronouns, they are transitive verbs—verbs that are used with a direct object. Study the following pairs of sentences.

Yo **acuesto** <u>a los niños</u>.	*I put the children to bed.*
Yo **me acuesto**.	*I go to bed.*
Los chicos **lavan** <u>el carro</u>.	*The boys are washing the car.*
Los chicos **se lavan**.	*The boys are washing up.*
¿Por qué no **acercas** <u>una silla</u>?	*Why don't you bring over a chair?*
¿Por qué no **te acercas**?	*Why don't you move closer?*
La madre **peinó** <u>a su hijita</u>.	*The mother combed her little daughter's hair.*
La madre **se peinó**.	*The mother combed her (own) hair.*

Here are some common verbs referring to aspects of one's daily routine. The verbs in the left column are transitive and express an action that one person does to another, as in the first example of each pair above. The verbs in the right column are reflexive and correspond to intransitive verbs in English.

acostar (o > ue) *to put (someone) to bed*	**acostarse (o > ue)** *to go to bed*
afeitar *to shave (someone)*	**afeitarse** *to shave*
arreglar *to arrange, fix (something)*	**arreglarse** *to get ready* (fix hair, clothing, etc.)
bañar *to bathe (someone)*	**bañarse** *to bathe, take a bath*
cansar *to tire (someone)*	**cansarse** *to get tired*
colocar *to place, put (something)*	**colocarse** *to get a job*
cortar *to cut (something)*	**cortarse** *to cut oneself*
cuidar *to take care of (someone)*	**cuidarse** *to take care of oneself*
desnudar *to undress (someone)*	**desnudarse** *to get undressed*
despertar (e > ie) *to wake (someone) up*	**despertarse (e > ie)** *to wake up*
duchar *to give (someone) a shower*	**ducharse** *to take a shower*
enfermar *to sicken, get sick*	**enfermarse** *to get sick*
lastimar *to hurt (someone)*	**lastimarse** *to hurt oneself*
lavar *to wash (someone/something)*	**lavarse** *to wash up*
levantar *to raise, pick up; get (someone)*	**levantarse** *to get up out of bed*
maquillar *to put makeup on (someone)*	**maquillarse** *to put on makeup*
peinar *to comb (someone's) hair*	**peinarse** *to comb one's hair*
pintar *to paint (something)*	**pintarse** *to put on makeup*
probar (o > ue) *to try, taste (something)*	**probarse (o > ue)** *to try on*
reunir *to join, gather (someone or something)*	**reunirse (con)** *to get together (with)*
vestir (e > i) *to dress (someone)*	**vestirse (e > i)** *to dress, get dressed*

Verbs referring to feelings and emotions can also be either reflexive or nonreflexive (transitive). The verbs in the left column below are transitive and express an action that one person does to another. The verbs in the right column are reflexive and correspond to intransitive verbs in English. In these verbs of emotion and feeling, the English equivalents often include *to be* or *to get* + the past participle.

aburrir *to bore (someone)*	**aburrirse** *to get/be bored*
alegrar *to make (someone) happy*	**alegrarse** *to be glad/happy*
animar *to cheer (someone) up, encourage (someone)*	**animarse** *to cheer up, take to heart, feel like doing something*
asustar *to frighten (someone)*	**asustarse** *to get scared*
calmar *to calm (someone) down*	**calmarse** *to calm down*
decidir *to decide (something)*	**decidirse a** *to make up one's mind*
divertir (e > ie) *to amuse (someone)*	**divertirse (e > ie)** *to have a good time*
emocionar *to move, touch, excite (someone)*	**emocionarse** *to be moved/touched, be/get excited*
enfadar *to make (someone) angry*	**enfadarse** *to get angry*
enojar *to make (someone) angry*	**enojarse** *to get angry*
entusiasmar *to excite, thrill, stir (someone)*	**entusiasmarse** *to get excited, feel thrilled*
exasperar *to exasperate, make (someone) lose patience*	**exasperarse** *to get exasperated, lose one's/his/her patience*
interesar *to interest (someone)*	**interesarse en** *to be interested in*
involucrar *to involve (someone)*	**involucrarse** *to be involved, be implicated*
irritar *to irritate (someone)*	**irritarse** *to get irritated*
marear *to make (someone) dizzy*	**marearse** *to get/feel dizzy*
molestar *to annoy, bother (someone)*	**molestarse** *to get annoyed*
ofender *to offend/insult/hurt (someone)*	**ofenderse** *to get offended/insulted; to feel hurt*
preocupar *to worry (someone)*	**preocuparse** *to worry*
relajar *to relax (someone)*	**relajarse** *to relax*
sorprender *to surprise (someone)*	**sorprenderse** *to be surprised*
tranquilizar *to calm (someone) down, reassure*	**tranquilizarse** *to calm down, stop worrying*

Many verbs of motion follow the same pattern. They occur in pairs: nonreflexive verbs that express an action that one person does to another and reflexive verbs that correspond to intransitive verbs in English.

acercar *to bring (something) closer/over*	**acercarse (a)** *to come closer, approach*
alejar *to move (something) away*	**alejarse (de)** *to move away from*
caer *to fall* (usually figurative)	**caerse** *to fall down*
correr *to move (something)*	**correrse** *to move over, make room for*
detener *to stop, bring (something) to a halt*	**detenerse** *to stop, come to a halt*
instalar *to install (something)*	**instalarse** *to move in*
levantar *to lift (something)*	**levantarse** *to get up, rise*
mover (o > ue) *to move (something)* (put in motion)	**moverse (o > ue)** *to move, stir, budge*
pasear *to take (something) for a walk, to walk*	**pasearse** *to stroll, go for a walk*
perder (e > ie) *to lose (something)*	**perderse (e > ie)** *to get lost*
sentar (e > ie) *to seat (someone)*	**sentarse (e > ie)** *to sit down*
tirar *to throw (something)*	**tirarse** *to jump, throw oneself; to lie down*
volcar (o > ue) *to knock (something) over*	**volcarse (o > ue)** *to get knocked over*

Some verbs change considerably in meaning when they become reflexive.

despedir (e > i) *to fire, dismiss*	**despedirse de** (e > i) *to say good-bye to*
dormir (o > ue) *to sleep*	**dormirse** (o > ue) *to fall asleep*
empeñar *to pawn*	**empeñarse** (en) *to insist (on), persist (in)*
ir *to go*	**irse** *to go away*
llevar *to carry, take*	**llevarse** *to take away;* **llevarse bien/mal con** *to get along / not get along with*
meter *to put in, insert*	**meterse** (en) *to meddle, butt in*
negar (e > ie) *to deny*	**negarse a** (e > ie) *to refuse to*
parar *to stop*	**pararse** *to stand up* (Spanish America)
parecer (yo **parezco**) *to seem*	**parecerse a** *to resemble*
quedar *to remain, be left*	**quedarse** *to stay, remain*
volver (o > ue) *to return*	**volverse** (o > ue) *to turn around*

There are some verbs that nearly always appear as reflexives, at least with the meanings given. Verbs marked with an asterisk have no nonreflexive form at all.

*acatarrarse *to catch a cold*
acordarse (o > ue) (de) *to remember*
apoderarse (de) *to take possession (of)*
apresurarse de *to hurry*
aprovecharse (de) *to take advantage (of)*
apuntarse a/para *to register, sign up for*
*arrepentirse de (e > ie) *to regret, repent*
*atreverse a *to dare to do (something)*
ausentarse *to be out/away*
burlarse de *to laugh at, make fun of*
casarse (con) *to get married (to)*
comprometerse *to get engaged*
*desmayarse *to faint*
*divorciarse *to get divorced*
echarse *to lie down*
enamorarse (de) *to fall in love (with)*
encararse con *to face, confront*
enterarse (de) *to find out (about)*
*equivocarse *to make a mistake*
escaparse *to escape*
fiarse de *to trust*
figurarse *to imagine*
fijarse (en) *to notice*
graduarse *to graduate*
inclinarse *to bend over*
*jactarse de *to boast about*
matricularse *to enroll, register*
mudarse *to move* (change residence)
ocuparse de *to take care of*
olvidarse (de) *to forget*
oponerse a *to oppose, be against*
ponerse de pie *to stand up* (Spain)

    portarse bien/mal *to behave well/badly*
  *****quejarse de** *to complain about*
    recostarse (o > ue) *to lie down*
    reírse (e > i) de *to laugh at*
  *****resfriarse** *to catch a cold*
    sentirse (e > ie) *to feel*
  *****suicidarse** *to commit suicide*

Here are some expressions that use reflexive verbs.

    darse cuenta (de) *to realize*
    darse prisa *to hurry*
    echarse a + infinitive *to begin to*
    hacerse daño *to hurt oneself*
    hacerse tarde *to get/grow late*
    ponerse a + infinitive *to begin to*
    ponerse de acuerdo *to agree, come to an agreement*
    quedarse con *to keep, hold onto*
    referirse (e > ie) a *to refer to*
    servirse (e > i) de *to use*
    tratarse de *to be about, be a question of*
    valerse de *to use*

A   *Complete each sentence with the correct form of the reflexive verb in parentheses for the tense indicated. ¡Ojo! Be sure the reflexive pronoun refers to the subject.*

Present

1. Yo _____ en forma. (ponerse)

2. Ud. _____ a las once. (acostarse)

3. Tú _____ en seguida. (dormirse)

4. Ella _____ elegantemente. (vestirse)

5. Ellos _____ temprano. (despertarse)

6. Nosotros _____. (relajarse)

Preterit

7. Ud. _____. (equivocarse)

8. Tú _____. (irse)

9. Yo _____. (tranquilizarse)

10. Uds. _____. (arrepentirse)

11. Él _____ de sus amigos. (despedirse)

12. Vosotros _____. (casarse)

Imperfect

13. Nosotros _____. (sorprenderse)

14. Ud. _____. (enamorarse)

15. Yo _____. (entusiasmarse)

16. Tú _____. (irse)

17. Ellos _____. (reunirse)

18. Silvia _____. (aburrirse)

Future

19. Yo _____. (decidirse)

20. Tú y yo _____ a su política. (oponerse)

21. Ellos _____. (detenerse)

22. Ricardo _____ bien. (sentirse)

23. Tú _____. (reírse)

24. Uds. _____ en la nueva casa. (instalarse)

Conditional

25. Tú _____ de todo. (acordarse)

26. Nosotras _____. (animarse)

27. Ud. _____. (correrse)

28. Yo _____ de su hacienda. (apoderarse)

29. Vosotros _____. (enfadarse)

30. Uds. _____ en forma. (mantenerse)

Present Perfect

31. Ellos _____. (sonreirse)

32. _____ tarde. (hacerse)

33. Uds. _____ patinando. (caerse)

34. Yo _____ del diccionario en línea. (servirse)

35. Tú _____ el pie. (romperse)

36. Nosotros _____ de pie. (ponerse)

B *Expand each reflexive sentence with the verb in parentheses. You will form verb + infinitive or verb + connector + infinitive constructions. Write each sentence in two ways. ¡Ojo! Retain the original tense of the verb.*

MODELO   Ella se arregla. (pensar)

     Piensa arreglarse.   Se piensa arreglar.

1. Él se colocó. (conseguir)

_____

2. Se interesan. (empezar a)

_____

3. Uds. se reúnen. (pensar)

_____

4. Te encararás con él. (tener que)

_____

5. No me involucraría en eso. (querer)

_____

6. Os preocupabais. (dejar de)

_____

7. Se divierte. (esperar)

_____

8. No nos decidiremos. (poder)

_____

9. Me paseaba. (ir a)

_____

10. Os vestís. (deber)

_____

11. Se quedaron. (preferir)

_____

12. Se cortaba. (temer)

_____

13. Te casas. (desear)

_____

14. Se duchó. (terminar de)

_____

C *Create sentences using the following strings of elements. Write all verbs in the preterit.*

MODELO   él / hacerse daño / jugando fútbol americano

Se hizo daño jugando fútbol americano.

1. yo / darse cuenta de / el problema

_____

2. Ud. / echarse a / correr

_____

3. nosotros / ponerse de acuerdo

_____

4. ellos / quedarse con / el dinero

   _____

5. tú / no fiarse de / tus socios

   _____

6. Uds. / darse prisa / al ver la hora

   _____

7. tratarse de / un asunto muy importante

   _____

8. ella / servirse de / unos libros de consulta

   _____

9. ¿vosotros / atreverse a / hablarles de esa manera?

   _____

10. él / ponerse a / reír

    _____

D **Translation.** *Express the following sentences in Spanish.*

1. *Each time Javier shaves, he cuts himself.*

   _____

2. *That's why he likes the barber to give him a shave.*

   _____

3. *I bathe my children before I put them to bed. Then I go to bed.*

   _____

4. *Today Marta and Daniela woke up at 7:30. They took a shower, dressed, put on makeup, and combed their hair.*

   _____

   _____

5. *I tell them not to worry. I want them to calm down and relax.*

   _____

6. *He persisted in meddling in our business.*

   _____

7. *Consuelo and Jaime graduated from college, fell in love, got engaged, and got married.*

   _____

   _____

8. *You (tú) caught a cold last week and you still feel bad?*

   _____

9. *She was approaching the house when she felt dizzy.*

   _____

10. *I regret being involved in their shady business (negocio turbio).*

    _____

11. *We'll register for the online business course.*

    _____

Reflexive Verbs with Reciprocal Meaning ("Each Other")

In the plural, reflexive verbs may convey a *reciprocal meaning* equivalent to English "each other."

Carlos y Eva **se quieren** mucho.	*Carlos and Eva love each other very much.*
Nos escribimos y **nos hablamos**.	*We write to each other and we talk to each other.*
Nos vemos mañana.	*We'll see each other tomorrow.*
¿Dónde **os conocisteis**?	*Where did you meet each other?*
¡Chicos! Pórtense bien. ¡No **se peguen**!	*Children! Behave yourselves. Don't hit each other!*

Spanish uses the phrase **el uno al otro** (or **uno a otro**) to emphasize or specify the meaning "each other." This phrase usually agrees with the gender and number of the people referred to: **el uno al otro / la una a la otra / los unos a los otros / las unas a las otras**.

Mis dos hermanos se ayudan **el uno al otro**.	*My two brothers help **each other**.*
Las chicas se miran **las unas a las otras**.	*The girls look at **each other**.*

The reflexive pronoun is not used to express "each other" with prepositions other than **a**.

Lola y Paula compran muchos regalos **la una para la otra**.	*Lola and Paula buy many gifts for each other.*

E Create sentences using the following strings of elements. Use the verbs reflexively to convey reciprocal meaning.

MODELO   tú y yo / hablar por teléfono

   Tú y yo nos hablamos por teléfono. _____

1. Claudia y yo / escribir mensajes electrónicos

   _____

2. Alejandro y Catalina / entender perfectamente

   _____

3. Miriám y Alejo / querer mucho

_____

4. David y yo / ver muy a menudo

_____

5. Diana y su hermana / ayudar mucho

_____

6. Miguel y Beatriz / comprar regalos

_____

7. Esteban y yo / decir muchas cosas

_____

8. Ud. y yo / llegar a conocer bien

_____

9. tú y yo / tutear (*address each other as* tú [informally])

_____

With many verbs, especially—but not only—verbs of motion, the switch from non-reflexive to reflexive shows a subtle shade of meaning that stresses the participation of the subject or an emotional, subjective reaction of the speaker. It is often difficult to capture the difference in meaning in English without completely altering the sentence. The reflexive forms are most common in informal language.

El niño **bajó** de su silla.	*The child got down from his chair.* *(This is an objective statement.)*
¡El niño **se bajó** de la silla!	*The child got down off his chair!* *(Isn't that amazing?)*
Salí porque era tarde.	*I left because it was late.*
Me enojé y **me salí**.	*I got angry and walked out.*
Ven conmigo.	*Come with me.*
Vente conmigo.	*Come along with me.*
No lo **creemos**.	*We don't believe it.*
No **nos** lo **creemos**.	*We can't believe it.*
Murió el rosal.	*The rosebush died.*
Se murió su padre.	*His father died. (And it was a terrible blow.)*
¿Qué **traes**?	*What are you bringing?*
¿Qué **te traes** entre manos?	*What are you up to?*
Sé el vocabulario.	*I know the vocabulary.*
Me sé el vocabulario.	*I (have studied and) know the vocabulary really well.*

When English uses reflexive pronouns (*myself, yourself, himself, herself, ourselves, yourselves, themselves*), the pronouns emphasize the fact that the subject performs the action upon himself. Spanish expresses this with **solo** or **mismo**.

—¿Su hijo ya se viste **solo**?	*"Can your son dress himself already?"*
—No, tiene solamente dos años. Yo lo visto.	*"No, he's only two. I dress him."*
—¿Dejas que te peine tu hermana?	*"Do you allow your sister to comb your hair?"*
—No, yo **misma** me peino.	*"No, I comb my own hair."*

How to Say "Become" in Spanish

In order to construct sentences containing the idea of *become* in Spanish, you have to select the appropriate verb or verbal phrase for the particular context.

To express *become* + an adjective, **ponerse** is usually used, especially for physical or emotional changes where no effort is implied.

—Siempre **te pones rojo** cuando hablo de María Elena.	*"You always get red when I talk about María Elena."*
—Y tú **te pones colorada** cuando yo menciono a Carlos.	*"And you blush when I mention Carlos."*
El jefe **se puso bravo** cuando oyó la noticia.	*The boss got angry when he heard the news.*
Cuando Laura descolgó el teléfono y oyó la voz de Pedro, **se puso pálida**.	*When Laura picked up the phone and heard Pedro's voice, she turned pale.*

Volverse can also be used with adjectives to imply a sudden, involuntary change, often a more profound one than that indicated by **ponerse**.

Si las cosas siguen así, **me voy a volver loco**.	*If things keep up like this, I will go crazy.*
Este niño **se ha vuelto imposible**.	*This child has gotten impossible.*
Nuestro barrio **se ha vuelto peligroso**.	*Our neighborhood has gotten dangerous.*
Los políticos **se vuelven** cada vez **más arrogantes**.	*The politicians are becoming more and more arrogant.*

To express *become* + a noun of profession or nationality, or an adjective indicating social or economic status, **hacerse** or **llegar a ser** is used. Both phrases imply effort on the part of the subject, with **hacerse** implying greater intent than **llegar a ser**. The phrase **pasar a ser** is used to stress the process of change rather than the effort required to bring it about.

Ese joven **se va a hacer rico**.	*That young man is going to get rich.*
Se dice que él **se hizo presidente de la República** por fraude electoral.	*They say that he became president of the country by voter fraud.*
Alicia y yo **nos hicimos amigas**.	*Alicia and I became friends.*
Luis **llegó a ser director** de la empresa.	*Luis became head of the firm.*
Él **pasó a ser tutor** de los hijos de su primo.	*He became the guardian of his cousin's children.*

However, when **hacerse** is followed by the definite article and an adjective, it means *to pretend to be, to act like*.

Cuando el profesor preguntó quién había escrito eso en la pizarra, Raúl **se hizo el desentendido**.	*When the teacher asked who had written that on the board, Raúl played dumb.*
Cuando le piden que ayude, **se hace la sorda**.	*When they ask her to help, she turns a deaf ear.*
Cuando vino la hora de ir a visitar a los vecinos, **me hice el dormido**.	*When the time came to go to visit the neighbors, I pretended to be asleep.*
No invitemos a Nicolás a la fiesta. Siempre **se hace el tonto** y molesta a los demás.	*Let's not invite Nicolás to the party. He always acts silly and annoys everyone.*

Quedarse can mean *to become*, especially with physical conditions.

Se quedó ciego a raíz del accidente.	*He went blind because of the accident.*
Si no bajas la radio, todos **nos vamos a quedar sordos**.	*If you don't turn down the radio, we're all going to go deaf.*

The phrases **convertirse (e > ie) en** and **transformarse en** are sometimes used to express the idea of *becoming*.

La industria petroquímica **se ha convertido en la base** de la economía de la región.	*The petrochemical industry has become the mainstay of the economy of the region.*
El sapo **se ha transformado en un príncipe**.	*The toad has been changed into a prince.*

The idea of *becoming* in Spanish is often expressed by a reflexive verb.

alegrarse *to become happy*
asustarse *to get scared*
cansarse *to get tired*
deprimirse *to get depressed*
emocionarse *to get excited*
enojarse *to get angry*
enredarse *to get entangled/involved*
entristecerse (yo entristezco) *to become sad*
entusiasmarse *to get excited*

Te cansas porque trabajas demasiado.	*You get tired because you work too much.*
Yo no tengo la culpa. **No se enojen** Uds. conmigo.	*I'm not to blame. Please don't get angry with me.*

Often the idea of *becoming* can be expressed by either a reflexive verb or by **hacerse/ponerse/volverse** + an adjective. The reflexive verb is more formal and literary.

enfurecerse (yo enfurezco) / ponerse furioso *to get furious*
enorgullecerse (yo enorgullezco) / volverse (o > ue) orgulloso *to become proud*
enriquecerse (yo enriquezco) / hacerse rico *to get rich*

El rey **se enfureció** cuando supo lo de la
rebelión de sus súbditos.

*The king got furious when he learned
of the rebellion of his subjects.*

Cuando se dio cuenta de que su hija había
vuelto a las tres de la madrugada,
su padre **se puso furioso.**

*When he realized that his daughter had
come home at three in the morning,
her father got furious.*

La dama **se enorgulleció** con el éxito de
sus fiestas.

*The lady prided herself on the success
of her parties.*

Ahora que tiene dinero **se ha vuelto muy
orgulloso.**

*Now that he has money, he has become
very haughty.*

Venezuela **se enriqueció** con sus
exportaciones de petróleo.

Venezuela got rich with its oil exports.

Javier **se hizo rico** invirtiendo dinero
en la Bolsa norteamericana.

*Javier got rich by investing money in the
U.S. stock market.*

For some adjectives, the idea of *becoming* can be expressed either by a nonreflexive verb
or by **ponerse/hacerse/volverse** + an adjective. The single verb is usually more formal
and literary, and it may also be more literal than the phrase with **ponerse/hacerse/
volverse.**

> **enflaquecer (yo enflaquezco) / ponerse flaco** *to get thin*
> **engordar / ponerse gordo** *to get fat*
> **enloquecer (yo enloquezco) / volverse (o > ue) loco** *to go crazy/mad*
> **enmudecer (yo enmudezco) / volverse (o > ue) mudo** *to become silent/speechless*
> **enriquecerse (yo me enriquezco) / hacerse rico** *to get rich*
> **ensordecer (yo ensordezco) / volverse (o > ue) sordo** *to go deaf*
> **envejecer (yo envejezco) / ponerse viejo** *to grow old*
> **palidecer (yo palidezco) / ponerse pálido** *to turn pale*

No como pasteles porque no quiero
engordar.

*I don't eat cake because I don't want
to get fat.*

Si comes tantos dulces **te vas a poner
gordo.**

*If you eat so many sweets, you're going
to get fat.*

Al saber que todos sus hijos habían
muerto en el terremoto, la mujer
enloqueció.

*When she found out that all her children
had died in the earthquake, the woman
went mad.*

¿A Paco le prestaste veinte mil dólares?
¿Qué te pasa? **¿Te has vuelto loco?**

*You lent Paco twenty thousand dollars?
What's wrong with you? Have you gone
crazy?*

Es difícil **envejecer** solo.

It's hard to grow old alone.

Mi madre no quiere salir mucho. **Se está
poniendo vieja.**

*My mother doesn't want to go out much.
She's getting/feeling old.*

F **Translation.** *Express the following sentences in Spanish.* **¡Ojo!** *Remember that there is more than one way to express* become *in Spanish.*

1. *The fans went crazy when they saw their favorite player.*

   _____

2. *Due to his good investments, he became rich.*

   _____

3. *Pablo and Amanda became friends.*

   _____

4. *The small town became a bustling* (bulliciosa) *international capital.*

   _____

   _____

5. *Paula is a timid girl who blushes frequently.*

   _____

6. *Jacobo was getting fat while his brother Cristóbal was getting thin.*

   _____

   _____

7. *They got angry when they saw that their dog had torn the rug.*

   _____

   _____

G **Translation.** *Express the following sentences in Spanish, using reflexive verbs to tell how these people reacted to events.*

1. *Aurelia cheered up.* _____

2. *I got excited.* _____

3. *Carlos got offended.* _____

4. *Pilar and I were touched.* _____

5. *They got angry.* _____

6. *You (tú) were annoyed.* _____

7. *You (Uds.) were exasperated.* _____

8. *You (Ud.) got bored.* _____

9. *You (vosotros) got irritated.* _____

10. *They got scared.* _____

11. *He got sad.* _____

12. *We were surprised.* _____

| BUILDING SENTENCES | **Sentences with the reflexive pronoun as indirect object** |

Certain reflexive verbs can appear with direct objects. In these cases the reflexive pronoun is an indirect object, not a direct object. The equivalent of the indirect object reflexive pronoun in English is usually a possessive adjective. Most of these verbs express actions that have an effect on articles of clothing or parts of the body.

| Me pongo el chaleco. | *I put on my vest.* |
| Los niños se ponen los zapatos. | *The children put on their shoes.* |

The reflexive pronoun in the examples above is closely related in function to the indirect object. If the indirect object reflexive pronoun is replaced by an indirect object referring to someone other than the subject, the relationship among the elements of the sentence changes.

| Le pongo el chaleco. | *I help him on with his vest.* |
| A los niños les ponemos los zapatos. | *We put the children's shoes on.* |

Study the following pairs of sentences. The first member of each pair has a reflexive pronoun to signal that the indirect object refers to the subject of the sentence.

Los chicos **se lavan la cara**.	*The children are washing their faces.*
A los chicos **les lavo la cara**.	*I am washing the children's faces.*
Mónica **se quitó el abrigo**.	*Mónica took off her coat.*
A Mónica **le quité el abrigo**.	*I helped Mónica off with her coat.*
Me voy a cortar el pelo.	*I'm going to get a haircut.*
Si quieres, **te corto el pelo**.	*If you want, I'll cut your hair.*

Here are some common reflexive verbs and expressions that use the same pattern as in the examples above.

ponerse + article of clothing *to put on*
quitarse + article of clothing *to take off*
romperse + article of clothing *to tear*

lavarse + part of the body *to wash*
quebrarse (e > ie) + part of the body *to break*
quemarse + part of the body *to burn*
romperse + part of the body *to break*

Here are some typical expressions using this pattern.

abrocharse la chaqueta / los zapatos / los cordones / el cinturón de seguridad
   to button one's jacket, tie one's shoes/shoelaces, buckle/fasten one's seat belt
amarrarse los zapatos / los cordones *to tie one's shoes/shoelaces*
atarse los zapatos / los cordones *to tie one's shoes/shoelaces*
cepillarse los dientes / el pelo *to brush one's teeth/hair*
cortarse el pelo *to get a haircut*
desabrocharse la chaqueta / los zapatos / los cordones / el cinturón de seguridad
   to unbutton one's jacket, untie one's shoes/shoelaces, unbuckle/unfasten one's seat belt
desamarrarse los zapatos / los cordones *to untie one's shoes/shoelaces*

desatarse los zapatos / los cordones *to untie one's shoes/shoelaces*
lastimarse el dedo *to hurt one's finger*
lavarse la cabeza *to wash one's hair*
limarse las uñas *to file one's nails*
limpiarse los dientes *to brush one's teeth*
maquillarse la cara *to put makeup on*
pintarse los labios *to put lipstick on*
secarse el pelo *to dry one's hair*
torcerse (o > ue) el tobillo *to twist one's ankle*

NOTE

Spanish uses a singular noun for articles of clothing and parts of the body, even with plural subjects, when each person has only one of the mentioned item. Only when each person has more than one of the mentioned item does Spanish use a plural noun.

Se quitaron **el gorro**.	*They took off their caps.*
Se quitaron **los guantes**.	*They took off their gloves.*

H *Rewrite each sentence, changing the direct object noun to a pronoun and making all necessary changes. ¡Ojo! Retain the original tense.*

MODELO   Pedro se rompió la pierna. <u>*Pedro se la rompió.*</u>

1. Roberto se torció el tobillo. _____

2. Eva y Ana se lavarán la cabeza. _____

3. Te probabas la camisa. _____

4. Pablo se ha roto el dedo meñique (*little finger*).

   _____

5. Me puse las medias. _____

6. Ud. se abrochó los zapatos. _____

7. Nos ponemos el suéter. _____

8. Os laváis las manos. _____

9. Iba a cortarme el pelo. _____

10. Acaba de lastimarse el codo. _____

11. Quiere pintarse los labios. _____

12. Necesitabas cepillarte el pelo. _____

13. Me he atado los cordones. _____

14. Se había limado las uñas. _____

15. Quiero que te seques el pelo. _____

16. Era necesario que nos abrocháramos el cinturón de seguridad.

    _____

The Imperative of Reflexive Verbs

Reflexive pronouns follow the same rules in commands as direct and indirect object pronouns. To review the placement of object pronouns with the imperative, see Chapter 9.

In negative commands, reflexive pronouns appear in their usual position before the verb.

No **te** quiebres el pie.	*Don't break your foot.*
No **se** preocupe Ud.	*Don't worry.*
No **nos** reunamos con ellos.	*Let's not get together with them.*
No **se** asusten Uds.	*Don't get scared.*
No **os** enojéis.	*Don't get angry.*
No **te** quites el anorak.	*Don't take off your ski jacket.*
No **te lo** quites.	*Don't take it off.*
No **se** rompa los pantalones.	*Don't tear your pants.*
No **se los** rompa.	*Don't tear them.*

In affirmative commands, reflexive pronouns are attached to the command form and an accent mark is added over the stressed syllable except in **vosotros** commands and in some two-syllable forms.

Levántate y **vístete** inmediatamente.	*Get up and get dressed immediately.*
Diviértase Ud.	*Have a good time.*
Acérquense Uds.	*Come closer.*
Animémonos.	*Let's cheer up.*
Calmaos.	*Calm down.*
Vete.	*Go away.*
Lávate la cabeza.	*Wash your hair.*
Lávatela.	*Wash it.*
Pruébese el traje.	*Try on the suit.*
Pruébeselo.	*Try it on.*

When the reflexive pronoun **nos** is added to a **nosotros** command form, the final **s** of the verb form drops.

Sentémonos en esta fila.	*Let's sit down in this row.*
Despidámonos de nuestros amigos.	*Let's say good-bye to our friends.*
Escribámonos todas las semanas.	*Let's write to each other every week.*
Pongámonos las botas.	*Let's put on our boots.*
Pongámonoslas.	*Let's put them on.*

As with other affirmative **nosotros** commands, the **vamos a** + infinitive construction often replaces the command form derived from the subjunctive.

Vamos a sentarnos en esta fila.	*Let's sit down in this row.*
Vamos a despedirnos de nuestros amigos.	*Let's say good-bye to our friends.*
Vamos a escribirnos todas las semanas.	*Let's write to each other every week.*
Vamos a ponérnoslas (**las** = **las botas**).	*Let's put them on.*

I ***Translation.*** *Express the following sentences in English. Write more than one translation for each sentence. **¡Ojo!** Focus on the indirect object pronoun and indirect object reflexive pronoun.*

1. Abrócheselo.

   _____

2. Pónganselas.

   _____

3. Lávasela.

   _____

4. Se los quitó.

   _____

5. Se la desabrocharon.

   _____

6. Va a cepillárselo.

   _____

7. Me las puse.

   _____

8. Debes limpiártelos.

   _____

J *Answer each question, using imperatives. Write an affirmative command and a negative command for each question. The cue in parentheses tells you whom to address. Change the direct object nouns to pronouns and make all necessary changes.*

MODELO   ¿Me quito los zapatos? (tú)

   Sí, quítatelos.

   No, no te los quites.

1. ¿Me pongo este traje de baño? (tú)

   _____

   _____

2. ¿Nos limpiamos los dientes? (Uds.)

   _____

   _____

3. ¿Me seco el pelo? (Ud.)

   _____

   _____

4. ¿Nos quitamos el suéter? (nosotras)

_____

_____

5. ¿Me pruebo las chaquetas de cuero? (tú)

_____

_____

6. ¿Nos lavamos las manos? (vosotros)

_____

_____

7. ¿Me corto el pelo? (Ud.)

_____

_____

8. ¿Nos desabrochamos los zapatos? (nosotros)

_____

_____

9. ¿Nos abrochamos el cinturón? (Uds.)

_____

_____

10. ¿Nos pintamos los labios? (vosotras)

_____

_____

K *Translation. Express the following sentences in Spanish.*

1. *I helped her on with her coat.*

_____

2. *He twisted his ankle during the football game.*

_____

3. *Let's move into the new house as soon as possible.*

_____

4. *Are you* (tú) *going to have your hair cut?*

_____

5. *Look! I had it cut yesterday.*

_____

6. *Should I try on this navy blue suit?*

_____

7. *Yes, try it on, and put on that gray one too.* (Ud.)

_____

8. *Let's calm down. Let's not worry.*

_____

9. *Here is your T-shirt. Put it on.* (tú)

_____

10. *You broke your foot. Don't break the other one!* (tú)

_____

11. *Dry them* (las lágrimas *tears*). (Ud.)

_____

12. *Dry them* (las lágrimas) *for her.* (Ud.)

_____

13. *Fasten (Buckle) your seat belts.* (Uds.)

_____

14. *Fasten your little girl's seat belt.* (Ud.)

_____

The Present Participle; The Progressive Tenses

Formation of the Present Participle

The Spanish present participle, or *gerund*, ends in **-ndo** and is a form parallel in many of its uses to the English present participle, which ends in *-ing*.

-Ar verbs form the present participle by removing the **-ar** of the infinitive and adding **-ando**. **-Er** and **-ir** verbs replace the **-er** and **-ir** of the infinitive with **-iendo** to form the present participle. However, **-er** and **-ir** verbs whose stems end in a vowel replace the ending **-iendo** with **-yendo** to form the present participle.

INFINITIVE	PRESENT PARTICIPLE
tomar	tomando
aprender	aprendiendo
abrir	abriendo
caer	cayendo
creer	creyendo
leer	leyendo
traer	trayendo
oír	oyendo
construir	construyendo

Stem-changing **-ir** verbs have the same vowel in the stem of the present participle as in the **él/ella/Ud.** form of the preterit.

INFINITIVE	**yo** FORM PRESENT TENSE	**él/ella/Ud.** FORM PRETERIT	PRESENT PARTICIPLE
sentir	siento	sintió	sintiendo
pedir	pido	pidió	pidiendo
servir	sirvo	sirvió	sirviendo
dormir	duermo	durmió	durmiendo
morir	muero	murió	muriendo

-Ir verbs with irregular preterit stems show the vowel of that form in the present participle.

INFINITIVE	**yo** FORM PRESENT TENSE	**él/ella/Ud.** FORM PRETERIT	PRESENT PARTICIPLE
decir	digo	dijo	diciendo
venir	vengo	vino	viniendo

Poder and **ir** have irregular present participles.

poder	**pudiendo**
ir	**yendo**

Object pronouns and reflexive pronouns are attached to the present participle in writing, and an accent mark is written over the **a** or **e** of the -**ndo** ending.

esperándolo
dándomelas
levantándose
viéndolos
trayéndosela
sintiéndose

The present participle often functions as an adverbial phrase or adverb clause beginning with *by, if, when, while,* or *because.* Some grammarians call the present participle a *gerund* in this function.

Los niños aprenden mucho **escuchando** la conversación de los mayores.	*Children learn a lot by listening to the conversation of adults.*
Se acatarró **caminando** bajo la lluvia.	*He caught a cold while walking in the rain.*

With verbs of perception, such as **ver, mirar, oír,** and **escuchar,** either the infinitive or the present participle can be used, as in English.

Los oímos cantar. Los oímos cantando.	*We heard them sing/singing.*
Siempre la veo pasear a su perro. Siempre la veo paseando a su perro.	*I always see her walk/walking her dog.*

A *Create sentences using **pasar** + the present participle. Include the time cue in parentheses to tell how long people spent doing their activities.*

MODELO ella / trotar (treinta minutos)
  Pasó treinta minutos trotando.

1. yo / hacer ejercicio (una hora)

   _____

2. tú / vestirse (diez minutos)

   _____

3. Juan Carlos / navegar en la Red (dos horas)

   _____

4. ellos / pasearse (media hora)

_____

5. nosotros / divertirse (el día entero)

_____

6. Uds. / instalarse en el condominio (una semana)

_____

7. Ignacio / oír música (cuarenta y cinco minutos)

_____

8. vosotros / discutir (mucho tiempo)

_____

9. Marisol / probarse ropa (toda la tarde)

_____

10. tú / dormir la siesta (veinte minutos)

_____

11. Uds. / leer (toda la mañana)

_____

12. nosotros / ver tele (menos de una hora)

_____

B *Write sentences using the following strings of elements. Use verbs of perception, and write two sentences for each item—one using the infinitive, the other using the gerund. Use the preterit for all verbs.*

MODELO   él / oír cantar / a Juan Diego
  Él lo oyó cantar.   Él lo oyó cantando.

1. Uds. / ver bailar ballet / a Cristina

_____

2. tú / escuchar hablar / a los locutores

_____

3. nosotros / mirar actuar / a las actrices

_____

4. Ud. / oír llorar / al niño

_____

5. yo / ver correr / los miembros del equipo

_____

6. vosotros / observar hacer gimnasia / a la gimnasta

_____

_____

7. ellos / oír silbar (*whistle*) una melodía / a mí

_____

_____

8. él / ver cruzar la calle / a nosotros

_____

The Progressive Tenses

The progressive tenses consist of any tense of **estar** + the present participle.

TENSE NAME	EXAMPLE SENTENCE	ENGLISH TRANSLATION
PRESENT PROGRESSIVE	Estoy leyendo una novela.	*I am reading a novel.*
IMPERFECT PROGRESSIVE	Estaba leyendo una novela.	*I was reading a novel.*
PRETERIT PROGRESSIVE	Estuve leyendo una novela hasta las dos de la tarde.	*I was reading a novel until two in the afternoon.*
FUTURE PROGRESSIVE	Estaré leyendo una novela.	*I will be reading a novel.*
CONDITIONAL PROGRESSIVE	Estaría leyendo una novela.	*I would be reading a novel.*

The progressive forms of **estar**, **ir**, and **venir** are rarely used.

The present, imperfect, future, and conditional progressives all emphasize that the action is, was, will be, or would be in progress. The preterit progressive, a less common tense, usually appears in a sentence where the end of the action is specified and, like all preterits, implies a completed action. It conveys the idea of an action going on in the past that ended.

Estuvieron bailando en la discoteca hasta el amanecer.	*They were dancing in the discotheque until dawn.*
Estuvo corriendo hasta que comenzó a llover.	*He was running until it began to rain.*
Estuve formateando hasta que mi computadora crasheó.	*I was formatting until my computer crashed.*

The progressive tenses may convey the idea of a temporary action or an action that represents a change from what the speaker is used to.

Tenemos que entrar. **Está lloviendo.**	*We have to go in. It has started to rain.*
¿Qué es esto? ¿Miguel **está fumando**?	*What's this? Miguel has started to smoke?*

There is often not much difference in meaning between the simple imperfect and the imperfect progressive.

¿Qué me **decías**?	
¿Qué me **estabas diciendo**?	*What were you telling me?*

However, the simple imperfect conveys a habitual action in the past. The imperfect progressive may convey the idea of a recently begun action or strongly imply that the action was interrupted, but not that it was a habitual one.

Elisa **trabajaba** en el centro.	*Elisa used to work downtown.*
Elisa **estaba trabajando** en el centro.	*Elisa was working downtown.*

The future and conditional progressives may be used to express probability or conjecture. As with the simple future and conditional of probability, the future progressive expresses probability or conjecture about the present, the conditional progressive about the past.

¿Qué **estarán haciendo**?	*I wonder what they are doing.*
¿No quisieron salir? **Estarían estudiando.**	*They didn't want to go out? They were probably studying.*

The Spanish present progressive is never used to refer to future time like the English present progressive commonly is. Spanish uses either the simple present, the **ir a** + infinitive construction, or the future tense.

El avión sale a las tres.	
El avión va a salir a las tres.	*The plane is leaving at three.*
El avión saldrá a las tres.	

The sentence **El avión está saliendo** can only mean *The plane is leaving (right now).*

In the progressive tenses, object pronouns and reflexive pronouns either precede the form of **estar** or follow the present participle and are attached to it in writing, in which case an accent mark is added over the **a** or **e** of the present participle ending.

Los chicos **se están levantando.**	
Los chicos **están levantándose.**	*The children are getting up.*

¿El café? **Lo estoy haciendo.**	
¿El café? **Estoy haciéndolo.**	*The coffee? I'm making it.*

Other Verbs Used in Progressive Constructions

Verbs other than **estar** are also used in progressive constructions.

The verb **seguir** is used with the present participle to mean *to be still doing something, to keep on doing something.*

¿**Sigues tomando** clases de español?	*Are you still taking Spanish classes?*
Siguen viviendo en la casa de sus padres.	*They still live in their parents' house.*

Ir is used with the present participle to convey the idea of *gradually* or *little by little.*

Nuestra empresa **va prosperando.**	*Our firm is gradually prospering.*
El pueblo **fue creciendo** poco a poco.	*The town was growing little by little.*

Andar is used with the present participle to convey the idea of *going around doing something* and may imply aimlessness.

Anda pidiendo préstamos.   *He goes around asking for loans.*
Andan buscando casa.   *They are constantly house hunting.*

The **llevar** + **-ndo** construction expresses actions that began in the past and are continuing into the present. It is the equivalent of **hace** + time expression + **que**.

Llevo una semana redactando el informe. ⎫
Hace una semana que redacto el informe. ⎬ *I've been writing up the report for a week.*
                                        ⎭

Verbs of motion such as **salir**, **entrar**, **subir**, and **bajar** can be used with present participles to specify how the motion was performed. English usually prefers to use a different verb for each type of motion, followed by an adverbial complement such as *out, in, into, up,* or *down.*

Salieron corriendo.   *They ran out.*
Un pájaro entró volando en la casa.   *A bird flew into the house.*
Subí la escalera cojeando.   *I limped up the stairs.*
El ascensor estaba descompuesto y por *The elevator wasn't working and that's*
  eso bajé caminando.   *why I walked down.*
Los niños bajaron la escalera saltando. *The kids jumped down the stairs.*

C *Rewrite each sentence, changing the verb from the present indicative to the present progressive. Change direct object nouns to pronouns and make all necessary changes. Write each sentence in two ways.* **¡Ojo!** *Focus on the placement of object pronouns and write accent marks as necessary.*

MODELO   Entra los datos.
         Está entrándolos.   Los está entrando.

1. Alquila el video.

   _____

2. Se divierten mucho.

   _____

3. Te pruebas las sandalias.

   _____

4. Les servimos las margaritas.

   _____

5. Imprime los documentos.

   _____

6. Le pongo el pañal (*diaper*) al bebé.

   _____

7. Nos pedís el iPod.

   _____

8. Leo el libro de cocina.

_____

9. Me escriben el correo electrónico.

_____

10. Os secáis las lágrimas (*tears*).

_____

11. Te rompes la camiseta.

_____

12. Enciende el fuego de campamento.

_____

13. Les consiguen los billetes.

_____

14. Se limpian los dientes.

_____

15. Nos comemos la torta de chocolate.

_____

D *Rewrite each sentence, changing the verb from the imperfect to the imperfect progressive. Change direct object nouns to pronouns and make all necessary changes. Write each sentence in two ways.* **¡Ojo!** *Focus on the placement of object pronouns and write accent marks as necessary.*

MODELO   Escribían el informe.
     Estaban escribiéndolo.   Lo estaban escribiendo.

1. Descargaba los ficheros.

_____

2. Me vestía.

_____

3. Le quitábamos el abrigo.

_____

4. Te cortabas el pelo.

_____

5. Nos decían lo ocurrido.

_____

6. Compartíais las ganancias.

_____

7. Nos reuníamos.

_____

8. Le traía la correspondencia.

_____

9. Me mostraban las fotos.

_____

10. Se lavaba las manos.

_____

11. Me ponía en forma.

_____

12. Se reían a carcajadas (*split one's sides laughing*).

_____

E *Rewrite each sentence, changing the verb either from the future to the future progressive or from the conditional to the conditional progressive. Change direct object nouns to pronouns and make all necessary changes. Write each sentence in two ways.*
¡Ojo! *Focus on the placement of object pronouns and write accent marks as necessary.*

MODELOS Prepararé la cena.
   Estaré preparándola.   La estaré preparando.

Prepararía la cena.
   Estaría preparándola.   La estaría preparando.

1. Terminará la tesis.

_____

2. Cuidarían a sus sobrinos.

_____

3. Nos registraremos (*to register*) en el hotel.

_____

4. Se acostaría.

_____

5. Me dirían su plan.

_____

6. Les harías las chuletas de cordero.

_____

7. Le pondré la chaqueta.

_____

8. Se atarán los cordones.

   _____

9. Te aburrirás.

   _____

10. Le entregaréis los disquetes.

    _____

F *Rewrite each sentence, changing the verb from the preterit to the preterit progressive and incorporating the phrase in parentheses. Change direct object nouns to pronouns and make all necessary changes. Write each sentence in two ways.* **¡Ojo!** *Focus on the placement of object pronouns and write accent marks as necessary.*

MODELO Hice la comida (hasta que vinieron las visitas).

      Estuve haciéndola hasta que vinieron las visitas.

      La estuve haciendo hasta que vinieron las visitas.

1. Practiqué el béisbol (hasta las cinco).

   _____

   _____

2. Se arregló (hasta que él llegó a recogerla).

   _____

   _____

3. Se instalaron (hasta el sábado).

   _____

   _____

4. Nos paseamos (hasta el anochecer).

   _____

   _____

5. Te lavaste la cabeza (hasta que sonó el teléfono).

   _____

   _____

6. Se reunieron (hasta que la presidenta [*chairwoman*] levantó [*adjourned*] la reunión).

   _____

   _____

7. Se portó mal (hasta que sus papás le riñeron).

   _____

   _____

8. Le contó los chismes (hasta que su amiga no pudo más [*couldn't stand it anymore*]).

_____

_____

G *Rewrite each sentence, using the* **llevar** + **-ndo** *construction.*

MODELO   Hace una hora que hago las maletas.
        Llevo una hora haciendo las maletas.

1. Hace cuarenta minutos que navego en la Red.

_____

2. Hace tres horas que juegan al golf.

_____

3. Hace un par de días que se siente mal.

_____

4. Hace varios años que nos interesamos en el arte.

_____

5. Hace quince minutos que te limas las uñas.

_____

6. Hace media hora que os probáis esos pantalones.

_____

7. Hace mucho tiempo que me mantengo en forma.

_____

8. Hace una semana que se reúnen en el congreso.

_____

H *Translation. Express the following sentences in English.*

1. Patricia seguía trabajando en los suburbios cuando di con ella.

_____

2. La empresa iba aumentando sus precios para crear los sitios Web.

_____

3. Uds. subían la escalera corriendo.

_____

4. Bajaste la escalera bailando.

_____

5. Llevamos media hora escribiéndonos mensajes instantáneos.

_____

6. Se resfriaron bebiendo en los vasos ajenos.

_____

7. Pasaron el fin de semana divirtiéndose.

_____

8. Carmen se lastimó el dedo cortando el pan.

_____

I   *Express the following sentences in Spanish. Use the progressive tenses where possible.*
¡Ojo! There might be more than one way to express some sentences.

1. *The chocolate ice cream? I'm serving it to them right now.*

_____

2. *Her coat? He's helping her on with it.*

_____

3. *They're combing their hair while we get dressed.*

_____

4. *The player tore his pants falling down.*

_____

5. *We were falling asleep when the phone rang.*

_____

6. *They're probably moving into their new house.*

_____

7. *I didn't see her dancing at the discotheque last night. I wonder what she was doing.*

_____

_____

8. *I hope you (tú) are getting ready so that we won't arrive late.*

_____

9. *Did you (Uds.) hear him coughing all night?*

_____

10. *We've been looking for a parking meter (el parquímetro) for twenty minutes.*

_____

11. *González was pitching very well until he twisted his ankle.*

_____

NEOGLISMS baseball terms

Baseball has had an enormous impact on many Spanish American societies, and as the sport was adopted, a lexicon for baseball came into being. Many English words were adopted into the language and reshaped according to Spanish pronunciation and grammar, and existing Spanish words took on new meanings to express features of the sport.

Here are some verbs borrowed from English and adapted to the Spanish language with Spanish synonyms in parentheses: **pitchear** (**lanzar**), **cachar** or **cachear** (**atrapar, coger, capturar**), **batear** and **jitear** (**palear**), **fildear**, and **embasar** *to put on base*. Note that these new verbs created in Spanish are integrated into the -**ar** conjugation, most of them with the -**ear** suffix.

BUILDING SENTENCES   **Word order in Spanish**

The basic Spanish word order pattern is like that of English: subject–verb–object.

Claudia compró el carro. *Claudia bought the car.*

A major difference between Spanish and English is that Spanish can omit the subject.

—¿Qué hizo Claudia ayer? *"What did Claudia do yesterday?"*
—Compró el carro. *"She bought the car."*

However, Spanish allows many variations in the basic word order that English does not. The two key aspects of Spanish word order are *focus* and *topicalization*. *Focus* refers to new information. *Topicalization* is the mechanism for setting up the topic of the sentence, or establishing what is being talked about. Both *focus* and *topicalization* entail changes in the basic word order pattern of subject–verb–object.

Focus

The final element of the sentence in Spanish is usually the one focused on, the one that conveys new information. Thus, when the subject of the verb adds new information, it is often moved from before the verb to after it. The Spanish response that follows show word order pattern of object–verb–subject.

—¿Juan compró el carro? *"Did Juan buy the car?"*
—No, lo compró **Claudia**. *"No, **Claudia** bought it."*

English does not change word order for focus. Instead, English spea¹ stress of the sentence to the new piece of information. Comp‑ stress on *Claudia* in these two sentences.

NEUTRAL STATEMENT *Claudia bought the car.*
NEW INFORMATION *(Did Juan buy the car?) N*‑

The element of a sentence that provides the in‑ *questions* usually appears at the end of the sentence

—¿Cuándo compró Juan el carro? *"When*
—Lo compró **ayer**. *"He bougʰ*

Spanish speakers also put information that corrects an erroneous position expressed in a *yes/no question* at the end of the response.

—¿Juan compró el carro en esta ciudad?   *"Did Juan buy the car in this city?"*
—No, lo compró en **su ciudad natal**.   *"No, he bought it in **his home town**."*

Topicalization

The topic of a Spanish sentence is placed at the beginning of the sentence. For instance, when the topic of the sentence is the location of various events of a party, the location information is placed first in the sentence.

En el jardín sirvieron entremeses.   *They served hors d'oeuvres **in the garden**.*

En la sala conversaron.   *They talked **in the living room**.*
En el patio de atrás bailaron.   *There was dancing **on the patio in back of the house**.*

En el comedor sirvieron la comida.   *They served dinner **in the dining room**.*

The time for each of the party events could also be the topic, which would place the phrases of time at the beginning of the sentence and move the phrases of location to their normal position after the verb.

A las nueve sirvieron entremeses **en el jardín**.   *At nine they served hors d'oeuvres **in the garden**.*
A las diez bailaron **en el patio de atrás**.   *At ten there was dancing **on the patio in back of the house**.*

A las once y media sirvieron la comida **en el comedor**.   *At eleven thirty they served dinner **in the dining room**.*

However, if any of the sentences about the party is an answer to an *information question*, then the element that provides the new information sought by the question appears at the end of the sentence.

—¿Qué sirvieron en el jardín?   *"What did they serve in the garden?"*
—En el jardín sirvieron **entremeses**.   *"They served **hors d'oeuvres** in the garden."*

—¿Dónde sirvieron entremeses?   *"Where did they serve hors d'oeuvres?"*
—Sirvieron entremeses **en el jardín**.   *"They served hors d'oeuvres **in the garden**."*

—¿A qué hora sirvieron entremeses?   *"At what time did they serve hors d'oeuvres?"*
—Sirvieron entremeses **a las nueve**.   *"They served hors d'oeuvres **at nine**."*

—¿Quiénes sirvieron los entremeses?   *"Who served the hors d'oeuvres?"*
—Los sirvieron **los anfitriones**.   ***"The host and hostess** served them."*

[A]n object noun can be topicalized by moving it to the beginning of the sentence [and placin]g the direct object pronoun that refers to it before the verb. The idea conveyed is *as far as X is concerned*. . . . Note the *reduplicated* object pronouns that are mandatory when the direct object is moved to topic position.

El carro lo compró Juan.	*Juan bought the car. (Juan is the one who bought the car.)*
La computadora la usaba Lurdes.	*Lurdes was using the computer.*
Al embajador lo entrevistó el periodista.	*The journalist interviewed the ambassador.*
A sus nietos los acuesta la abuela.	*The grandmother is putting her grandchildren to bed.*
A la gerenta de publicidad la conocimos nosotros.	*We met the advertising manager.*

Topicalization of the direct object is especially common in correcting someone's impression. It adds specification.

—¿Sirvieron toda la comida en la casa?	*"Did they serve all the food in the house?"*
—No. **Los entremeses los** sirvieron en el jardín y **la cena la** sirvieron en el comedor.	*"No, they served the hors d'oeuvres in the garden and they served dinner in the dining room."*

Note that in the response for the example above, the phrases **en el jardín** and **en el comedor** add new information (focus) and are therefore placed at the end of their clauses. **Los entremeses** and **la cena** are the topics of their clauses, clarifying aspects of *la comida,* and are therefore placed at the beginning of their clauses.

J *Answer each yes/no question in the negative, using the new information in parentheses in your response. Change direct object nouns to pronouns and make all necessary changes.* **¡Ojo!** *Remember that the final element of the sentence in Spanish is usually the one that conveys new information.*

MODELO   ¿Lola preparó la comida? (Diana)
    <u>No, la preparó Diana.</u>

1. ¿El equipo Azul ganó el campeonato? (el equipo Rojo)

———————————————————————————————————

2. ¿Rodrigo se torció el tobillo? (Raimundo)

———————————————————————————————————

3. ¿Ud. se quemó la mano? (mi amigo)

———————————————————————————————————

4. ¿Los analistas se reunieron? (los consultores)

———————————————————————————————————

5. ¿Abrirán una frutería en la esquina? (una pastelería)

———————————————————————————————————

6. ¿Ellos hacían preguntas? (nosotros)

_____

7. ¿Verónica está probándose el vestido blanco? (Miriám)

_____

8. ¿Esta sucursal busca dependientes? (la otra sucursal)

_____

K *Rewrite each sentence, topicalizing the direct object noun and moving
it to the beginning of the sentence.* **¡Ojo!** *Remember to add the reduplicated
direct object pronoun.*

MODELO   Susana entregó el documento.
          El documento lo entregó Susana.

1. Sara cobró los cheques.

_____

2. Antonio y yo hicimos la lista.

_____

3. Tú preparabas el guacamole.

_____

4. Inés ha cuidado a sus hermanitos.

_____

5. Yo pagué las cuentas.

_____

6. Ellos usarán mi cámara digital.

_____

7. El enfermero tranquilizó a los pacientes nerviosos.

_____

8. Andrés llevó a Lorena a un concierto.

_____

9. Uds. han impreso el informe.

_____

10. El dueño del negocio despidió al empleado insolente.

_____

The Preposition **a** and Word Order

Since subjects frequently follow their verbs in Spanish, the preposition **a** helps you determine whether a noun that follows the verb is a subject or an object when that noun refers to a person. Compare the following pairs of sentences.

Le escribió Fernando.	*Fernando wrote to him.*
Le escribió **a** Fernando.	*He wrote to Fernando.*

In the first sentence above, **Fernando** is the subject of **escribió**. In the second, **Fernando** is the indirect object, labeled by the preposition **a** as referring to the same person as the indirect object pronoun **le**.

With direct objects, the personal **a** also helps to distinguish a direct object from a subject placed after the verb, but it is not the only distinguishing factor. The direct object pronoun is not used (except dialectally) when the direct object noun follows the verb.

Lo vio Fernando.	*Fernando saw him.*
Vio a Fernando.	*He saw Fernando.*

However, when the direct object is topicalized (moved to the beginning of the sentence), then the personal **a** does become the sole factor distinguishing the subject from the object.

Fernando lo vio.	*Fernando saw him.*
A Fernando lo vio.	*He saw Fernando.*

Thus, the word **a**—whether as a preposition marking the indirect object or a personal **a** marking the direct object—labels animate nouns as "oblique," the grammatical term for a noun playing a role other than that of subject in a sentence.

L **Translation.** *Express the following sentences in Spanish. ¡Ojo! There might be more than one way to express some sentences.*

1. *Victoria met him.* _____

2. *He met Victoria.* _____

3. *Isabel told it* (lo) *to her.* _____

4. *She told (it) to Isabel.* _____

5. *Jorge and Rita saw you* (la). _____

6. *You* (Ud.) *saw Jorge and Rita.* _____

7. *Martín showed them* (las) *to them.* _____

8. *They showed them to Martín.* _____

9. *Miguel read to her.* _____

10. *She read to Miguel.* _____

15

Passive Constructions; Reverse Construction Verbs

The Passive Voice

The passive voice in Spanish is similar in formation to the passive voice in English. It consists of a subject and a form of **ser** + the past participle. In the passive voice, the participle functions like an adjective and agrees with the subject in gender and number.

Aquella casa **fue construida** en el siglo XVIII.	*That house was built in the eighteenth century.*
Relaciones diplomáticas entre los dos países **serán establecidas**.	*Diplomatic relations between the two countries will be established.*

The function of the passive voice is to deemphasize the performer of the action and to shift the focus of the sentence to the action expressed by the verb and the direct object. To understand this, it is helpful to see passive sentences as deriving from active ones.

El duque **construyó** aquella casa en el siglo XVIII.	*The duke built that house in the eighteenth century.*
Los gobiernos **establecerán** relaciones diplomáticas entre los dos países.	*The governments will establish diplomatic relations between the two countries.*

In the sentences above, the subject is the performer of the action. When speakers wish to divert attention from the performer of the action, they remove it from the sentence, turn the direct object into the grammatical subject, and change the verb from active to passive.

The performer of the action may be added to a passive sentence in a phrase beginning with **por**. This is called the *agent*.

Aquella casa fue construida **por el duque** en el siglo XVIII.	*That house was built by the duke in the eighteenth century.*
Relaciones diplomáticas entre los dos países serán establecidas **por sus gobiernos**.	*Diplomatic relations between the two countries will be established by their governments.*

Both **ser** and **estar** can occur with the past participle in Spanish to form passive constructions: **ser** emphasizes the action of the verb, while **estar** focuses on the result of the action.

Las puertas **fueron abiertas**.	*The doors were opened. (the passive expression of* **Alguien abrió las puertas**.*)*
Las puertas **estaban abiertas**.	*The doors were open. (expresses the result of the action)*

An agent phrase with **por** is not used with **estar** + the past participle.

English has various ways of deemphasizing the performer of the action. Compare the following sentences.

Articles were written.
One wrote articles.
They wrote articles.
You wrote articles.
We wrote articles.
People wrote articles.

The pronouns *they, you,* and *we* in the above sentences are general rather than specific in reference. They are therefore unstressed. All of the above sentences focus on the act of writing articles without focusing on who wrote them.

Although the passive voice in English is one of the most common ways of deemphasizing the performer of the action, in Spanish it is more characteristic of formal written language than of everyday speech.

A   *Rewrite each sentence, changing it from active to passive. Retain the tense of the original sentence. ¡Ojo! Make sure that each verb agrees with its new subject.*

     MODELO   El terremoto destruyó el pueblo entero.

         El pueblo entero fue destruido por el terremoto.

1. El técnico reparó la computadora.

   _____

2. Una empresa alemana abrirá una cadena de perfumerías.

   _____

3. El mozo derramó el vino.

   _____

4. Unos estudiantes de informática escriben la revista electrónica.

   _____

5. Este equipo de arquitectos hará los planes.

   _____

6. El electricista desenchufó (*unplugged*) los aparatos eléctricos.

   _____

7. Estos programadores instalarán el software.

_____

8. El director inglés rueda la película en Barcelona.

_____

9. El presidente ha dado la conferencia.

_____

10. Los soldados detuvieron a los terroristas.

_____

11. Una pastelera de la academia de artes culinarias hizo estas tortas.

_____

12. El periódico publicó una serie de artículos sobre la guerra.

_____

B   *Rewrite each sentence, changing it from active to passive. Then derive a sentence from each one that shows the result of the action.*

   MODELO   El cocinero preparó los platos.

   Los platos fueron preparados por el cocinero.

   Los platos estaban preparados.

1. El asesor escribió el informe.

_____

_____

2. La directora suspendió la reunión.

_____

_____

3. Los voceros (*spokesmen*) pronunciaron los discursos.

_____

_____

4. El administrador de Web redactó las páginas Web.

_____

_____

5. La psicóloga resolvió los problemas.

_____

_____

6. El compositor francés compuso la sinfonía.

   _____

   _____

7. El jugador de béisbol rompió la ventana.

   _____

   _____

8. Los legisladores aprobaron la ley.

   _____

   _____

9. Los exploradores fundaron las colonias.

   _____

   _____

10. La enfermera cuidó a los pacientes.

    _____

    _____

C   *Translation.*   *Express the following sentences in Spanish.*

1. *The pizzas were home delivered* (a domicilio) *by the deliveryman* (el repartidor).

   _____

2. *The banks were closed by the managers.*

   _____

3. *The furniture was put in the living room by the movers* (cargadores).

   _____

4. *The walls were painted by our painter.*

   _____

5. *The car was rented by the tourists.*

   _____

6. *The car was rented.* [result of the action]

   _____

7. *The politicians of the two parties were interviewed by the press* (la prensa).

   _____

8. *The politicians were interviewed.* [result of the action]

   _____

9. *The gift was wrapped up by us.*

_____

10. *The gift was wrapped up.* [result of the action]

_____

11. *My friend got the tickets on the Internet.*

_____

12. *The tickets were bought.* [result of the action]

_____

Other Passive Constructions: The **se** Construction

Spanish uses a construction consisting of **se** + the verb in the third person to deemphasize the performer of the action. The noun that is logically the direct object of the verb becomes the grammatical subject of the sentence. The verb in this construction is either third-person singular or third-person plural, depending on whether the grammatical subject is singular or plural. No agent phrase can be used in this construction. In English, this **se** construction (**se** + verb) has many possible translations.

Singular Subjects

Se escucha el discurso del presidente.	*People are listening to the president's speech.*
Se va a construir un rascacielos en el centro.	*They are going to build a skyscraper downtown.*
Eso no se hace en nuestro país.	*That's not done in our country.*

Plural Subjects

Nunca **se limpian las calles** de esta ciudad.	*The streets of this city are never cleaned.*
Por fin **se solucionaron todos los problemas**.	*All the problems were finally solved.*
Todos estos platos se preparan con ají.	*You prepare all these dishes with chile pepper.*

An agent phrase with **por** is not used with the **se** construction.

D *Rewrite each sentence, using the* **se** *construction. Retain the tense of the original sentence.*

MODELO   El botones bajó el equipaje.
Se bajó el equipaje.

1. Nuestros amigos servían platos tejanomexicanos.

   _____

2. Esta florería vende flores exquisitas.

   _____

3. La compañía de alta tecnología necesita programadores.

   _____

4. Haremos tres copias del documento.

   _____

5. Realizaron el proyecto.

   _____

6. Estás organizando los archivos.

   _____

7. Hablan español en todas estas tiendas.

   _____

8. Leímos las obras clásicas.

   _____

9. Firmé el contrato.

   _____

10. Van a enviar el correo electrónico pronto.

    _____

11. No pueden hacer preguntas todavía.

    _____

12. Debes visitar ese sitio Web.

    _____

13. El panadero quemó el pan.

    _____

14. Necesitan almacenar los datos.

    _____

Intransitive verbs may also appear in the **se** construction. An intransitive verb in the **se** construction is always in the third-person singular. The English equivalents of these sentences may have nouns where Spanish has verbs in the **se** construction.

Intransitive Verbs

Se vive bien en este país.	*You live well in this country. (Life is good.)*
Por aquí no **se entra**.	*This is not the way in.*
¡Qué bien **se está** aquí!	*How comfortable one feels here.*

When an infinitive is the subject of a **se** construction, the verb is third-person singular.

Se debe comer frutas y legumbres frescas.	*You should eat fresh fruits and vegetables.*
Se puede subir al restaurante giratorio en aquel ascensor.	*One can go up to the revolving restaurant in that elevator.*
Se prohíbe tomar drogas.	*Taking drugs is forbidden.*

Transitive Verbs Used Intransitively

¡Qué bien **se come** en Italia!	*You eat so well in Italy! (How good the food is in Italy!)*
No se cruza aquí.	*You don't cross here.*
¡Qué rápido **se habla** en esta ciudad!	*How fast people talk in this city!*

Reflexive verbs cannot be used in the impersonal **se** construction. To express an impersonal subject, use **uno** (or **una** if the reference is specifically feminine) as the subject of the third-person singular form of the reflexive verb.

Uno se divierte mucho en Madrid.	*People have a great time in Madrid.*
Uno se acuesta más tarde durante las vacaciones.	*You go to bed later during vacation.*
A los doce años **una no debe maquillarse**.	*At twelve you shouldn't put on makeup.*

E *Write sentences using the **se** construction with intransitive verbs.*

MODELO   Leemos en la biblioteca.
         Se lee en la biblioteca.

1. Trabajan en equipo.

   _____

2. Navegamos en la Red.

   _____

3. Vives en una sociedad de información.

   _____

4. Compran y venden en un mercado global.

   _____

5. Puede hablar por teléfono móvil.

   _____

6. Deben llegar antes de las cuatro.

   _____

7. Entran por la puerta principal.

   _____

8. Salimos al jardín por aquí.

   _____

9. Suben en este elevador.

   _____

10. Bajas por la escalera trasera (*back*).

    _____

11. Charlan en el canal de conversación (*chat room*).

    _____

12. Buscamos el cajero automático (*ATM*).

    _____

Other ways of expressing the deemphasized performer of the action in Spanish are the following:

- **La gente** can serve as the subject, always with a third-person singular verb. This construction is especially common in the Caribbean.

La gente critica mucho a los políticos.	*People criticize politicians a lot.*
La gente sale mucho los domingos.	*People go out a lot on Sundays.*

- The third-person plural verb without an expressed subject can convey the impersonal subject, much like unstressed *they* in English.

Dicen que habrá una guerra.	*They say there will be a war.*
En esa tienda **cobran** demasiado.	*They charge too much in that store.*
Lo **entrevistaron** para ese puesto.	*They interviewed him for that position. (He was interviewed for that position.)*

- **Tú** can be used as an impersonal subject, much like unstressed *you* in English. This usage in Spanish is characteristic of informal speech.

Cuando **eres** pobre, todo es difícil.	*When you're poor, everything is difficult.*
Trabajas y **trabajas** y no **sales** adelante.	*You work and work and you don't get ahead.*

Other *se* Constructions

With many verbs, a **se** construction can be followed by an animate direct object that is preceded by the personal **a**. The verb is always in the third-person singular, whether the direct object is singular or plural.

Se mató a dos personas.	*Two people were killed.*

Such a construction removes the potential ambiguity of the more typical **se** construction when the subject is animate.

Se mataron dos personas.	*Two people killed themselves / got killed / were killed.*

Se mató a dos personas can only mean that the two people were killed by somebody else. Here are some additional examples.

Se liberó a los prisioneros.	*The prisoners were freed.*
Se detuvo a los terroristas.	*The terrorists were arrested.*
Se rescató al rehén.	*The hostage was ransomed.*
Se encarceló a los criminales.	*The criminals were jailed.*
Se destituyó a tres senadores.	*Three senators were removed from office.*

The direct objects in these sentences are replaced by **le, les**, not **lo, la, los, las**.

Se rescató al rehén. → **Se le rescató.**
Se encarceló a los criminales. → **Se les encarceló.**

F *Translation. Express the following sentences in Spanish.*

1. *English is spoken here.*

   _____

2. *One should take the one o'clock train.*

   _____

3. *People worry too much.*

   _____

4. *You can live very well in this city.*

   _____

5. *The apartments are being shown between ten and six.*

   _____

6. *The employees were hired by the manager.*

   _____

7. *These products were made by an English company.*

   _____

8. *People wake up late on the weekend.*

_____

9. *How do you (How does one) say "the Net" in Spanish?*

_____

10. *You* [impersonal] *fasten your seat belt when you travel by car.*

_____

11. *Did the terrorists get killed?*

_____

12. *Yes, they got killed. And many others were jailed.*

_____

Reverse Construction Verbs

Some verbs in Spanish typically occur with an indirect object pronoun. **Gustar** *to like* is one of the most common of this class of verbs. In the English translations of sentences with such verbs, the Spanish subject usually corresponds to the English direct object. The English subject corresponds to the Spanish indirect object.

I like cookies.

Me gustan las galletas.

I is the subject of the English sentence; **las galletas** is the subject of the Spanish sentence. *Cookies* is the direct object in the English sentence; **me** is the indirect object of the verb **gustan** in the Spanish sentence. It is useful to think of these verbs as *reverse construction verbs*, since the grammatical functions of the elements of the sentences are reversed.

Study the complete paradigm of **gustar** in the present tense. Note that the verb agrees with the subject of the Spanish sentence—**torta** or **galletas**.

Me gusta la torta. *I like the cake.*
Me gustan las galletas. *I like the cookies.*

Nos gusta la torta. *We like the cake.*
Nos gustan las galletas. *We like the cookies.*

Te gusta la torta. *You like the cake.*
Te gustan las galletas. *You like the cookies.*

Os gusta la torta. *You like the cake.*
Os gustan las galletas. *You like the cookies.*

Le gusta la torta. *He/She likes / You like the cake.*
Le gustan las galletas. *He/She likes / You like the cookies.*

Les gusta la torta. *You/They like the cake.*
Les gustan las galletas. *You/They like the cookies.*

When the grammatical subject of a verb like **gustar** is an infinitive, the verb is always in the third-person singular.

—**Me encanta patinar** sobre el hielo.   *"I love to ice skate."*
—A mí **me gusta** más **esquiar.**   *"I like skiing better."*

Here are some other verbs and verbal phrases that function like **gustar.**

agradarle a uno *to like something, find something pleasing*
caerle bien/mal a uno *to like/dislike (usually a person)*
convenirle a uno *to suit someone, be good for someone*
desagradarle a uno *to dislike something, find something unpleasant*
disgustarle a uno *to dislike something, find something unpleasant*
encantarle a uno *to love something*
entusiasmarle a uno *to be excited about something*
faltarle a uno *to be missing something, not have something; to be short* (money)
fascinarle a uno *to be fascinated (by something)*
hacerle falta a uno *to need something*
importarle a uno *to care about something; to mind; to matter*
interesarle a uno *to be interested in something*
quedarle a uno *to have something left*
sobrarle a uno *to have more than enough of something*
tocarle a uno *to be someone's turn*
urgirle a uno *to be urgent for someone to do something*

NOTE

The usual way to express *to like/dislike a person* in Spanish is **caerle bien/mal a uno. Gustarle a uno** often implies a romantic attraction when referring to people. **Gustar** may, however, be used to refer to a person as professional or to refer to children.

Me gusta aquella escritora.   *I like that writer.*
Nos gustan los hijos de los Peña.   *We like the Peñas' children.*

—**¿Te importa** acompañarme al museo?   *"Would you mind accompanying me
    to the museum?"*

—**Me encantaría. Me interesa** mucho   *"I'd love to. I'm very interested in art."*
el arte.

—Creo que **te convendría** salir un poco.   *"I think it would be good for you to go
    out a little."*

—Sé que **me hace falta,** pero **me sobra**   *"I know I need to, but I have too much
trabajo.   work."*

—Parece que no **te entusiasma** mucho   *"It seems that you're not very excited
este juego.   about this game."*
—Cada vez que **me toca a mí,** pierdo.   *"Every time it's my turn, I lose."*

When speakers want to focus on or contrast the indirect object pronouns, they add a phrase consisting of **a** + the corresponding stressed pronoun to the sentence. This prepositional phrase is also used for "short responses," that is, responses that are not complete sentences.

—¿Cuánto dinero nos queda?	*"How much money do we have left?"*
—A mí me quedan doscientos dólares. **¿Y a ti?**	*"I have two hundred dollars left. How about you?"*
—Chicos, ¿a quién le gusta la torta de chocolate?	*"Kids, who likes chocolate cake?"*
—**¡A mí! ¡A mí! ¡A mí!**	*"I do! I do! I do!"*

The phrase **¿Y a ti?** is short for **Y a ti, ¿cuánto dinero te queda?** The phrase **¡A mí!** is short for **A mí me gusta la torta de chocolate.**

G *Change the subject from singular to plural in each sentence. Retain the tense of the original sentence. ¡Ojo! Remember to make all necessary changes.*

MODELO   Me gusta el libro.

Me gustan los libros.

1. Le gusta esta marca.

   _____

2. ¿Te interesa mi idea?

   _____

3. Nos encantó el concierto.

   _____

4. Me entusiasmaba su plan.

   _____

5. Les quedaba el examen oral.

   _____

6. Os fascinará el pianista.

   _____

7. Les agrada la exposición.

   _____

8. Nos ha caído bien ese profesor.

   _____

9. Le falta un dólar.

   _____

10. Me haría falta un disquete.

   _____

H *Expand each sentence by adding the* **ir a** + infinitive *construction.*

MODELO   Me gusta la película.

Me va a gustar la película.

1. No te conviene meterte (*meddle*) en sus asuntos.

   _____

2. No nos importa el qué dirán (*what others say*).

   _____

3. Me toca a mí hacer la compra.

   _____

4. Les sobra tiempo.

   _____

5. Le desagrada tu actitud.

   _____

6. Os disgustan sus costumbres.

   _____

7. Le interesan esas pinturas.

   _____

8. Te encantan los postres.

   _____

9. Nos urge contactarlos.

   _____

10. Me agrada pasar las vacaciones en Ibiza.

   _____

I **Translation.** *Express the following sentences in Spanish. Use reverse construction verbs.*

1. *Whose turn is it?*

   _____

2. *She likes these perfumes.*

   _____

3. *We were excited about the baseball game.*

   _____

4. *It will be good for them to wait.*

   _____

5. *Would you (Uds.) be interested in it?*

   _____

6. *She is not going to like them.* [Use **caer.**]

   _____

7. *Frankly, I don't care.*

   _____

8. *Would you (tú) like to go out to eat?*

   _____

9. *I would love it.*

   _____

10. *What do you (Ud.) need?*

    _____

11. *I don't need anything.*

    _____

12. *Do you (vosotros) not have enough money?*

    _____

13. *No, we have more than enough.*

    _____

14. *I would find them unpleasant.*

    _____

BUILDING SENTENCES	**Se le construction for unplanned occurrences**

The indirect object pronoun can be added to a **se** construction with certain verbs to express *unplanned occurrences*. These constructions focus on the object affected rather than on the person involved.

acabársele a uno *to run out of*
averiársele a uno *to get damaged, break down, fail*
caérsele a uno *to drop*
descomponérsele a uno *to have something break down*
ocurrírsele a uno *to dawn on, get the idea of*
olvidársele a uno *to forget*
perdérsele a uno *to lose*
quebrársele a uno *to break*
quedársele a uno *to leave something behind*
rompérsele a uno *to break*

—Veo que **se te rompieron** los anteojos.   *"I see that you broke your glasses."*
—Sí, **se me cayeron** en la calle.   *"Yes, I dropped them in the street."*

—¿Cómo **se les ocurrió** venir ayer?   *"How did they get the idea to come*
   yesterday?"

—**Se les había olvidado** que la reunión   *"They had forgotten that the meeting*
era mañana.   *was tomorrow."*

—**Se nos está acabando** la gasolina.   *"We're running out of gas. We have to buy*
Tenemos que comprar.   *some."*
—Ay, **se me quedó** la tarjeta de crédito   *"Oh, I left my credit card at home."*
en casa.

Many other verbs can be used with this construction.

¡Cuidado! **Se te va a subir** la sopa.   *Careful! Your soup is going to boil over.*
Se nos fue la chica au pair.   *The au pair left us.*
Se me murió el perro.   *My dog died.*

The equivalent of the English imperative of these verbs is an indirect command in Spanish.

¡**Que no se te caigan** los platos!   *Don't drop the dishes!*
¡**Que no se les ocurra** hacer eso!   *Don't get it into your heads to do that!*

J   *Write sentences that express unplanned occurrences, using the following strings of elements. Use the preterit for all verbs.*

    MODELO   él / rompérsele / el tobillo
               Se le rompió el tobillo.

1. Ud. / perdérsele / los anteojos

2. yo / ocurrírsele / una cosa increíble

3. ellos / descomponérsele / el aire acondicionado

4. ella / quebrársele / dos dedos

5. tú / caérsele / los platos

6. nosotros / quedársele en casa / la llave del coche

7. Uds. / acabársele / la paciencia

8. vosotros / olvidársele / hacer la llamada

_____

9. él / averiársele / los frenos del coche

_____

10. yo / olvidársele / mi clave personal (*PIN*)

_____

11. ellas / perdérsele / la libreta de cheques

_____

12. Ud. / acabársele / el jugo de naranja

_____

K **Translation.** *Express the following sentences in Spanish, using the* **se le** *construction for unplanned occurrences.*

1. *He left his cell phone at the office.*

_____

2. *It hasn't occurred to anyone yet?*

_____

3. *Their computer is breaking down.*

_____

4. *Have you (tú) forgotten that her birthday is tomorrow?*

_____

5. *Who left these gloves here?*

_____

6. *How did you (Ud.) break your foot?*

_____

7. *I broke it playing soccer.*

_____

8. *We're running out of bread.*

_____

9. *I dropped the vase* (el florero).

_____

10. *Did it break?*

_____

Answer Key

Chapter 1
The Present Tense of Regular Verbs

A 1. mando 2. estudia 3. tomamos 4. entran 5. escuchas 6. habláis 7. toca
8. llevo 9. navegan 10. regresan 11. alquila 12. miramos 13. llegan 14. trabaja
15. guardas 16. viajamos 17. enseña 18. estacionan 19. esperáis 20. charlan
21. paso 22. cambia 23. entrega 24. doblas 25. funciona 26. dura
27. desayunamos 28. necesita

B 1. a. Nosotros buscamos las llaves. b. Él busca su teléfono móvil. c. Uds. buscan la tienda
de videos. 2. a. Yo compro unos libros de texto. b. Vosotros compráis un condominio.
c. Ud. compra zapatos de tenis. 3. a. Tú estudias informática. b. Ella estudia
programación. c. Tú y yo estudiamos mercadeo. 4. a. Uds. graban una película.
b. Ellas graban un programa de televisión. c. Él graba una canción francesa.
5. a. Ud. habla inglés. b. Vosotras habláis italiano. c. Ellos hablan chino. 6. a. Tú llevas
una maleta. b. Yo llevo mi portafolio. c. Uds. llevan el equipaje.

C 1. Alquiláis el video. 2. Escuchan las noticias. 3. Tomáis café en Starbucks.
4. Telecargan los documentos. 5. Estacionáis detrás del banco. 6. Cambian de opinión.
7. Averiguan la información. 8. Mandáis el correo electrónico. 9. Pulsan el botón.
10. Llegáis a las siete.

D 1. Crean un sitio Web. 2. Regresan al anochecer. 3. Ganan una beca.
4. Aprovechan la oferta. 5. Arrastran el ratón. 6. Compran jeans en una tienda GAP.
7. Trabajan en el centro. 8. Preparan los sándwiches. 9. Llevan una computadora
portátil. 10. Desarrollan un plan.

E 1. Acepta 2. Averiguamos 3. Saco 4. Practican 5. firmas 6. preparáis 7. Escucha
8. Descarga 9. Marca 10. Crean 11. Celebra 12. Bailamos 13. Contesta 14. Trotan
15. Llevan

F 1. nosotros/nosotras 2. Uds./ellos/ellas 3. yo 4. Ud./él/ella 5. tú 6. Ud./él/ella
7. vosotros/vosotras 8. Uds./ellos/ellas 9. yo 10. tú 11. Ud./él/ella
12. nosotros/nosotras 13. yo 14. vosotros/vosotras 15. tú

G 1. comen 2. leo 3. asistimos 4. imprime 5. metes 6. discuten 7. vende 8. escribe
9. corréis 10. comparten 11. tose 12. beben 13. vivo 14. aprendemos 15. subís
16. comprenden 17. recibe 18. ocurre 19. creen 20. interrumpen 21. insistes
22. debes 23. transmite 24. resiste 25. abre

H 1. tú 2. Ud./él/ella 3. nosotros/nosotras 4. yo 5. Uds./ellos/ellas 6. vosotros/vosotras
7. nosotros/nosotras 8. Ud./él/ella 9. vosotros/vosotras 10. Uds./ellos/ellas 11. yo
12. tú 13. nosotros/nosotras 14. tú 15. Ud./él/ella

I 1. Discuto la idea con ellos.   2. Viven en esta vecindad.   3. Vende cosas en eBay.
4. Abrimos las maletas.   5. Bebéis vino con la carne.   6. Aprende latín y griego.
7. Suben en la escalera mecánica.   8. No comprendes la teoría.   9. Comparten una pizza.
10. Debe una fuerte cantidad de dinero.   11. Comemos de todo.   12. ¿Asistís al partido
de fútbol?   13. Leemos varias revistas electrónicas.   14. Prende las luces.
15. Escribes un artículo para el periódico.

J 1. sigues   2. escojo   3. exijo   4. construye   5. recojo   6. huyen   7. consiguen
8. corrige   9. cogéis   10. elige   11. destruye   12. protege   13. extinguimos   14. persigue
15. dirige   16. acogemos   17. surgen   18. distingo   19. diluyes   20. urge

K 1. ¿Cuánto tiempo hace que Carolina navega en la Red? Hace dos horas que navega
en la Red. Navega en la Red hace dos horas.   2. ¿Cuánto tiempo hace que estudias
administración de empresas? Hace un año que estudio administración de empresas.
Estudio administración de empresas hace un año.   3. ¿Cuánto tiempo hace que Uds. viven
en Londres? Hace cuatro años que vivimos en Londres. Vivimos en Londres hace cuatro
años.   4. ¿Cuánto tiempo hace que los Soriano viajan por Europa? Hace seis semanas
que viajan por Europa. Viajan por Europa hace seis semanas.   5. ¿Cuánto tiempo hace
que vosotros asistís a estas conferencias? Hace un par de meses que asistimos a estas
conferencias. Asistimos a estas conferencias hace un par de meses.   6. ¿Cuánto tiempo
hace que Ud. descarga los documentos? Hace media hora que descargo los documentos.
Descargo los documentos hace media hora.   7. ¿Cuánto tiempo hace que discutimos
los trámites? Hace una semana que discutimos los trámites. Discutimos los trámites hace
una semana.   8. ¿Cuánto tiempo hace que exijo la colaboración de todos? Hace varios
días que exige/exiges la colaboración de todos. Exige/Exiges la colaboración de todos hace
varios días.

L 1. ¿Trabajas en la oficina mañana?   2. No, paso el día en casa.   3. ¿Asiste al concierto
esta noche?   4. Sí, y antes ceno con unos amigos.   5. ¿Cuánto tiempo hace que construyen
la casa?   6. Hace un año que construimos la casa. / Construimos la casa hace un año.
7. ¿Cuánto tiempo hace que están en los Estados Unidos? / ¿Cuánto tiempo llevan en los
Estados Unidos? / ¿Cuánto tiempo tienen en los Estados Unidos?   8. Hace quince años que
están aquí. / Llevan quince años aquí. / Tienen quince años aquí.   9. ¿Desde cuándo prosigue
(OR sigue con) sus estudios?   10. Curso (OR Tomo clases de) ingeniería desde enero.

M 1. transitive   2. intransitive   3. transitive   4. transitive   5. transitive   6. intransitive
7. transitive   8. intransitive   9. transitive   10. transitive   11. transitive   12. intransitive
13. transitive   14. transitive   15. intransitive

N 1. Tú cantas afinadamente.   2. Los atletas corren en la carrera.   3. Pablo tose mucho.
4. ¿Uds. viven en las afueras?   5. Yo regreso la semana entrante.   6. El módem funciona
bien.   7. Nosotros subimos al tercer piso.   8. Los habitantes huyen del terremoto.
9. Yo troto por el parque.   10. El gerente trabaja de lunes a viernes.   11. ¿Vosotros llegáis
en tren?   12. Tú viajas por el sudoeste del país.   13. ¿Mercedes y Sofía estornudan por
su alergia?   14. Un conflicto surge entre los socios.   15. Ud. baja por la escalera.
16. Nosotros participamos en el foro de debate.   17. ¿Qué opinan Uds. de la facultad
de educación?

O 1. Roberto y yo ahorramos dinero.   2. Yo rijo la empresa.   3. Los jefes concluyen su conversación.   4. ¿Ud. consigue sus billetes electrónicos?   5. Tú guardas el secreto. 6. Uds. compran una cámara digital.   7. Vosotros imprimís el informe.   8. Beatriz y Alicia comparten la computadora.   9. Ud. lee la página Web.   10. Nosotras creamos unas carpetas.   11. Marco Antonio aprende las fechas de memoria.   12. ¿Vosotros marcáis el número de teléfono?   13. Yo consigo los boletos.   14. Los programadores instalan un programa de gráficas.   15. Tú recibes revistas de informática.   16. El director de la junta interrumpe la reunión.

P 1. Alberto y Daniela esperan un taxi.   2. ¿Ud. asiste al congreso?   3. Tú y yo escuchamos estos discos compactos.   4. La jefa renuncia a su puesto.   5. El ingeniero entra los datos. 6. Vosotras miráis los sitios Web.   7. Uds. salen del hotel.   8. Los jugadores pisan el césped.   9. Rafael y yo jugamos (al) fútbol.   10. Yo entro al / en el centro comercial. 11. Mi hermana sube su ropa al dormitorio.   12. Los vecinos comentan las noticias del barrio.   13. Los turistas visitan los monumentos.   14. ¿Vosotros aprobáis el plan económico?   15. ¿Tú buscas las llaves?

Q 1. Solicito este puesto.   2. Virginia mira su correo electrónico.   3. ¿Aprovechas las rebajas? 4. Asistimos a ese concierto.   5. Entran a/en la librería.   6. Entra datos.   7. Esteban renuncia al proyecto.   8. ¿Qué buscan?

R 1. No, no usamos una calculadora de bolsillo.   2. No, no habla por teléfono celular. 3. No, no echamos las cartas al buzón.   4. No, no prendo el ordenador. 5. No, no compartimos los gastos.   6. No, no transmiten el documental esta noche. 7. No, no corrijo las faltas en el manuscrito.   8. No, no renuncia a su puesto de contable. 9. No, no extinguen el fuego de campamento.   10. No, no influimos en la decisión.

S 1. No, no solicitamos nada.   2. No, no grita nadie. / No, nadie grita.   3. No, no salen a bailar nunca/jamás. / No, nunca/jamás salen a bailar.   4. No, no exijo nada. 5. No, no espero a nadie.   6. No, no lloran nunca/jamás. / No, nunca/jamás lloran. 7. No, no llega puntualmente nunca/jamás. / No, nunca/jamás llega puntualmente. 8. No, no montamos a caballo nunca/jamás. / No, nunca/jamás montamos a caballo. 9. No, no trasnochan nunca/jamás. / No, nunca/jamás trasnochan.   10. No, no llega tarde nunca/jamás. / No, nunca/jamás llega tarde.

T 1. ¿Ya no trasnochas?   2. No reparamos la computadora mucho / muchas veces / a menudo. 3. Jaime todavía no guarda los archivos.   4. Uds. nunca/jamás cenan antes de las ocho. / Uds. no cenan nunca/jamás antes de las ocho.   5. No miran nada. 6. Nadie aprovecha la oportunidad.   7. No pasa (OR ocurre) nada.   8. Yo no escojo (OR elijo) nada.   9. Muchas veces / A menudo alquilamos videos.   10. A veces / Algunas veces miran (OR ven) los partidos de béisbol en la computadora.   11. Alguien te busca. 12. Ella nunca interrumpe a nadie.

Chapter 2
Stem-changing Verbs; Special Verbs Ending in **-iar** and **-uar**

A 1. quiero 2. pensamos 3. comienza 4. entiendes 5. recomienda 6. pierden
7. encendéis 8. gobierna 9. desciendes 10. empiezo 11. cierran 12. Nieva
13. atravesamos 14. defienden 15. asciende 16. hiela 17. despierta 18. sientan

B 1. vuelven 2. encuentro 3. envolvemos 4. almuerzas 5. devuelve 6. cuesta
7. merendáis 8. demuestra 9. llueve 10. puede 11. probamos 12. recuerdan
13. huele 14. resuelvo 15. vuelan 16. muestra 17. acuestas 18. acordáis

C 1. Uds. juegan (al) béisbol. 2. Yo juego en un equipo de tenis. 3. Los jugadores juegan
limpio. 4. Él juega sucio. 5. Tú juegas (al) baloncesto. 6. Nosotros jugamos (al) fútbol
americano en otoño. 7. Vosotros jugáis juegos electrónicos. 8. Los campeones juegan
el partido el sábado.

D 1. siento 2. prefieres 3. divierten 4. refiere 5. hierve 6. mentimos 7. convierte
8. advierten

E 1. piden 2. sirve 3. visten 4. despido 5. sigues 6. reímos 7. impedís 8. sonríe
9. repite 10. medimos 11. consigo 12. persiguen

F 1. duermo 2. duermes 3. duermen 4. dormimos 5. duermen 6. duerme
7. duerme 8. dormís

G 1. confiamos 2. envían 3. continúas 4. gradúo 5. varían 6. resfría 7. insinuáis
8. fía 9. evaluamos 10. guía 11. efectúan 12. esquío 13. acentúas 14. vacían
15. actúa 16. espían 17. criáis 18. rocía

H 1. Logramos ahorrar mucho dinero. 2. No pueden averiguar nada. 3. Siento interrumpir
su conversación. 4. Suele llover por aquí en abril. 5. Consigue escribir el informe en
un solo día. 6. Hacen construir unos rascacielos. 7. ¿Teméis manejar en la autopista?
8. Procuras volver lo antes posible. 9. Quiero comprar un organizador personal.
10. Espera no perder el tren. 11. Prometen no mentir más. 12. Pienso aprovechar las
rebajas navideñas. 13. ¿Prefieres beber el vino tinto o el blanco? 14. Olvida pedir los
billetes electrónicos. 15. No recuerdan encender la videocasetera. 16. Prohíben aparcar
en esta zona en hora punta. 17. Decidimos correr en el maratón. 18. Ese carro debe
costar una fortuna. 19. ¿Sabéis crear sitios Web? 20. Escojo enviar el paquete por
el FedEx.

I 1. Quiero navegar por Internet (OR por la Red). 2. Esperamos comenzar el proyecto
la semana que viene. 3. Puede leer su correo electrónico en el cibercafé. 4. ¿Piensan viajar
por avión o por tren? 5. Suelen pasar los fines de semana en Nueva York. 6. No debes
interrumpir la reunión. 7. Prefiere comprar ropa en los grandes almacenes.
8. ¿Sabéis descargar/bajar música?

J 1. X 2. A 3. X 4. a 5. al 6. a 7. X 8. A 9. a 10. X 11. a 12. a 13. X
14. a 15. X 16. a 17. a 18. a 19. X 20. a 21. X 22. al

K 1. ¿A quién quieres invitar al baile? 2. Piensan ver al ingeniero. 3. Isabel no ayuda
a nadie. 4. Espero a alguien. 5. La empresa debe contratar programadores. 6. ¿Conocen
a Roberto Murillo? 7. Buscamos a nuestro perro. 8. El restaurante necesita un cocinero.
9. ¿A cuántos jugadores de fútbol conoce? 10. No conozco a ninguno. / No conozco
a ningún jugador de fútbol. 11. Señor, ¿Ud. me busca? 12. No, señorita, no la busco.

Chapter 3
Irregular Verbs (Part I)

A 1. salimos, ponen   2. hace, tenemos   3. cae, hace   4. oyes, oigo   5. tengo, hago
6. vienen, caen   7. oyen, digo, oímos, dices   8. pones, traigo   9. venís, tenemos
10. sale, tiene   11. dicen, hace   12. cae, salgo   13. tiene, ponen   14. ponemos, vale
15. pongo, haces, valgo

B 1. Oigo hablar del nuevo centro comercial.   2. Vienen en taxi.   3. Tiene veintiséis años.
4. Pospongo la reunión un par de días.   5. Traemos dos botellas de vino a la fiesta.
6. ¿Quién dice tal cosa?   7. Salgo para la oficina temprano.   8. En otoño las hojas caen
de los árboles.   9. ¿Sales al cine esta noche?   10. No valgo para esas cosas.   11. Hago clic
al botón.   12. ¿Oye las noticias?

C 1. caer, cae   2. hacer, hago   3. venir, vienes   4. poner, ponen   5. tener, tiene
6. decir, dice   7. oír, oímos   8. salir, salís   9. traer, traigo   10. valer, vale   11. tener, tiene
12. hacer, hace

D 1. conozco   2. tuerce   3. vencen   4. permanecemos   5. introduzco   6. favorece
7. cuezo   8. conduces   9. obedecen   10. amanecéis   11. ofrezco   12. produce
13. agradezco   14. aparece   15. reduzco   16. traduzco   17. ejerce   18. resplandecen
19. reproduzco   20. establece

E 1. ¿Toca la flauta Mirián?   2. ¿Ellos traducen los informes?   3. ¿Hacen la cena Raquel
y Daniel?   4. Uds. oyen música clásica?   5. ¿Vienes en taxi tú?   6. ¿Pongo la mesa yo?
7. ¿Jorge conduce un coche deportivo?   8. ¿Hace una pregunta Ud.?   9. ¿Traemos la torta
Julia y yo?   10. ¿El cumpleaños de Miguel cae en viernes?

F 1. Miguel busca un sitio para aparcar, ¿no es cierto?   2. Uds. hacen una excursión el
domingo, ¿no?   3. Tú no conoces nuestro barrio, ¿verdad?   4. Pilar tiene confianza en
sí misma, ¿no es verdad?   5. Aquellos terrenos pertenecen a tu familia, ¿no?   6. Yo no
necesito pagar con contante, ¿verdad?   7. Nosotros debemos digitalizar los documentos,
¿no es cierto?   8. Ud. no consigue convencerlo, ¿verdad?

G 1. ¿Dónde / En qué ciudad viven?   2. ¿Cuántos hijos tiene(s)?   3. ¿Cuál es la capital de
Puerto Rico?   4. ¿Adónde van?   5. ¿Qué/Cuál libro lee(s)?   6. ¿Qué es la ofimática?
7. ¿A quién conocen/conocéis?   8. ¿Cómo salen las cosas?   9. ¿Para dónde salen?
10. ¿Por dónde camina?   11. ¿Qué es el comercio electrónico?   12. ¿Cuánto cuesta esta
cámara digital?   13. ¿Quiénes llegan?   14. ¿De quién son los disquetes?   15. ¿A qué hora
vuelve(s)?   16. ¿Cuál es la fecha de hoy?   17. ¿Con quién quiere Nicolás bailar?
18. ¿Por qué no van/vais a la playa?   19. ¿Dónde / En qué avenida está el cibercafé?
20. ¿Cómo expresan sus ideas?   21. ¿Qué estudia Juan Ramón?   22. ¿Cuántas tarjetas
telefónicas compran?

H 1. ¿Cuándo / ¿Qué día tiene lugar la reunión?   2. ¿Qué necesitas comprar?   3. ¿Cuál marca
prefieres?   4. ¿Adónde vas esta noche?   5. ¿Qué estudia Elena?   6. ¿Con quién vas a la
fiesta?   7. ¿Trabajas el viernes?   8. ¿Haces ejercicio ahora?   9. ¿Mañana salimos de paseo?
10. ¿Conduces tú?   11. ¿A qué hora debemos ir?   12. ¿Vamos a estar de vuelta para las seis?

I 1. ¿De dónde vienen?   2. ¿Cuál es la capital de España?   3. ¿Con quién haces planes?
4. ¿En qué mes salen de viaje?   5. ¿Qué tiempo hace?   6. ¿Hace sol?   7. ¿Vale la pena?
8. ¿Por qué tiene tanta prisa?   9. ¿Qué es el telemercadeo?   10. ¿Hago clic / Cliqueo en
el enlace?

Chapter 4
Irregular Verbs (Part II)

A 1. va, ir   2. vemos, ver   3. doy, dar   4. cabe, caber   5. saben, saber   6. voy, ir
7. sabe, saber   8. quepo, caber   9. ve, ver   10. da, dar   11. Dan, dar   12. veo, ver
13. dais, dar   14. vas, ir   15. veis, ver   16. sé, saber   17. dais, dar   18. vais, ir
19. sabemos, saber   20. ves, ver   21. vamos, ir   22. Caben, caber

B 1. conoce, sé   2. conoces, conozco   3. sabe, sé   4. conoces, conozco, sé
5. conocen, conocemos   6. sabéis, conocemos   7. sabe, sabe   8. saben, saben

C 1. Hay una función el sábado a las dos.   2. Hay que hacer clic en el icono.   3. Hay que ser
un buen ciudadano.   4. No hay necesidad de quedarse.   5. Hay conferencias en la feria
del libro.   6. Hay una megatienda tecnológica en esta carretera.   7. Hay que pasar por
la aduana.   8. ¿Hay alguna dificultad en realizar el proyecto?   9. Hay que invertir en varias
industrias.   10. Hay que entrevistar a los candidatos.

D 1. de   2. con   3. que   4. a   5. en   6. a   7. en   8. a   9. con   10. de   11. que   12. de
13. a   14. a   15. en   16. a   17. en   18. en   19. por/en   20. de   21. por   22. de

E 1. X   2. en   3. X   4. a   5. en   6. X   7. de   8. X   9. a   10. X   11. X   12. con   13. por
14. en   15. de   16. a   17. X   18. en   19. de   20. a

F 1. Hay un teléfono celular en la mesa.   2. Hay que saber inglés en el mercado global.
3. Acaban de salir a cenar.   4. Sergio vuelve a llamar.   5. ¿Ud. empieza/comienza a escribir
el informe?   6. No conozco al nuevo programador.   7. ¿Saben su número de teléfono?
8. Sé descargar (OR bajar) los ficheros.   9. Quedamos/Consentimos en ir en carro.
10. Ana cuenta con ver a Federico en la fiesta.   11. Te esfuerzas por/en triunfar en la vida.
12. Me alegro de verlos.

Chapter 5
Ser and Estar

A 1. es   2. son   3. soy   4. son   5. somos   6. es   7. eres   8. es   9. sois   10. son

B 1. Yo soy de los Estados Unidos. Soy de origen inglés.   2. Matías es de Polonia. Es de origen
ruso.   3. Tú eres de España. Eres de origen italiano.   4. Nosotros somos de Taiwán. Somos
de origen chino.   5. Ud. es de la India. Es de origen hindú.   6. Jacobo y Sara son de Israel.
Son de origen turco.   7. Uds. son de Vietnám. Son de origen tailandés.   8. Vosotros sois
de Australia. Sois de origen coreano.   9. María Luisa es de Chile. Es de origen alemán.
10. Los Madero son de Francia. Son de origen kosovano.

C 1. estás   2. está   3. están   4. estoy   5. están   6. estamos   7. está   8. están   9. estáis
10. está

D 1. Los grandes almacenes están a la vuelta de la esquina.   2. El club de jazz está por esta
avenida.   3. El parqueo está detrás del teatro.   4. Los hoteles más lujosos están en frente
del jardín público.   5. La piscina del condominio de tiempo compartido está en el patio.
6. La estación de tren está en la zona oeste de la ciudad.   7. Los sillones están delante
de la ventana.   8. Los dormitorios están en el segundo piso.   9. La librería técnica está
a dos cuadras de aquí.   10. Los monumentos históricos están en la ciudad vieja.
11. La tienda de videos está al lado de la pizzería.   12. Los centros comerciales están
en las afueras.

E 1. es   2. estamos   3. es   4. son   5. están   6. es   7. está   8. son   9. estoy   10. estáis   11. somos   12. soy   13. estás   14. sois   15. eres   16. está   17. somos   18. está   19. Son   20. ser   21. son   22. es   23. son   24. estar   25. estás   26. están

F 1. Yo soy ingeniero genético. ¿Cuál es su profesión?   2. Son las siete y media de la mañana. ¿Qué hora es?   3. El cine Mediaplex está al lado de un bar. ¿Dónde está el Cine Mediaplex? 4. Los mensajes electrónicos son para Eva. ¿Para quién son los mensajes electrónicos? 5. Los aficionados de béisbol están entusiasmados y nerviosos. ¿Cómo están los aficionados de béisbol?   6. Hoy es el veintitrés de junio. ¿Cuál es la fecha de hoy?   7. Estas llaves de coche son de Marcelo. ¿De quién son estas llaves de coche?   8. El euro está a noventa centavos de dólar. ¿A cuánto está el euro hoy?   9. Los gemelos de Hugo y Silvia son consentidos y malcriados. ¿Cómo son los gemelos de Hugo y Silvia?   10. Nosotros somos de Canadá. ¿De dónde son Uds.? (OR ¿Cuál es su nacionalidad?)

G 1. El coche está descompuesto. ¿Está descompuesto el coche?   2. Su ropa es elegante. ¿Es elegante su ropa?   3. Estos platos de comida fusión están ricos. ¿Están ricos estos platos de comida fusión?   4. Las clases de finanzas son fáciles. ¿Son fáciles las clases de finanzas? 5. Los analistas son superinteligentes. ¿Son superinteligentes los analistas?   6. Su nuevo abrigo es azul marino. ¿Es azul marino su nuevo abrigo?   7. El museo de arte está abierto. ¿Está abierto el museo de arte?   8. Los mozos están ocupados. ¿Están ocupados los mozos? 9. La chica es simpática. ¿Es simpática la chica?   10. Las tiendas están cerradas. ¿Están cerradas las tiendas?   11. Aquellos hoteles son lujosos. ¿Son lujosos aquellos hoteles? 12. Los directores están reunidos. ¿Están reunidos los directores?   13. Su buzón de correo electrónico está lleno. ¿Está lleno su buzón de correo electrónico?

H 1. Esteban es programador.   2. Están de vacaciones en este momento.   3. Son las nueve y cuarto (OR quince).   4. El estreno de la película va a ser en Nueva York.   5. Alicia está preocupada y cansada.   6. El programa es aburrido y los televidentes están aburridos. 7. Lo más interesante de la exposición (OR la exhibición) son los cuadros.   8. Julia es/está casada con Miguel. Su hermana es/está divorciada.   9. ¿Están rotas las ventanas? 10. ¿Cómo son tus vecinos?   11. ¿Cómo están Uds.?   12. Son de origen inglés. 13. Los duraznos están verdes todavía.   14. Todas estas camisetas son de algodón. 15. Soy del sudoeste.

I 1. Sí, los uso.   2. Sí, la hago.   3. Sí, los toma.   4. Sí, las reparan.   5. Sí, las leen. 6. Sí, los entramos.   7. Sí, lo conocemos.   8. Sí, la aprovecho.   9. Sí, lo busca. 10. Sí, la felicitan.   11. Sí, las espero.   12. Sí, lo traemos.   13. Sí, los imprimen. 14. Sí, los oigo.   15. Sí, la conduzco.

J 1. Quiero comprarlo. Lo quiero comprar.   2. ¿Acabas de grabarla? ¿La acabas de grabar? 3. Vamos a analizarlos. Los vamos a analizar.   4. Ud. debe conocerla. Ud. la debe conocer. 5. ¿Comienzas a comprenderlas? ¿Las comienzas a comprender?   6. Los aficionados piensan verlo. Los aficionados lo piensan ver.   7. Los usuarios no saben utilizarlas. Los usuarios no las saben utilizar.   8. Ramón corre a buscarlos. Ramón los corre a buscar.   9. Aprendo a tocarlo. Lo aprendo a tocar.   10. Tratamos de ganarla. La tratamos de ganar.

K 1. ¿Pides el plato de carne como de costumbre?   2. Sí, si lo encuentro en la carta. 3. ¿Vas a esperarme? / ¿Me vas a esperar?   4. Sí, te veo después de la conferencia. 5. ¿Uds. quieren oír estas canciones?   6. No, acabamos de oírlas. / No, las acabamos de oír.   7. ¿Cristina es la mejor bailarina?   8. Sí, lo es.   9. ¿Adónde lleva a los consultores (OR asesores)?   10. Los llevo a conocer a la jefa.   11. Veo a Mauricio allí. ¿Lo ves? 12. A Laura la veo pero a Mauricio, no.

Chapter 6
The Preterit

A 1. Ud./él/ella, vender 2. yo, celebrar 3. nosotros/nosotras, imprimir 4. Uds./ellos/ellas, aprender 5. Ud./él/ella, patinar 6. vosotros/vosotras, vivir 7. nosotros/nosotras, correr 8. Uds./ellos/ellas, ahorrar 9. yo, aprender 10. tú, insistir 11. vosotros/vosotras, beber 12. vosotros/vosotras, saludar 13. Ud./él/ella, compartir 14. nosotros/nosotras, disfrutar 15. yo, escribir 16. tú, hablar 17. tú, romper 18. Uds./ellos/ellas, transmitir 19. Ud./él/ella, utilizar 20. yo, añadir

B 1. regresaste 2. asistí 3. corrimos 4. transmitieron 5. aceptó 6. recibisteis 7. aprendiste 8. discutimos 9. tosió 10. viajaron 11. abrí 12. tomaron 13. vendieron 14. insistió 15. alquilé 16. bebieron 17. rompió 18. viviste 19. compró 20. grabamos 21. dibujasteis 22. compartieron 23. comió 24. prendió

C 1. Volvieron 2. Pensé 3. Nos divertimos 4. perdió 5. Encontraste 6. probó 7. pidieron 8. Servisteis 9. Nevó 10. Entendí 11. se vistió 12. Tronó 13. Cerraron 14. llovió 15. riñeron 16. Medisteis 17. se convirtió 18. siguieron 19. sintió 20. se derritió 21. hirvió 22. Prefirieron 23. mintió 24. murió 25. Patrocinamos

D 1. Ya lo marqué. 2. Ya jugué al béisbol. 3. Ya almorcé. 4. Ya navegué en la Red. 5. Ya lo aparqué. 6. Ya la aplacé. 7. Ya los conjugué. 8. Ya la expliqué. 9. Ya lo realicé. 10. Ya la entregué. 11. Ya adelgacé. 12. Ya lo toqué. 13. Ya lo practiqué. 14. Ya las fregué. 15. Ya los actualicé. 16. Ya los organicé. 17. Ya los colgué. 18. Ya lo agregué. 19. Ya la arranqué. 20. Ya las apagué.

E 1. Los muchachos tiñeron las camisetas de rojo. 2. La guerra destruyó el país. 3. Los consumidores no distinguieron entre los dos productos. 4. Ana consiguió la maestría en salud pública. 5. Unas empresas reconstruyeron los barrios bajos. 6. ¿Ud. oyó la noticia? 7. El soldado cayó en la batalla. 8. Los usuarios leyeron las páginas Web. 9. Los habitantes oprimidos huyeron de la dictadura. 10. ¿Por qué riñeron todo el día? 11. Uds. siguieron por la autopista. 12. Los hombres de negocios concluyeron la negociación del contrato. 13. La pastelera hiñó la masa. 14. Todo el mundo creyó sus relatos.

F 1. Ud./él/ella, hacer 2. Uds./ellos/ellas, poder 3. Ud./él/ella, ser AND ir 4. tú, decir 5. yo, estar 6. nosotros/nosotras, saber 7. Uds./ellos/ellas, producir 8. yo, ver 9. vosotros/vosotras, andar 10. yo, venir 11. nosotros/nosotras, querer 12. yo, ser AND ir 13. tú, tener 14. Uds./ellos/ellas, caber 15. Ud./él/ella, traer 16. yo, dar

G 1. Pusiste fin a la discusión. 2. Tuvieron mucho éxito con su compañía. 3. Hice clic al botón. 4. ¿Ud. vino en taxi? 5. No dijimos nada. 6. ¿Cómo lo supiste? 7. No pude entender su actitud. 8. Quisimos salir a comer. 9. Nos trajeron unos regalos. 10. Fui la directora del equipo. 11. Vio a Verónica en el cibercafé. 12. Hubo grandes ofertas en las tiendas. 13. El compositor compuso una canción. 14. Me dieron las gracias. 15. Fui de compras. 16. ¿Por qué intervinieron en el conflicto? 17. Conduje a setenta millas por hora. 18. ¿Qué les atrajo? 19. Tradujimos los documentos al inglés. 20. No cupo nadie más en el aula.

H 1. ¿Quién puso la mesa? 2. La puse yo. 3. ¿Qué hizo ayer? 4. Jugué al tenis y luego di un paseo. 5. ¿Adónde fuiste anoche? 6. Fui al cine. 7. ¿Viste a nuestros amigos? 8. No, llegué tarde y no pude encontrarlos. 9. ¿Sabe la dirección (OR casilla) electrónica de Susana? 10. Sí, la supe la semana pasada.

I   1. Tú les mostraste tu iPod.   2. Uds. me enviaron un e-mail.   3. Carolina le pidió un favor.
4. Yo les expliqué el concepto.   5. Ellos os hicieron una buena comida.   6. Nosotros le
dijimos el motivo.   7. Ud. les leyó las instrucciones.   8. Vosotros nos vendisteis el coche.
9. Carlos Manuel te recordó la fecha de la conferencia.   10. Yo les entregué los papeles.
11. Juan e Isabel le escondieron los regalos de cumpleaños.   12. Tú les ocultaste tu
desilusión.

J   1. Tú les escribiste unos mensajes electrónicos a los directores.   2. Él le contó el
argumento de la película a su amigo.   3. Uds. les enviaron unos paquetes a los soldados.
4. Nosotros le compramos el quitanieves al vecino.   5. La anfitriona les sirvió comida
italiana a los invitados.   6. Ud. le devolvió la calculadora de bolsillo a su amiga.
7. Los jefes le ofrecieron el puesto al programador.   8. Nuestro equipo le ganó el partido
al equipo suyo.   9. La niña les quitó los cubos a los otros niños.   10. Yo le mostré
mis maletas al guardia de seguridad.

K   1. I looked for the programmers everywhere.   2. The Red Sox won the World Series
from the Cardinals.   3. We returned the videos to the store employee.   4. The mother
told her children a fairy tale.   5. Did you send an e-mail to Pedro or did you call him?
6. Martita walked her dog in the park. There a big dog took her dog's toys away from him.

L   1. Le entregué el informe a mi jefe.   2. Mi jefe me solicitó el otro informe.   3. Adrián le
pidió prestado el carro a Jaime.   4. Jaime le dijo que sí.   5. El ladrón le robó al hombre su
reloj de oro.   6. El hombre le arrebató/arrancó el reloj al ladrón.   7. Les trajimos manzanas
y uvas a los niños.   8. Nos dieron las gracias./Nos agradecieron.   9. ¿Le enseñaste/
mostraste tu nuevo vestido a Claudia?   10. Sí, y les enseñé/mostré el vestido a mis otras
amigas también.   11. La moza le sirvió la torta de chocolate al cliente.   12. El cliente
le pidió un tenedor a la moza.

Chapter 7
The Imperfect; The Imperfect vs. the Preterit

A   1. yo/Ud./él/ella   2. Uds./ellos/ellas   3. nosotros/nosotras   4. yo/Ud./él/ella
5. Uds./ellos/ellas   6. nosotros/nosotras   7. vosotros/vosotras   8. tú   9. vosotros/vosotras
10. yo/Ud./él/ella   11. tú   12. tú   13. Uds./ellos/ellas   14. yo/Ud./él/ella
15. nosotros/nosotras   16. Uds./ellos/ellas   17. nosotros/nosotras   18. vosotros/vosotras

B   1. trabajaban   2. leíamos   3. vivían   4. corría   5. jugaban   6. subían   7. estábamos
8. decíais   9. ponías   10. esperaba   11. rodaba   12. tenía   13. abría   14. hacían
15. tomabais   16. era   17. aprendía   18. escribías   19. hablaba   20. preferían
21. bebíais   22. salíamos   23. iba   24. veían   25. Nevaba   26. funcionaban

C   1. Quería acompañarlos.   2. Envolvían los paquetes.   3. ¿Qué decían Uds.?   4. Solía nevar
en enero.   5. Te divertías muchísimo.   6. Algo olía mal.   7. Pedía los billetes electrónicos
por computadora.   8. Íbamos a caballo en la hacienda.   9. Comenzaba a estudiar.
10. Volvían para las diez de la noche.   11. Les daba la bienvenida.   12. Se despertaban
tarde los fines de semana.   13. ¿Servías carne o pescado?   14. Soñaban con ser millonarios.
15. Fingía no entender el chiste.   16. Contaba con el apoyo de su familia.   17. No podían
tranquilizarse.   18. No entendía el por qué.   19. Eran muy serios.   20. Uds. se vestían
muy bien.   21. Concluían la presentación.   22. Tenía mucho interés en el proyecto.

D 1. Eran las diez y media cuando llegué a la oficina.   2. Hacía sol cuando comenzó la comida campestre.   3. Cuando vinieron era mediodía ya.   4. Nevaba cuando salí para la pista de esquí.   5. Eran las siete treinta cuando despegó el avión.   6. Tronaba y había relámpagos cuando aterrizamos.   7. Era la madrugada cuando sonó mi teléfono celular. 8. Llovía a cántaros cuando los novios fueron a la iglesia.   9. Hacía muy buen tiempo cuando los recién casados salieron de la iglesia.   10. Había montones de nieve en el parque cuando saqué a mi perro a retozar.   11. Había tormenta cuando le devolvieron el coche de alquiler al agente.   12. Cuando los jóvenes se durmieron era ya tardísimo.   13. Estaba nublado y hacía viento cuando llegamos a la cumbre de la montaña.   14. Eran las dos en punto cuando empezó la función de la tarde.

E 1. Siempre les traía bombones a los abuelos.   2. De costumbre al terminar el trabajo los compañeros tomaban una copa.   3. Todos los sábados Daniela salía con Federico a bailar. 4. A menudo Paco le pedía prestado el coche a su hermano.   5. Cada semana nadabas en la piscina del gimnasio universitario.   6. Todos los inviernos íbamos a la sierra de Guadarrama para esquiar.   7. Generalmente los chicos llegaban hambrientos a la casa. 8. Muchas veces pasábamos un par de horas en el centro comercial.   9. Veían a sus primos italianos todos los veranos.   10. ¿Hacíais un viaje de negocios todos los meses?

F 1. Ignacio les informó que buscaba trabajo.   2. Laura anunció que iba a casarse. 3. Ellos insistieron en que sabían hacerlo.   4. Les escribí que hacía un viaje en mayo. 5. Nos avisaron que no podían llegar puntual a la cita.   6. Me advirtieron que el ordenador estaba descompuesto.   7. Los jefes notificaron que despedían a muchos empleados. 8. Pedro y Consuelo me contaron que eran felices.

G 1. Eran, salieron   2. Había, pude   3. conoció, estudiaba   4. veías, corrimos 5. pensaba, vino   6. sabíamos, dijo   7. Hubo, trabajabas   8. dabais, dio   9. nació, era 10. estábamos, marcó   11. era, logré   12. huyó, dormían   13. enseñaba, inició 14. dio, viajaba   15. prestaba, riñó   16. pagué, comían   17. aparecieron, conocíamos 18. consiguió, tenía   19. presentó, necesitaban   20. llegaron, preparaban

H 1. ¿Cuánto (tiempo) hacía que vivían en Nueva York cuando compraron un condominio? 2. Hacía dos años que vivíamos en la ciudad.   3. ¿Cuánto (tiempo) hacía que estudiabas español en Madrid cuando decidiste volver a tu universidad estadounidense?   4. Hacía seis semanas que estaba allí.   5. ¿Cuánto (tiempo) hacía que Julia usaba su computadora cuando cambió de marca?   6. Hacía tres años que la tenía.   7. ¿Desde cuándo trabajaba Jaime de asesor?   8. Desde el año pasado cuando consiguió su maestría en administración de empresas.

I 1. Se las expliqué.   2. Se lo pidió.   3. Nos lo enseñaban.   4. Me la devuelve. 5. ¿Te lo ofrecieron?   6. Os las sirven.   7. Se los regalamos.   8. Se lo envío. 9. Se la mandó.   10. Nos la recomiendan.   11. Se lo vendimos.   12. Me la dijo. 13. Te lo prestamos.   14. ¿Nos lo demostráis?   15. Se los dio.   16. Os lo suben. 17. Se las trajisteis.   18. Se los hice.   19. Se lo comentaban.   20. Me las entregó.

J 1. a. Ricardo gave them to you/him/her/them. b. You/He/She gave them to Ricardo.
2. a. The consultants described it to you/him/her/them. b. You/They described it to
the consultants.   3. a. Ofelia repeated them to you/him/her/them. b. You/He/She repeated
them to Ofelia.   4. a. You ask him/her/them for it. b. He/She asks you for it.   5. a. Sarita
was going to send them to you/him/her/them. b. I was / You were / He/She was going to send
them to Sarita.   6. a. Our colleagues want to show it to you/him/her/them. b. You/They
want to show it to our colleagues.   7. a. The professor wasn't able to explain it to you/
him/her/them. b. You weren't / He/She wasn't able to explain it to the professor.
8. a. These lawyers have just asked you/him/her/them for them. b. You/They have just
asked these lawyers for them.

K 1. ¿Puedes prestarme tu cámara digital?   2. Se la presté a Esteban la semana pasada.
Puedes pedírsela a él.   3. Compré este suéter para regalárselo a alguien.   4. ¿A quién
quieres dárselo? / ¿A quién se lo quieres dar?   5. Les escribíamos mensajes electrónicos
todos los días.   6. ¿Todavía se los mandan tan a menudo?   7. ¿Ya les hicieron la cena?
8. Vamos a hacérsela pronto.   9. Daniel nos escribió que iba a darle una sortija a su novia.
10. ¿Dijo cuándo pensaba dársela? / ¿Dijo cuándo se la pensaba dar?   11. Julia les entregó
su tesis a los profesores anteayer.   12. ¿No tenía que entregársela el semestre pasado?
13. ¿Cuánto (tiempo) hacía que trabajaban para la empresa cuando el jefe les dio un
aumento de sueldo?   14. Hacía seis meses que hacían programación / programaban cuando
se lo dio. / Hacían programación / Programaban hacía seis meses cuando se lo dio.

Chapter 8
The Past Participle; The Present Perfect; The Pluperfect

A 1. hemos   2. hablado   3. han   4. entendido   5. has   6. leído   7. ha   8. dicho
9. he   10. ha   11. discutido   12. mirado   13. llegado   14. escrito   15. habido

B 1. Tú has hablado por teléfono móvil.   2. Nuestro equipo ha ganado el partido.
3. Ellos han puesto la mesa.   4. Ud. ha recibido la correspondencia.   5. Gerardo ha hecho
un login.   6. Yo he leído los titulares.   7. Nuestra familia ha vivido bien.   8. Uds. han
tenido mucha experiencia.   9. Tú has descargado el fichero.   10. Vosotros no habéis
comprendido el asunto.   11. Nosotros hemos sido muy felices.   12. Nadie ha dicho nada.
13. ¿Quién ha roto la ventana?   14. Nora y Daniela han ido de compras.   15. ¿Ud. ha oído
esta orquesta?   16. Yo he escrito el informe.   17. Nosotros hemos resuelto el conflicto.
18. ¿Cómo han estado Uds.?   19. La cocinera ha frito el pescado.   20. Ellos no han querido
molestar.   21. Vosotros habéis impreso los papeles.   22. Los electrodomésticos han
funcionado bien.

C 1. Han almorzado en la cafetería.   2. Ha llovido todo el día.   3. Han hecho construir una
casa.   4. Ha perdido el tren esta mañana.   5. Ha habido mucha congestión en Internet.
6. Este libro ha sido un éxito de librería.   7. Han vuelto del viaje de negocios.
8. El director ha rodado la película en Texas.   9. Los niños han querido ver los dibujos
animados.   10. Jorge ha conseguido trabajar en la seguridad nacional y la ciberseguridad.
11. El armario ha olido mal.   12. Los ha despertado.   13. Te lo he dicho.   14. Se las hemos
devuelto.   15. Han preferido dársela. / Se la han preferido dar.   16. No se lo he podido
recomendar. / No he podido recomendárselo.   17. ¿Has tratado de enviárnoslos? /
¿Nos los has tratado de enviar?   18. Te la han pensado regalar. / Han pensado regalártela.
19. Ha vuelto a pedírmelas. / Me las ha vuelto a pedir.   20. ¿Por qué habéis necesitado
recordárselo? / ¿Por qué se lo habéis necesitado recordar?

D 1. Ya lo he probado.   2. Ya ha empezado.   3. Ya los hemos visitado.   4. Ya lo ha rellenado.
5. Ya los ha lanzado.   6. Ya lo he repetido.   7. Ya la han emprendido.   8. Ya la he comido.
9. Ya la ha estudiado.   10. Ya lo hemos realizado.   11. Ya las hemos hecho.   12. Ya me
la han mostrado.   13. Ya nos los han contado.   14. Ya se la ha entregado.   15. Ya nos
las han servido.   16. Ya lo he leído.

E 1. No, había corrido en la carrera en abril.   2. No, lo habíamos visto hace un mes.
3. No, la habían hecho el primer fin de semana de mayo.   4. No, la habían abierto hace tres
semanas.   5. No, había vuelto de vacaciones anteayer.   6. No, la habían comprado el año
pasado.   7. No, se la pidió el Día de los Enamorados.   8. No, lo había celebrado el primero
del mes.   9. No, la había llamado para invitarla a la fiesta el martes.   10. No, se lo
habíamos dado en noviembre.

F 1. Cuando tú nos llamaste, nosotros ya habíamos ido de compras.   2. Cuando yo llegué
al cine, Nicolás y Mari ya habían visto la mitad de la película.   3. Cuando los invitados
vinieron, Isabel ya había puesto la mesa.   4. Cuando Paco comenzó a trotar, los otros
jugadores ya habían corrido cinco millas.   5. Cuando Uds. me invitaron, yo ya había hecho
planes para ese día.   6. Cuando nosotros fuimos en lancha, ya había habido tempestad.
7. Cuando vosotros pasasteis la aspiradora, Susana ya había sacudido el polvo.   8. Cuando
Toni solucionó el problema, Ud. ya lo había resuelto.   9. Cuando Vicente le pidió la cuenta
a la moza, Enrique ya la había pagado.   10. Cuando yo volví a la tienda de antigüedades,
alguien ya había comprado la estatua.

G 1. a. comprada b. alquilado c. amueblados d. pintadas e. vendido f. construido
g. rehechas   2. a. entrados b. introducida c. bajadas d. cargado e. telecargados
f. transmitidos   3. a. frito b. cocidos c. hervida d. asadas e. hecha f. hecha
4. a. visto b. visitado c. concurrido d. navegado e. diseñado f. creado   5. a. animadas
b. entusiasmadas c. aburridas d. agradecidas e. enfurecidas f. casadas g. vestidas
6. a. dichas b. escritas c. expresadas d. pronunciadas e. traducidas f. oídas

H 1. está frita   2. estamos mojados   3. está metido   4. están dormidos   5. está comida
6. están hechas

I 1. Yo he escrito los poemas. Los poemas están escritos.   2. Marcia ha teñido la tela.
La tela está teñida.   3. Nosotros hemos cubierto los gastos. Los gastos están cubiertos.
4. La abuela ha acostado a sus nietos. Sus nietos están acostados.   5. Patricio ha fotocopiado
las cartas. Las cartas están fotocopiadas.   6. Tú has hecho las galletas. Las galletas están
hechas.   7. Ud. ha apagado el fuego. El fuego está apagado.   8. Vosotros habéis perdido
la plata. La plata está perdida.   9. Uds. han tirado la basura. La basura está tirada.
10. Alguien ha estacionado el coche. El coche está estacionado.   11. Perla ha enloquecido
a sus amigas. Sus amigas están enloquecidas.   12. Ellos han atravesado el puente. El puente
está atravesado.   13. Los soldados han caído. Los soldados están caídos.   14. Yo he resuelto
el problema. El problema está resuelto.   15. Nosotros hemos impreso la tesis. La tesis
está impresa.   16. Lorenzo ha roto sus pantalones. Sus pantalones están rotos.
17. El arquitecto ha rehecho estas casas. Estas casas están rehechas.   18. La directora ha
pospuesto la reunión. La reunión está pospuesta.   19. La cocinera ha frito las croquetas.
Las croquetas están fritas.   20. El dramaturgo ha terminado el guión. El guión está
terminado.

J 1. Supimos que ya habías vuelto de tu viaje de negocios.   2. Cuando estalló la guerra en su país, los Reyes ya habían huido a los Estados Unidos.   3. Escrita la novela exitosa, la autora empezó a escribir la segunda.   4. He dicho lo más importante. / Tengo lo más importante dicho.   5. ¿La videocámara? Eva se la ha prestado.   6. Los invitados están sentados a la mesa. La comida y el vino están servidos.   7. ¿Han oído las noticias en la radio? Ha habido un maremoto.   8. ¿El dinero? Se lo he pedido a Andrés pero él no ha querido devolvérmelo.   9. ¿Ha hecho las maletas?   10. Sí, las maletas están hechas.   11. ¿Has enchufado la computadora?   12. No, no está enchufada porque funciona con pilas.

Chapter 9
The Imperative

A 1. Arregle el cuarto. No arregle el cuarto.   2. Cierre la puerta. No cierre la puerta.   3. Corra en el maratón. No corra en el maratón.   4. Lea el artículo. No lea el artículo.   5. Cuente lo que pasó. No cuente lo que pasó.   6. Comparta los gastos. No comparta los gastos.   7. Riña al chico. No riña al chico.   8. Siga por el río. No siga por el río.   9. Pruebe la sopa. No pruebe la sopa.   10. Encienda la luz. No encienda la luz.   11. Vaya con nosotros. No vaya con nosotros.   12. Busque al perro. No busque al perro.   13. Imprima el informe. No imprima el informe.   14. Beba el jugo. No beba el jugo.   15. Despierte al niño. No despierte al niño.   16. Pague la cuenta. No pague la cuenta.   17. Vea ese programa. No vea ese programa.   18. Juegue al tenis. No juegue al tenis.   19. Descargue el fichero. No descargue el fichero.   20. Dé un paseo. No dé un paseo.

B 1. Lleven los paquetes.   2. Aparquen en este parqueo.   3. Pidan el helado de coco.   4. Hagan una lista.   5. Organicen estos papeles.   6. Toquen jazz.   7. No gasten tanto dinero.   8. No digan tonterías.   9. Asistan al concierto.   10. No rechacen su idea.   11. No sean desagradables.   12. Empiecen a programar.   13. No vuelquen el florero.   14. Lleguen a las ocho.   15. Sonrían.   16. Consigan los billetes.   17. No tengan miedo.   18. No caigan por la casa sin llamar.   19. Vengan lo antes posible.   20. Introduzcan los datos.

C 1. Sí, alquilemos un video. Sí, vamos a alquilar un video.   2. Sí, naveguemos en la Red. Sí, vamos a navegar en la Red.   3. Sí, comamos algo. Sí, vamos a comer algo.   4. No, no volvamos a ese balneario.   5. Sí, comencemos el proyecto. Sí, vamos a comenzar el proyecto.   6. Sí, juguemos al béisbol. Sí, vamos a jugar al béisbol.   7. Sí, oigamos música. Sí, vamos a oír música.   8. Sí, salgamos al cine. Sí, vamos a salir al cine.   9. No, no hagamos planes.   10. Sí, escojamos un postre. Sí, vamos a escoger un postre.   11. No, no vayamos al centro comercial.   12. Sí, demos una vuelta. Sí, vamos a dar una vuelta.   13. Sí, reduzcamos nuestros gastos. Sí, vamos a reducir nuestros gastos.   14. No, no envolvamos el regalo.   15. No, no subamos en el telesquí.   16. Sí, traigamos una botella de vino. Sí, vamos a traer una botella de vino.   17. No, no sirvamos arroz con pollo.   18. No, no mezamos al bebé.   19. Sí, sigamos por esta calle. Sí, vamos a seguir por esta calle.   20. Sí, conozcamos al nuevo asesor. Sí, vamos a conocer al nuevo asesor.

D 1. Escribe en el disquete. No escribas en el disquete.   2. Lee los cuentos. No leas los cuentos.
3. Repite el plato. No repitas el plato.   4. Haz un clic en el icono. No hagas un clic en el
icono.   5. Envía un fax. No envíes un fax.   6. Cuelga el cartel en esta pared. No cuelgues
el cartel en esta pared.   7. Exige más de ellos. No exijas más de ellos.   8. Pon un anuncio
en el periódico. No pongas un anuncio en el periódico.   9. Pide un aumento de sueldo.
No pidas un aumento de sueldo.   10. Di que sí. No digas que sí.   11. Ve el sitio Web.
No veas el sitio Web.   12. Sé interesado. No seas interesado.   13. Analiza la información.
No analices la información.   14. Sal a pasear. No salgas a pasear.   15. Ve a caballo.
No vayas a caballo.   16. Llega temprano. No llegues temprano.   17. Ven al cibercafé.
No vengas al cibercafé.   18. Tiñe la camisa. No tiñas la camisa.   19. Crea una base de
datos. No crees una base de datos.   20. Ten confianza en ellos. No tengas confianza en ellos.

E 1. Estudiad mercadeo. No estudiéis mercadeo.   2. Vended vuestro coche. No vendáis
vuestro coche.   3. Abrid el baúl. No abráis el baúl.   4. Recoged las uvas. No recojáis las
uvas.   5. Sed agresivos. No seáis agresivos.   6. Seguid nuestros consejos. No sigáis
nuestros consejos.   7. Haced cola. No hagáis cola.   8. Venid en taxi. No vengáis en taxi.
9. Dormid la siesta. No durmáis la siesta.   10. Publicad vuestras memorias. No publiquéis
vuestras memorias.   11. Id al dentista. No vayáis al dentista.   12. Tragad rápidamente.
No traguéis rápidamente.   13. Salid a bailar. No salgáis a bailar.   14. Aplazad la reunión.
No aplacéis la reunión.   15. Medid las cortinas. No midáis las cortinas.   16. Oíd las
noticias. No oigáis las noticias.   17. Traed el cheque. No traigáis el cheque.   18. Buscad el
cajero automático. No busquéis el cajero automático.   19. Decid la clave personal. No digáis
la clave personal.   20. Invertid en esta industria. No invirtáis en esta industria.

F 1. Yo no quiero. Que haga los quehaceres ella.   2. Yo no quiero. Que compren la cerveza
ellos.   3. Yo no quiero. Que aprenda a bailar salsa ella.   4. Yo no quiero. Que lleve
a mi novia al cine más a menudo ella.   5. Yo no quiero. Que practique todos los días él.
6. Yo no quiero. Que busquen trabajo ellos.   7. Yo no quiero. Que lo llame él.   8. Yo no
quiero. Que vaya él a ver el partido de tenis.

G 1. Enjoy this marvelous art exhibit.   2. Have everybody see this marvelous art exhibit.
3. Have him go to get the ink cartridges.   4. Have the secretary send the e-mail messages
right now.   5. Have the customers line up at the box office.   6. Don't let anyone
interrupt the meeting of the heads of state.   7. Let the rest participate in the event.
8. Have somebody notify us as soon as possible.

H 1. Seguir derecho.   2. No pisar el césped.   3. Utilizar nuestra banca electrónica.
4. Reservar sus billetes en línea.   5. Agregar una cucharadita de canela.   6. Abrir una
cuenta corriente.   7. Guardar las recetas en su PDA.   8. Para más información llamar
al teléfono 182329.   9. Para mayores informes enviar un e-mail a esta dirección.
10. Calentar el guisado a fuego lento.   11. Abrocharse el cinturón de seguridad.
12. No tocar los cables de electricidad.   13. Interesados ponerse en contacto con el
director.   14. Alojarse en el Hotel Caribe.

I 1. Haga el favor de volver más tarde.   2. Favor de esperarnos en la oficina.
3. Tengan la bondad de sentarse en la sala.   4. Favor de hacerme una copia de seguridad.
5. Tenga la bondad de pulsar el botón.   6. Hagan el favor de explicármelo.
7. Favor de reunirse la semana próxima.   8. Haga el favor de no meterse en este asunto.
9. Favor de no oponerse al plan.   10. Tengan la bondad de no decírselo a nadie.

J 1. No, no lo pulses/pulse. 2. No, no lo pisen/piséis/pisemos. 3. No, no la hagas/haga. 4. No, no las coman/comáis/comamos. 5. No, no me llames mañana. 6. No, nos ayude con los cajones. 7. No, no lo traigan/traigáis/traigamos. 8. No, no se la regalen/regaléis/regalemos. 9. No, no nos los manden. 10. No, lo paseen/paseéis/paseemos. 11. No, no me busquen esta noche. 12. No, no se las enseñes/enseñe. 13. No, no nos lo cuentes. 14. No, no se la solicites/solicite. 15. No, no nos las expliquéis. 16. No, no me lo des ahora.

K 1. Sí, escríbelo/escríbalo. 2. Sí, ciérrala/ciérrela. 3. Sí, alquílenlos/alquiladlos/alquilémoslos. 4. Sí, diríjanla/dirigidla/dirijámosla. 5. Sí, recógenos/recójanos en el museo. 6. Sí, páguensela/pagádsela/paguémosela. 7. Sí, díganmelo. 8. Sí, házselo/hágaselo. 9. Sí, devuélvannoslos. 10. Sí, vístanlos/vestidlos/vistámoslos. 11. Sí, recuérdenmela/recordádmela. 12. Sí, muéstrenmelas. 13. Sí, sírveselos/sírvaselos. 14. Sí, pídanselo/pedídselo/pidámoselo. 15. Sí, espéranos en el bar. 16. Sí, véndemelo.

L 1. Go and see him/it. (ir, tú; ver, tú) 2. Show it to him/her/them. (mostrar, Ud.) 3. Send them to him/her/them. (enviar, Uds.) 4. Take them up for us. (subir, vosotros) 5. Give it to him/her/them. (dar, tú) 6. Bring it to us. (traer, Uds.) 7. Don't hide them from him/her/them. (ocultar, tú) 8. Don't say it to me. (decir, Ud.) 9. Let's ask him/her/them for them. / Let's order them from him/her/them. (pedir, nosotros) 10. Make/Do it for him/her/them. (hacer, Uds.)

M 1. ¿El teléfono celular? Dámelo. 2. ¿La computadora? Muéstrennosla. / Enséñennosla. 3. ¿Los paquetes? Envuélvamelos. 4. ¿Tus preguntas? Hacédselas. 5. ¿La noticia? Escribámosela. / Vamos a escribírsela. 6. ¿Esa marca? No se la pidamos. 7. Si la comida está hecha, sírvenosla. 8. Si el informe está impreso, léaselo. 9. ¿La raqueta de tenis? Ofrézcasela. 10. Ten paciencia. No vayas todavía.

Chapter 10
The Future and the Conditional;
The Future Perfect and the Conditional Perfect

A 1. Compraremos muchas cosas en una tienda virtual. 2. Contarán con nosotros para llevarlo a cabo. 3. Aprenderás los lenguajes de programación. 4. Nevará pasado mañana. 5. ¿A qué hora vendrán? 6. Gabriela estudiará enfermería pediátrica. 7. No les diré nada. 8. Tendréis mucho que hacer. 9. Habrá millones de navegantes en línea. 10. Marcos efectuará grandes cambios. 11. No podrán vernos hasta la semana entrante. 12. Jaime hará el papel del protagonista. 13. Estarán muy emocionados por la noticia. 14. Oirás la música mejor desde esta fila. 15. La situación irá de mal en peor. 16. Nos pondremos los zapatos. 17. Cabrán quinientas personas en el salón de actos. 18. Querremos pintar unos paisajes. 19. Perseguirán al culpable. 20. Empezaréis a acostumbraros al horario.

B 1. Virginia cumplirá veintitrés años el lunes.   2. Ellos nos pondrán al día.
3. Profundizaremos el tema.   4. Haré un login.   5. Formatearán el documento.
6. ¿No cabrá más memoria en el ordenador?   7. La boda será en un hotel céntrico.
8. Estos jóvenes tendrán mucho éxito.   9. Lloverá toda la temporada.   10. Habrá
un simulacro de incendio esta tarde.   11. Su cumpleaños caerá en un miércoles.
12. Sus esfuerzos valdrán la pena.   13. Saldrán ganando como siempre.
14. Los cursos satisfarán los requisitos.   15. ¿Nos los traeréis?   16. Querremos dársela.
17. Podré informarte mañana.   18. Vendrán lo antes posible.   19. Lo sabré pronto.
20. La oirás cantar en la comedia musical.

C 1. Los empleados habrán salido de la oficina para la hora de la cena.   2. Diana y yo
habremos vuelto del museo a eso de las cuatro.   3. Rogelio habrá conseguido la maestría en
comunicaciones para fines del semestre.   4. Yo se lo habré hecho para la semana que viene.
5. Uds. habrán reservado los billetes electrónicos antes de las vacaciones de verano.
6. Ud. les habrá enviado el correo después de verlos.   7. Tú habrás resuelto el problema
antes de la reunión.   8. Vosotros nos las habréis dado para mediados de enero.
9. Nosotros los habremos visto para el Día de la Independencia.   10. Ellos habrán
mandado los impuestos para el quince de abril.

D 1. tendrías   2. tomaríamos   3. querría   4. tratarían   5. oirían   6. haría   7. traería
8. añadiría   9. se lo exigiría   10. se lo diríais

E 1. vendrían   2. cabrán   3. habría   4. aceptaría   5. sabría   6. compraremos   7. podrías
8. estaría   9. hará   10. aterrizaría   11. le interesaría   12. les encantarán

F 1. Tú no habrías mentido.   2. Ud. no los habría invitado a comer en un restaurante caro.
3. Nosotros no habríamos caído en una trampa.   4. Ellos no habrían dicho nada sin querer.
5. Yo no habría comido comida basura. / Yo no la habría comido.   6. Uds. no habrían
puesto al cantante por las nubes. / Uds. no lo habrían puesto por las nubes.   7. Vosotros no
habríais repetido el plato de carne. / Vosotros no lo habríais repetido.   8. Isaac no habría
visto el programa de realidad. / Isaac no lo habría visto.   9. Daniela y Alfredo no les habrían
regalado a los novios esa cámara digital. / Daniela y Alfredo no se la habrían regalado.
10. Tú no habrías utilizado una chuleta en el examen. / Tú no la habrías utilizado.

G 1. Habrá celos entre las cuñadas.   2. La noche caerá pronto.   3. Los gemelos tendrán
veintiún años.   4. Querrán bailar el tango.   5. Los aficionados estarán entusiasmados.
6. Su sortija de diamantes valdrá mucho.   7. ¿Lloverá mañana?   8. Será la una y media.

H 1. ¿Cuándo llegarán?   2. ¿Qué hora será?   3. ¿Quién sabrá su número de teléfono?
4. ¿Dónde será (OR tendrá lugar) la reunión?   5. ¿Qué tiempo hará esta semana?
6. ¿Cómo estarán?

I 1. Habría treinta invitados en la fiesta.   2. Sería un verano muy caluroso.   3. Tendría
veintinueve años.   4. Las joyas costarían un ojo de la cara.   5. Estarían de viaje.
6. Haría mucho frío.   7. ¿Nevaría mucho en la sierra?   8. Él estaría contentísimo.

J 1. ¿Qué hora sería cuando nos llamaron?   2. Serían las nueve y media.   3. ¿Por qué estaría
tan cansada?   4. Sería por el vuelo largo y difícil.   5. Habría un problema con su carro.
6. Estaría descompuesto.

K 1. Habrán reñido por una tontería.   2. Habrá nevado toda la noche.   3. El perro habrá
tragado la pelota.   4. Los bomberos habrán llegado muy rápidamente para apagar el
incendio.   5. No habrán sacado la basura.   6. Emilio no habrá reciclado los periódicos
en seis meses.

L 1. ¿Cuándo vendrán a vernos? / ¿Cuándo deben (de) venir a vernos?   2. Serían las once
cuando llegué a la estación de tren. / Debían (de) ser las once cuando llegué a la estación
de tren.   3. Los habrán visto en la fiesta. / Deben (de) haberlos visto en la fiesta.
4. El Ferrari les habrá costado un dineral. / El Ferrari debe (de) haberles costado un
dineral. / El Ferrari les costaría un dineral. / El Ferrari debía (de) costarles un dineral.
5. ¡Increíble! Él no habría dicho una cosa tan espantosa.   6. Cuando conocimos a Irene
tendría unos veintidós años. / Cuando conocimos a Irene debía (de) tener unos veintidós
años.   7. Me habrás mandado/enviado un e-mail mientras estabas en el cibercafé. /
Debes (de) haberme mandado/enviado un e-mail mientras estabas en el cibercafé.
8. ¿Qué hora será?   9. ¿Por qué habrá salido Carlos sin avisarnos?   10. Habrá ocurrido
algo imprevisto. / Debe (de) haber ocurrido algo imprevisto.   11. Todo el mundo habrá
leído *El código Da Vinci.* / Todo el mundo debe (de) haber leído *El código Da Vinci.*
12. Tendrán ganas de ir al cine.   13. Será demasiado tarde ya.   14. Ya no habrá función.

Chapter 11
The Subjunctive (Part I): The Present Subjunctive

A 1. tenemos   2. hagan   3. está   4. encargue   5. conozcas   6. es   7. viene   8. salga
9. discutamos   10. utilizáis   11. diga   12. va   13. lleguen   14. ocupo   15. rechaces

B 1. impida   2. veas   3. almuercen   4. sean   5. traigan   6. ponga   7. haya   8. pagues
9. esté   10. aparezca   11. vayamos   12. critiques   13. juegue   14. salga   15. invirtamos
16. sepa   17. dé   18. oigan   19. vuelvan   20. sigamos

C 1. Es importante que ellos sigan una dieta equilibrada.   2. Es útil que Ud. tenga palanca.
3. Es mejor que yo espere un par de días.   4. Es preciso que Uds. hagan clic en el enlace.
5. Es imprescindible que tú entiendas la política exterior.   6. Urge que él envíe el correo
electrónico.   7. Es obligatorio que nosotros asistamos a la reunión.   8. Más vale que
Uds. vayan a pie.   9. Hace falta que vosotros descarguéis los documentos.   10. Es bueno
que nuestra familia viva cómodamente.   11. Es inútil que Anita busque su billetera.
12. Es malo que Pedro no devuelva el dinero prestado.

D 1. Es bueno que haya tantos adelantos tecnológicos.   2. Es cierto que yo trabajo para
una compañía de alta tecnología.   3. No es evidente que tengan interés en el proyecto.
4. No es dudoso que el dueño de la empresa abre otras sucursales.   5. Es que no conocemos
bien el interior del país.   6. Es obvio que los novios están enamorados.   7. No es seguro
que seáis de origen irlandés.   8. Es una lástima que nadie quiera ayudarlos.   9. Está mal
que la cosa no salga bien.   10. Es triste que el huracán haga tanto daño.

E 1. Queremos que nuestros hijos sean felices.   2. El programador necesita bajar el programa.
3. Me alegro de hacer el patinaje sobre hielo.   4. Le aconsejas a Francisca que sirva
entremeses.   5. Temen que haya piratas informáticos en Internet.   6. Duda que ellos sepan
utilizar la hoja de cálculo electrónica.   7. Les gusta que Paco estudie urbanización.
8. Deseáis practicar deportes acuáticos.   9. No creo que Ramón tenga don de gentes.
10. No piensan hacer pintar la casa este año.   11. Tienen miedo de que un virus infecte
su computadora.   12. Le pides a la agencia virtual que te mande dos billetes electrónicos
de ida y vuelta.   13. No deja hablar.   14. Sienten que no las veamos.   15. Insiste en llegar
antes que nadie.

F 1. Esperamos que Uds. puedan asistir a la conferencia esta noche. 2. ¿El informe? Es imprescindible que Ud. se lo dé ahora mismo. 3. Me alegro de que vayan de vacaciones con nosotros. 4. Es necesario / Es preciso / Hace falta que hagamos las maletas la noche anterior. 5. Le aconsejan que le pida un aumento de sueldo a su jefe. 6. Han sugerido que busquemos la marca en los grandes almacenes. 7. ¿No tiene miedo de que / No teme que suprimas todos los ficheros? 8. En la tienda virtual nos dicen que pongamos (OR coloquemos) nuestras compras en el carrito y que vayamos (OR pasemos) a la caja. 9. Es importante disfrutar (OR gozar) de la vida. ¡Que disfruten (OR gocen) de la vida! 10. Ojalá (que) / Espero que triunfes (OR tengas éxito) en la vida.

G 1. interesa 2. esfuerce 3. sepa 4. tengan 5. sean 6. da 7. crea 8. atraiga 9. guste 10. haga 11. esté 12. tiene

H 1. hojees 2. saque 3. pidan 4. salimos 5. haya 6. traiga 7. comenzó 8. asistimos 9. veas 10. devuelvan 11. instale 12. vengan

I 1. No creo que quieras ver esta película. 2. Es necesario / Es preciso que les envíe un mensaje electrónico (OR un e-mail). 3. Es útil que hagamos nuestras investigaciones en la Red (OR por Internet). 4. Me alegro de que vengan a vernos este fin de semana. 5. Buscamos una casa que tenga seis dormitorios. 6. Necesitan un director que conozca la empresa muy bien. 7. Ojalá (que) / Espero que nuestro equipo gane el partido el domingo. 8. ¡Que te diviertas! (OR ¡Que lo pases bien!) 9. No hay ningún sándwich en la carta que me guste. 10. Consigamos los billetes electrónicos tan pronto como / en cuanto / luego que yo haga el login (OR la conexión). 11. Te muestro (OR Te mostraré OR Te voy a mostrar) el sitio Web de viajes para que / a fin de que puedas escoger un paquete turístico. 12. ¿Quieren comer algo antes de que comience la comedia (OR la obra de teatro)? 13. Te compraremos un recuerdo cuando lleguemos a Granada. / Te compraremos un recuerdo al llegar a Granada. 14. No vale la pena organizar la tertulia a menos que todos nuestros amigos puedan venir (OR ir).

J 1. Yo la invité al concierto pero ella no pudo ir. 2. No puede tomar el seminario de ciencias políticas a las once porque cursa literatura mundial a la misma hora. 3. O llegas puntualmente o no te dejan entrar. 4. Terminó de mandar el correo electrónico e hizo el logoff. 5. No lo encontramos ni en casa ni en la oficina así que lo llamamos por teléfono móvil. 6. Él no sólo se ocupa de los quehaceres domésticos sino que hace la jardinería también. 7. Te afirmo que son dignos de confianza. 8. Ellos fueron corriendo de tal modo que Ud. no consiguió alcanzarlos. 9. Pasaron por mí a las seis de manera que logramos llegar al aeropuerto con tiempo de sobra. 10. El avión iba a despegar conque los pasajeros se abrocharon el cinturón de seguridad.

K 1. No sólo canta sino que baila también. 2. O los llamaremos por teléfono (OR O los telefonearemos) hoy o les hablaremos cuando los veamos. 3. ¿Ud. confirma que ha recibido los billetes electrónicos? 4. Juro que yo no tengo la culpa. 5. Va a pasar sus vacaciones en San Francisco porque sus padres viven allí. 6. Prende la computadora de modo que / de manera que / de forma que yo pueda ver tu sitio Web. 7. Así que / Conque / De tal modo que / De tal manera que / De tal forma que no había nadie cuando llegaron. 8. Ellos fueron al cine pero nosotros decidimos alquilar una película. 9. Fuimos a las grandes almacenes de modo que pudimos comprarles un regalo para inaugurar la casa. 10. Ella hizo el logon y fue a su sitio Web primero. 11. Sé que esos archivos ya están formateados y almacenados. 12. Quieren que viajemos (OR hagamos un viaje) con ellos, pero los encontramos muy aburridos.

Chapter 12
The Subjunctive (Part II): The Present Perfect Subjunctive; The Imperfect Subjunctive; The Pluperfect Subjunctive

A 1. Es probable que se hayan divertido mucho.   2. Dudo que Antonio y Nora hayan sido novios.   3. Es útil que yo se lo haya explicado.   4. Estamos furiosos que él haya mentido. 5. Es una lástima que no hayan tenido una vida privada.   6. Me sorprende que Ud. no la haya visto.   7. Es posible que el avión haya despegado.   8. Es bueno que los rescatadores los hayan encontrado sanos y salvos.   9. Niego que me hayan dicho eso.   10. No es cierto que hayan llegado a casa achispados.   11. Es malo que haya habido un fallo del sistema. 12. Sienten que su gato haya muerto.   13. Espera que hayamos hecho algo interesante. 14. Es importante que hayas tecleado correctamente la palabra clave.   15. No nos gusta que no haya contribuido nada a la caridad.

B 1. Dudo que Rebeca haya encontrado su pendiente de oro.   2. Es bueno que hayan resuelto su problema.   3. No nos gusta que hayan caído por la casa sin llamar.   4. Es útil que hayas descargado (OR bajado) los ficheros.   5. ¿Le sorprende que no le hayan ofrecido a Carlos un aumento de sueldo?   6. Me alegro de que te haya salido bien.   7. No es cierto que Isabel haya renunciado a su puesto.   8. Está furioso que el perro haya hecho pedazos la alfombra. 9. Sienten que las cosas hayan ido de mal en peor.   10. Es probable que ya le hayáis devuelto el paraguas.

C 1. realizaras/realizases   2. se metiera/se metiese   3. hiciera/hiciese   4. se especializara/ se especializase   5. anduvieran/anduviesen   6. cupieran/cupiesen   7. leyeran/leyesen 8. pasarais/pasaseis   9. estuviéramos/estuviésemos   10. redujéramos/redujésemos 11. entrara/entrase   12. trajeras/trajeses   13. diera/diese   14. conociera/conociese 15. se dedicara/se dedicase   16. gustara/gustase   17. corrigiera/corrigiese 18. fuéramos/fuésemos   19. pidiera/pidiese   20. quisiera/quisiese

D 1. Esperábamos que trajeras tu cámara digital a la fiesta.   2. Le aconsejé que comprara la blusa blanca de seda.   3. No había nada que los entusiasmara.   4. Mariana les pidió que pusieran la mesa.   5. Nos habían mandado los videos sin que los pagáramos. 6. Preferiríamos que no se lo dijera.   7. Querían una computadora que funcionara bien. 8. Llevaba mi teléfono móvil por todas partes para que / a fin de que mis hijos pudieran llamarme a toda hora.   9. Ojalá llegaran hoy.   10. Le gustaría que le regaláramos un iPod. 11. Ojalá se tranquilizaran (OR se calmaran).   12. Ojalá te quedaras.

E 1. Me alegré de que hubiéramos hecho un viaje a Santa Fe.   2. Era importante que nos hubieran puesto al día.   3. Esperábamos que ella hubiera hecho la comida.   4. Nos extrañó que no se lo hubieras dicho a nadie.   5. Fue imposible que hubiera pasado una cosa así. 6. Nos gustó que hubierais leído tantos libros.   7. Fue probable que ellos hubieran impreso los documentos.   8. Ojalá (que) lo hubiéramos sabido lo antes posible.   9. Temían que la computadora hubiera tenido un gusano.   10. Les sorprendió que yo hubiera conseguido unos billetes electrónicos tan baratos.

F 1. No era cierto que Angélica hubiera roto con su novio.   2. Negó que ellos hubieran dicho palabrotas.   3. Se alegró de que hubiéramos oído los discos compactos.   4. Contestó como si no hubiera entendido la pregunta.   5. Ojalá hubieran podido pasar todo el verano con nosotros.   6. Nos sorprendió que no hubieras asistido a la reunión.   7. Era malo que hubiera llovido antes de la carrera.   8. Era posible que hubieran tratado de telefonearnos (OR llamarnos por teléfono).   9. ¿Dudaban que yo les hubiera dicho la verdad? 10. No creía que les hubiera escrito todavía.

G 1. voy, haré   2. saldremos, nieva   3. explica, procuraré   4. llevará, decide   5. es, pondrá   6. matriculará, hay   7. vienen, verán   8. meriendas, tendrás   9. querré, riegas   10. optan, podrán

H 1. fueras, iría   2. podríamos, tuviéramos   3. hubiera, quedarían   4. preocuparan, serían   5. tendría, fuera   6. pasaríamos, hiciera   7. siguieran, perderían   8. pidieras, perdonarían   9. dormiría, tomara   10. trajeras, daría

I 1. hubieras navegado, habrías/hubieras visto   2. habría/hubiera conseguido, hubiera estudiado   3. hubieran recibido, habrían/hubieran tenido   4. habría/hubiera sacado, hubiera jugado   5. hubiéramos leído, habríamos/hubiéramos sabido   6. hubieran vivido, habrían/hubieran echado   7. habría/hubiera visto, hubieras vuelto   8. hubierais aprovechado, habríais/hubierais ahorrado   9. habrían/hubieran conocido, hubieran ido   10. hubiera habido, habrías/hubieras perdido   11. habrían/hubieran tenido, hubieran prendido   12. te hubieras olvidado, habría/hubiera recibido

J 1. Si lo vemos en el partido, lo saludaremos por ti (OR de tu parte).   2. Compartirían los gastos si pudieran.   3. La empresa la habría/hubiera contratado si ella hubiera tenido cinco años de experiencia.   4. Si no lloviera, daríamos un paseo.   5. Si Ud. me hubiera dado el contrato, yo lo habría/hubiera firmado.   6. Los esperaría si no tuviera que coger el tren de las seis.   7. Esquiarán este fin de semana si hace buen tiempo.   8. Si nuestros colegas fueran más trabajadores, nosotros no tendríamos tanto que hacer.   9. Si quisieras usar el coche, te lo prestaríamos.   10. Si ella les hubiera pedido un iPod, ellos se lo habrían/hubieran regalado.   11. Yo habría/hubiera tomado el vuelo de medianoche de San Diego a Nueva York si hubiera tenido que asistir a una reunión a las nueve de la mañana.   12. Si Uds. compran (OR hacen las compras) en línea, ahorrarán tiempo y dinero.

Chapter 13
Reflexive Verbs

A 1. me pongo   2. se acuesta   3. te duermes   4. se viste   5. se despiertan   6. nos relajamos   7. se equivocó   8. te fuiste   9. me tranquilicé   10. se arrepintieron   11. se despidió   12. os casasteis   13. nos sorprendíamos   14. se enamoraba   15. me entusiasmaba   16. te ibas   17. se reunían   18. se aburría   19. me decidiré   20. nos opondremos   21. se detendrán   22. se sentirá   23. te reirás   24. se instalarán   25. te acordarías   26. nos animaríamos   27. se correría   28. me apoderaría   29. os enfadaríais   30. se mantendrían   31. se han sonreído   32. Se ha hecho   33. se han caído   34. me he servido   35. te has roto   36. nos hemos puesto

B 1. Consiguió colocarse. Se consiguió colocar.   2. Empiezan a interesarse. Se empiezan a interesar.   3. Piensan reunirse. Se piensan reunir.   4. Tendrás que encararte con él. Te tendrás que encarar con él.   5. No querría involucrarme en eso. No me querría involucrar en eso.   6. Dejabais de preocuparos. Os dejabais de preocupar.   7. Espera divertirse. Se espera divertir.   8. No podremos decidirnos. No nos podremos decidir.   9. Iba a pasearme. Me iba a pasear.   10. Debéis vestiros. Os debéis vestir.   11. Prefirieron quedarse. Se prefirieron quedar.   12. Temía cortarse. Se temía cortar.   13. Deseas casarte. Te deseas casar.   14. Terminó de ducharse. Se terminó de duchar.

C 1. Me di cuenta del problema.   2. Se echó a correr.   3. Nos pusimos de acuerdo.   4. Se quedaron con el dinero.   5. No te fiaste de tus socios.   6. Se dieron prisa al ver la hora.   7. Se trata de un asunto muy importante.   8. Se sirvió de unos libros de consulta.   9. ¿Os atrevisteis a hablarles de esa manera?   10. Se puso a reír.

D 1. Cada vez que Javier se afeita se corta.   2. Por eso le gusta que el barbero lo afeite.
3. Yo baño a mis hijos antes de acostarlos. Luego yo me acuesto.   4. Hoy Marta y Daniela
se despertaron a las siete y media. Se ducharon, se vistieron, se maquillaron (OR se pintaron)
y se peinaron.   5. Les digo que no se preocupen. Quiero que se tranquilicen (OR se calmen)
y que se relajen.   6. Se empeñaba en meterse en nuestros asuntos.   7. Consuelo y Jaime
se graduaron en la universidad, se enamoraron, se comprometieron y se casaron.
8. ¿Te acatarraste (OR Te resfriaste) la semana pasada y todavía te sientes mal?
9. Se acercaba a la casa cuando se mareó.   10. Me arrepiento de involucrarme en su negocio
turbio.   11. Nos matricularemos (OR Nos apuntaremos) para el curso de administración
en línea.

E 1. Claudia y yo nos escribimos mensajes electrónicos.   2. Alejandro y Catalina se entienden
perfectamente.   3. Miriám y Alejo se quieren mucho.   4. David y yo nos vemos muy
a menudo.   5. Diana y su hermana se ayudan mucho.   6. Miguel y Beatriz se compran
regalos.   7. Esteban y yo nos decimos muchas cosas.   8. Ud. y yo llegamos a conocernos
bien.   9. Tú y yo nos tuteamos.

F 1. Los aficionados se volvieron locos al ver a su jugador favorito.   2. Debido a sus buenas
inversiones, se hizo / llegó a ser rico.   3. Pablo y Amanda se hicieron / llegaron a ser amigos.
4. El pequeño pueblo se convirtió en / se transformó en una bulliciosa capital internacional.
5. Paula es una muchacha tímida que se pone roja/colorada con frecuencia.   6. Jacobo se
ponía gordo / engordaba mientras su hermano Cristóbal se ponía flaco / enflaquecía.
7. Se pusieron furiosos / Se enfurecieron al ver (OR cuando vieron) que su perro había roto
la alfombra.

G 1. Aurelia se alegró.   2. Yo me entusiasmé.   3. Carlos se ofendió.   4. Pilar y yo nos
emocionamos.   5. Ellos se enojaron / se enfadaron.   6. Tú te molestaste.   7. Uds. se
exasperaron.   8. Ud. se aburrió.   9. Vosotros os irritasteis.   10. Ellos se asustaron.
11. Él se entristeció.   12. Nosotros nos sorprendimos.

H 1. Roberto se lo torció.   2. Eva y Ana se la lavarán.   3. Te la probabas.   4. Pablo se lo
ha roto.   5. Me las puse.   6. Ud. se los abrochó.   7. Nos lo ponemos.   8. Os las laváis.
9. Iba a cortármelo. / Me lo iba a cortar.   10. Acaba de lastimárselo. / Se lo acaba de lastimar.
11. Quiere pintárselos. / Se los quiere pintar.   12. Necesitabas cepillártelo. / Te lo necesitabas
cepillar.   13. Me los he atado.   14. Se las había limado.   15. Quiero que te lo seques.
16. Era necesario que nos lo abrocháramos.

I 1. Fasten/Button/Tie it. / Fasten/Button/Tie it for him/her/them.   2. Put them on. /
Put them on for him/her/them.   3. Wash it for him/her/them.   4. You/He/She took them
off. / You/He/She took them off for him/her/you/them.   5. You/They unbuttoned/
unbuckled it. / You/They unbuttoned/unbuckled it for him/her/you/them.   6. He/She is /
You are going to brush it. / He/She is / You are going to brush it for him/her/you/them.
7. I put them on.   8. You should clean them.

J 1. Sí, póntelo. No, no te lo pongas.   2. Sí, límpienselos. No, no se los limpien.
3. Sí, séqueselo. No, no se lo seque.   4. Sí, quitémonoslo. No, no nos lo quitemos.
5. Sí, pruébatelas. No, no te las pruebes.   6. Sí, laváoslas. No, no os las lavéis.
7. Sí, córteselo. No, no se lo corte.   8. Sí, desabrochémonoslos. No, no nos los
desabrochemos.   9. Sí, abróchenselo. No, no se lo abrochen.   10. Sí, pintáoslos.
No, no os los pintéis.

K 1. Le puse el abrigo. 2. Él se torció el tobillo durante el partido de fútbol americano.
3. Instalémonos / Vamos a instalarnos en la casa nueva lo antes posible. 4. ¿Vas a cortarte
el pelo? 5. ¡Mira! Me lo corté ayer. 6. ¿Debo probarme este traje azul marino?
7. Sí, pruébeselo y póngase ese gris también. 8. Tranquilicémonos./Calmémonos. No nos
preocupemos. 9. Aquí tienes tu camiseta. Póntela. 10. Te quebraste / Te rompiste el pie.
¡No te quiebres / No te rompas el otro! 11. Séqueselas. 12. Séqueselas. 13. Abróchense
el cinturón de seguridad. 14. Abróchele el cinturón de seguridad a su hijita (OR niñita).

Chapter 14
The Present Participle; The Progressive Tenses

A 1. Pasé una hora haciendo ejercicio. 2. Pasaste diez minutos vistiéndote. 3. Pasó dos
horas navegando en la Red. 4. Pasaron media hora paseándose. 5. Pasamos el día entero
divirtiéndonos. 6. Pasaron una semana instalándose en el condominio. 7. Pasó cuarenta
y cinco minutos oyendo música. 8. Pasasteis mucho tiempo discutiendo. 9. Pasó toda
la tarde probándose ropa. 10. Pasaste veinte minutos durmiendo la siesta. 11. Pasaron
toda la mañana leyendo. 12. Pasamos menos de una hora viendo tele.

B 1. Uds. la vieron bailar ballet. Uds. la vieron bailando ballet. 2. Tú los escuchaste hablar.
Tú los escuchaste hablando. 3. Nosotros las miramos actuar. Nosotros las miramos
actuando. 4. Ud. lo oyó llorar. Ud. lo oyó llorando. 5. Yo los vi correr. Yo los vi
corriendo. 6. Vosotros la observasteis hacer gimnasia. Vosotros la observasteis haciendo
gimnasia. 7. Ellos me oyeron silbar una melodía. Ellos me oyeron silbando una melodía.
8. Él nos vio cruzar la calle. Él nos vio cruzando la calle.

C 1. Está alquilándolo. Lo está alquilando. 2. Están divirtiéndose. Se están divirtiendo.
3. Estás probándotelas. Te las estás probando. 4. Estamos sirviéndoselas. Se las estamos
sirviendo. 5. Está imprimiéndolos. Los está imprimiendo. 6. Estoy poniéndoselo.
Se lo estoy poniendo. 7. Estáis pidiéndonoslo. Nos lo estáis pidiendo. 8. Estoy leyéndolo.
Lo estoy leyendo. 9. Están escribiéndomelo. Me lo están escribiendo. 10. Estáis
secándooslas. Os las estáis secando. 11. Estás rompiéndotela. Te la estás rompiendo.
12. Está encendiéndolo. Lo está encendiendo. 13. Están consiguiéndoselos. Se los están
consiguiendo. 14. Están limpiándoselos. Se los están limpiando. 15. Estamos
comiéndonosla. Nos la estamos comiendo.

D 1. Estaba descargándolos. Los estaba descargando. 2. Estaba vistiéndome. Me estaba
vistiendo. 3. Estábamos quitándoselo. Se lo estábamos quitando. 4. Estabas cortándotelo.
Te lo estabas cortando. 5. Estaban diciéndonoslo. Nos lo estaban diciendo. 6. Estabais
compartiéndolas. Las estabais compartiendo. 7. Estábamos reuniéndonos. Nos estábamos
reuniendo. 8. Estaba trayéndosela. Se la estaba trayendo. 9. Estaban mostrándomelas.
Me las estaban mostrando. 10. Estaba lavándoselas. Se las estaba lavando. 11. Estaba
poniéndome en forma. Me estaba poniendo en forma. 12. Estaban riéndose a carcajadas.
Se estaban riendo a carcajadas.

E 1. Estará terminándola. La estará terminando. 2. Estarían cuidándolos. Los estaría
cuidando. 3. Estaremos registrándonos en el hotel. Nos estaremos registrando en el hotel.
4. Estaría acostándose. Se estaría acostando. 5. Estarían diciéndomelo. Me lo estarían
diciendo. 6. Estarías haciéndoselas. Se las estarías haciendo. 7. Estaré poniéndosela.
Se la estaré poniendo. 8. Estarán atándoselos. Se los estarán atando. 9. Estarás
aburriéndote. Te estarás aburriendo. 10. Estaréis entregándoselos. Se los estaréis
entregando.

F 1. Estuve practicándolo hasta las cinco. Lo estuve practicando hasta las cinco.
2. Estuvo arreglándose hasta que él llegó a recogerla. Se estuvo arreglando hasta que
él llegó a recogerla.   3. Estuvieron instalándose hasta el sábado. Se estuvieron instalando
hasta el sábado.   4. Estuvimos paseándonos hasta el anochecer. Nos estuvimos paseando
hasta el anochecer.   5. Estuviste lavándotela hasta que sonó el teléfono. Te la estuviste
lavando hasta que sonó el teléfono.   6. Estuvieron reuniéndose hasta que la presidenta
levantó la reunión. Se estuvieron reuniendo hasta que la presidenta levantó la reunión.
7. Estuvo portándose mal hasta que sus papás le riñeron. Se estuvo portando mal hasta
que sus papás le riñeron.   8. Estuvo contándoselos hasta que su amiga no pudo más.
Se los estuvo contando hasta que su amiga no pudo más.

G 1. Llevo cuarenta minutos navegando en la Red.   2. Llevan tres horas jugando al golf.
3. Lleva un par de días sintiéndose mal.   4. Llevamos varios años interesándonos en el arte.
5. Llevas quince minutos limándote las uñas.   6. Lleváis media hora probándoos esos
pantalones.   7. Llevo mucho tiempo manteniéndome en forma.   8. Llevan una semana
reuniéndose en el congreso.

H 1. Patricia was still working in the suburbs when I ran into her.   2. The company
was gradually raising its prices to create Web sites.   3. You were running up the stairs.
4. You danced down the stairs.   5. We've been writing instant messages to each other
(OR We've been instant messaging to each other) for half an hour.   6. They caught a cold
drinking from other people's glasses.   7. They spent the weekend having fun (OR a good
time).   8. Carmen hurt her finger cutting the bread.

I 1. ¿El helado de chocolate? Estoy sirviéndoselo / Se lo estoy sirviendo ahora mismo.
2. ¿Su abrigo? Él está poniéndoselo. / Él se lo está poniendo.   3. Ellos están peinándose /
Ellos se están peinando mientras nosotros estamos vistiéndonos / nosotros nos estamos
vistiendo.   4. El jugador se rompió los pantalones (OR el pantalón) cayéndose.
5. Estábamos durmiéndonos cuando sonó el teléfono.   6. Estarán instalándose en su casa
nueva.   7. No la vi bailando en la discoteca anoche. ¿Qué estaría haciendo?   8. Espero
que estés arreglándote / te estés arreglando para que no lleguemos tarde.   9. ¿Uds. lo oyeron
tosiendo toda la noche?   10. Llevamos veinte minutos buscando un parquímetro.
11. González estuvo lanzando (OR pitcheando) muy bien hasta que se torció el tobillo.

J 1. No, lo ganó el equipo Rojo.   2. No, se lo torció Raimundo.   3. No, se la quemó mi
amigo.   4. No, se reunieron los consultores.   5. No, abrirán en la esquina una pastelería.
6. No, las hacíamos nosotros.   7. No, está probándoselo Miriám.   8. No, los busca la otra
sucursal.

K 1. Los cheques los cobró Sara.   2. La lista la hicimos Antonio y yo.   3. El guacamole
lo preparabas tú.   4. A sus hermanitos los ha cuidado Inés.   5. Las cuentas las pagué yo.
6. Mi cámara digital la usarán ellos.   7. A los pacientes nerviosos los tranquilizó el
enfermero.   8. A Lorena la llevó a un concierto Andrés.   9. El informe lo han impreso
Uds.   10. Al empleado insolente lo despidió el dueño del negocio.

L 1. Victoria lo conoció. / Lo conoció Victoria.   2. Él conoció a Victoria. / A Victoria la
conoció él.   3. Isabel se lo dijo. / Se lo dijo Isabel.   4. Ella se lo dijo a Isabel.   5. Jorge y Rita
la vieron. / La vieron Jorge y Rita.   6. Ud. vio a Jorge y a Rita. / A Jorge y a Rita los vio Ud.
7. Martín se las mostró. / Se las mostró Martín.   8. Se las mostraron a Martín.
9. Miguel le leyó. / Le leyó Miguel.   10. Le leyó a Miguel.

Chapter 15
Passive Constructions; Reverse Construction Verbs

A 1. La computadora fue reparada por el técnico.   2. Una cadena de perfumerías será abierta por una empresa alemana.   3. El vino fue derramado por el mozo.   4. La revista electrónica es escrita por unos estudiantes de informática.   5. Los planes serán hechos por este equipo de arquitectos.   6. Los aparatos eléctricos fueron desenchufados por el electricista.   7. El software será instalado por estos programadores.   8. La película es rodada en Barcelona por el director inglés.   9. La conferencia ha sido dada por el presidente.   10. Los terroristas fueron detenidos por los soldados.   11. Estas tortas fueron hechas por una pastelera de la academia de artes culinarias.   12. Una serie de artículos sobre la guerra fue publicada por el periódico.

B 1. El informe fue escrito por el asesor. El informe estaba escrito.   2. La reunión fue suspendida por la directora. La reunión estaba suspendida.   3. Los discursos fueron pronunciados por los voceros. Los discursos estaban pronunciados.   4. Las páginas Web fueron redactadas por el administrador de Web. Las páginas Web estaban redactadas.   5. Los problemas fueron resueltos por la psicóloga. Los problemas estaban resueltos.   6. La sinfonía fue compuesta por el compositor francés. La sinfonía estaba compuesta.   7. La ventana fue rota por el jugador de béisbol. La ventana estaba rota.   8. La ley fue aprobada por los legisladores. La ley estaba aprobada.   9. Las colonias fueron fundadas por los exploradores. Las colonias estaban fundadas.   10. Los pacientes fueron cuidados por la enfermera. Los pacientes estaban cuidados.

C 1. Las pizzas fueron entregadas a domicilio por el repartidor.   2. Los bancos fueron cerrados por los gerentes.   3. Los muebles fueron puestos (OR colocados) en la sala por los cargadores.   4. Las paredes fueron pintadas por nuestro pintor.   5. El coche fue alquilado por los turistas.   6. El coche estaba alquilado.   7. Los políticos de los dos partidos fueron entrevistados por la prensa.   8. Los políticos estaban entrevistados.   9. El regalo fue envuelto por nosotros.   10. El regalo estaba envuelto.   11. Mi amigo/amiga consiguió los billetes en la Red (OR por Internet).   12. Los billetes estaban comprados.

D 1. Se servían platos tejanomexicanos.   2. Se venden flores exquisitas en esta florería.   3. Se necesitan programadores en esta compañía de alta tecnología.   4. Se harán tres copias del documento.   5. Se realizó el proyecto.   6. Se están organizando los archivos.   7. Se habla español en todas estas tiendas.   8. Se leyeron las obras clásicas.   9. Se firmó el contrato.   10. Se va a enviar el correo electrónico pronto.   11. No se puede hacer preguntas todavía.   12. Se debe visitar ese sitio Web.   13. Se quemó el pan.   14. Se necesita almacenar los datos.

E 1. Se trabaja en equipo.   2. Se navega en la Red.   3. Se vive en una sociedad de información.   4. Se compra y se vende en un mercado global.   5. Se puede hablar por teléfono móvil.   6. Se debe llegar antes de las cuatro.   7. Se entra por la puerta principal.   8. Se sale al jardín por aquí.   9. Se sube en este elevador.   10. Se baja por la escalera trasera.   11. Se charla en el canal de conversación.   12. Se busca el cajero automático.

F 1. Se habla inglés aquí.   2. Se debe tomar el tren de la una.   3. Uno se preocupa demasiado.   4. Se puede vivir muy bien en esta ciudad.   5. Se muestran (OR Se enseñan) los apartamentos entre las diez y las seis.   6. Los empleados fueron contratados por el gerente.   7. Estos productos fueron hechos por una empresa inglesa.   8. Uno se despierta tarde los fines de semana.   9. ¿Cómo se dice "the Net" en español?   10. Uno se abrocha el cinturón de seguridad cuando se viaja en coche.   11. ¿Se mató a los terroristas? 12. Sí, se les mató. Y se encarceló a muchos otros.

G 1. Le gustan estas marcas.   2. ¿Te interesan mis ideas?   3. Nos encantaron los conciertos.
4. Me entusiasmaban sus planes.   5. Les quedaban los exámenes orales.   6. Os fascinarán
los pianistas.   7. Les agradan las exposiciones.   8. Nos han caído bien esos profesores.
9. Le faltan unos dólares.   10. Me harían falta unos disquetes.

H 1. No te va a convenir meterte en sus asuntos.   2. No nos va a importar el qué dirán.
3. Me va a tocar a mí hacer la compra.   4. Les va a sobrar tiempo.   5. Le va a desagradar
tu actitud.   6. Os van a disgustar sus costumbres.   7. Le van a interesar esas pinturas.
8. Te van a encantar los postres.   9. Nos va a urgir contactarlos.   10. Me va a agradar pasar
las vacaciones en Ibiza.

I 1. ¿A quién le toca?   2. Le gustan estos perfumes.   3. Nos entusiasmó el partido de béisbol.
4. Les convendrá esperar.   5. ¿Les interesaría?   6. No le van a caer bien. / Le van a caer
mal.   7. Francamente no me importa.   8. ¿Te gustaría salir a comer ?   9. Me encantaría.
10. ¿Qué le hace falta?   11. No me hace falta nada.   12. ¿Os falta dinero?   13. No, nos
sobra.   14. Me desagradarían. / Me disgustarían.

J 1. Se le perdieron los anteojos.   2. Se me ocurrió una cosa increíble.   3. Se les descompuso
el aire acondicionado.   4. Se le quebraron dos dedos.   5. Se te cayeron los platos.
6. Se nos quedó la llave del coche en casa.   7. Se les acabó la paciencia.   8. Se os olvidó
hacer la llamada.   9. Se le averiaron los frenos del coche.   10. Se me olvidó mi clave
personal.   11. Se les perdió la libreta de cheques.   12. Se le acabó el jugo de naranja.

K 1. Se le quedó su teléfono celular en la oficina.   2. ¿Todavía no se le ha ocurrido a nadie?
3. Se les está descomponiendo/averiando su computadora.   4. ¿Se te ha olvidado que
su cumpleaños es mañana?   5. ¿A quién se le quedaron estos guantes aquí?   6. ¿Cómo se
le quebró/rompió el pie?   7. Se me quebró/rompió jugando al fútbol.   8. Se nos está
acabando el pan.   9. Se me cayó el florero.   10. ¿Se te rompió/quebró?

Index

About the Authors

Ronni L. Gordon, Ph.D., is a prominent author of foreign language textbooks, reference books, and materials for multimedia. She is co-author of the acclaimed *The Ultimate Spanish Review and Practice: Mastering Spanish Grammar for Confident Communication* and *The Big Red Book of Spanish Verbs: 555 Fully Conjugated Verbs*. She is Vice President of Mediatheque Publisher Services, a leader in the development of foreign language instructional materials. She received a Ph.D. in Spanish language and Spanish and Latin American history and literature from Rutgers University, and taught at Harvard University and Boston University. She has read for the National Endowment for the Humanities and founded the Committee for Quality Education, an organization devoted to the improvement of academic standards in the public schools. She is an education consultant specializing in curriculum development in foreign languages, literature, and history, and in teacher training. She is an associate scholar of a Philadelphia-based think tank.

David M. Stillman, Ph.D., is a well-known writer of foreign language textbooks, multimedia courses, and reference books. He is co-author of the acclaimed *The Ultimate Spanish Review and Practice: Mastering Spanish Grammar for Confident Communication* and *The Big Red Book of Spanish Verbs: 555 Fully Conjugated Verbs*. He is President of Mediatheque Publisher Services, a leader in the development of foreign language instructional materials. He received a Ph.D. in Spanish linguistics from the University of Illinois and taught at Harvard University, Boston University, and Cornell University. He has been appointed to national committees devoted to the improvement of teacher training. He teaches at The College of New Jersey, where he has given courses in Spanish, French, Italian, and Hebrew, and supervises conversation hours in French, German, Italian, Chinese, Japanese, and Arabic.